IN WITH THE IN CROWD

American Made Music Series

Advisory Board

David Evans, General Editor
Barry Jean Ancelet
Edward A. Berlin
Joyce J. Bolden
Rob Bowman
Curtis Ellison
William Ferris
John Edward Hasse
Kip Lornell
Bill Malone
Eddie S. Meadows
Manuel H. Peña
Wayne D. Shirley
Robert Walser

IN WITH THE IN CROWD

Popular Jazz
in 1960s Black America

Mike Smith

University Press of Mississippi / Jackson

The University Press of Mississippi is the scholarly publishing agency of the Mississippi Institutions of Higher Learning: Alcorn State University, Delta State University, Jackson State University, Mississippi State University, Mississippi University for Women, Mississippi Valley State University, University of Mississippi, and University of Southern Mississippi.

www.upress.state.ms.us

The University Press of Mississippi is a member of the Association of University Presses.

Any discriminatory or derogatory language or hate speech regarding race, ethnicity, religion, sex, gender, class, national origin, age, or disability that has been retained or appears in elided form is in no way an endorsement of the use of such language outside a scholarly context.

Copyright © 2024 by University Press of Mississippi
All rights reserved

∞

Library of Congress Cataloging-in-Publication Data

Names: Smith, Mike (Music educator), author.
Title: In with the in crowd : popular jazz in 1960s Black America / Mike Smith.
Other titles: American made music series.
Description: Jackson : University Press of Mississippi, 2024. | Series: American made music series | Includes bibliographical references and index.
Identifiers: LCCN 2023056338 (print) | LCCN 2023056339 (ebook) | ISBN 9781496851147 (hardback) | ISBN 9781496851154 (trade paperback) | ISBN 9781496851161 (epub) | ISBN 9781496851178 (epub) | ISBN 9781496851185 (pdf) | ISBN 9781496851192 (pdf)
Subjects: LCSH: Jazz—1961–1970—History and criticism. | Jazz—1961–1970—Analysis, appreciation. | Jazz—Social aspects—United States—History—20th century | Sound recording industry—United States—History—20th century. | Music and race—United States—History—20th century.
Classification: LCC ML3508 .S65 2024 (print) | LCC ML3508 (ebook) | DDC 781.650973—dc23/eng/20240131
LC record available at https://lccn.loc.gov/2023056338
LC ebook record available at https://lccn.loc.gov/2023056339

British Library Cataloging-in-Publication Data available

CONTENTS

vii   **ACKNOWLEDGMENTS**

3   **INTRODUCTION**
Where's Nancy?

19   **CHAPTER ONE**
Who's Afraid of Eddie Harris?—Why the Story of Jazz in the Sixties Is Almost Always Misrepresented

37   **CHAPTER TWO**
Serenade to a Soul Sister—Nancy Wilson and the Popular Jazz Divas

53   **CHAPTER THREE**
"The Sidewinder"—The Groove That Launched a Thousand Clones

65   **CHAPTER FOUR**
33s and 45s—The Record Labels That Put the Sounds in the Grooves

91   **CHAPTER FIVE**
The "In" Crowd Goes to the Club—Bars, Taverns, Nightclubs, and the Live Scene

113   **CHAPTER SIX**
"When You Go, Let 'Em Know That Daddy-O Told You So"—Black Radio and the DJs That Spread the Sounds

123   **CHAPTER SEVEN**
Pulling out All the Stops—Organ Jazz, the Quintessential Sound of Sixties Jazz

135 **CHAPTER EIGHT**
Mean Greens, Fried Neckbones, and Home Cookin' at the Greasy Spoon—Black Cultural Identity and Popular Jazz

149 **CHAPTER NINE**
"Why Am I Treated So Bad?"..."Compared to What?"—Popular Jazz and Civil Rights

171 **CHAPTER TEN**
How Did We Forget, Why Did We Forget?—The Revising of the Sixties Jazz Narrative

183 **APPENDIX A**
1960s Popular Jazz Listening Guide

187 **NOTES**

203 **BIBLIOGRAPHY**

209 **INDEX**

ACKNOWLEDGMENTS

There are so many people who have been influential in my musical journey. I would like to thank William B. McClelland, Aaron Horne, Kenneth Singleton, Richard Mayne, Jonathan Bellman, Jim White, and Charlotte Mills, all of whom have been influential educators (Bellman's book, *A Short Guide to Writing about Music*, is invaluable!). I would also like to thank Edgar B. Gangware, J. Fred McDonald, Elza Doherty, Zilner T. Randolph, and Kelan Phil Cohran, all of whom have passed on, but all of them have left their mark on my musical thinking.

I would like to acknowledge numerous professional colleagues throughout the years and particularly William T. (Ted) McDaniel, my former colleague at the Ohio State University, who is the model professor/scholar I try to emulate in my work. To my numerous jazz band/concert band/marching band director friends—thanks for all the great work that you do. You are keeping the tradition alive and pointing the way forward for music in the future. And to all of the musicians with whom I have played in bands and orchestras throughout the years—thank you for the honor of making music with you. When it's good, there is nothing better than making music!

To all of my friends (and especially my Green Street family)—thanks for the love and friendship throughout the years. It is cool to have a forum to tell all your friends that you appreciate and love them! To all of my former and present students—thank you for letting me teach you how to make music and for making music with me.

To my family scattered across the country in Mississippi, Tennessee, Texas, Louisiana, California, Missouri, and of course Chicago (and suburbs)—hope you like this! Love you all.

To Moleska (my sister)—all that drum banging throughout the house that you always complained about wasn't just for nothing—I told you that it would pay off! Love you sis, but you know that (so does Alanna, my niece)!

To Juliet (my kids' mom)—you provided years of inspiration, both musically and personally, and I am forever grateful.

To Jasmine and Miles—I have no idea how I got to be so lucky to have you as my kids. You are both great musicians and even better people, and your dad is so proud!! Could not love you more if I tried!!

To Sadie, my mom—there are not words to properly express my love. I am who I am because of you and Dad, and I am aware every day that you set me on this path. You asked me one day when I was seventeen why I spent all my money on albums and drum accessories. Well . . . this!

This book is dedicated to Franklin Roosevelt Smith (1933–2018), my old man. I wish that he was here to read this book and to see that I really was paying attention to all his stories as he was playing the music that is central to this book. To a large degree, this is his book, and he wrote it through me. There were numerous times as I was writing this book that I thought, "Damn it, I wish Frank was here so I could ask him about this!!" Most of those times, I was chuckling as I thought it, but there were a couple when I teared up at the thought. Truth be told, just about everything that I do musically can be traced back to my dad. He taught me about music, and he taught me how to be a good man. I miss him every day.

IN WITH THE IN CROWD

INTRODUCTION

Where's Nancy?

On April 14, 1967, almost exactly one year before his assassination, Dr. Martin Luther King Jr. delivered a speech at Stanford University titled "The Other America." It was a topic that he returned to on many occasions in that last year of his life. In the speech, Dr. King contrasted two Americas—one which was "beautiful . . . and overflowing with the milk of prosperity and the honey of opportunity,"[1] while the other America "has a daily ugliness about it . . . an arena of blasted hopes and shattered dreams."[2] Dr. King mentions that there are many groups in that second America, "but probably the largest group in this other America in proportion to its size in the population is the American Negro."[3] While it might be considered a somewhat drastic representation, Dr. King's observation of two Americas can be seen as a metaphor for many aspects of American life and culture as lived and viewed contrastingly by white and Black Americans. Since the beginnings of this country, there have been many moments where those contrasts have been observed, and quite often that metaphorical view has dominated the way Black American life in the 1960s is historically represented.

In the world of jazz, there have been numerous times when the two Americas have diverged, times where one can see separate approaches and perceptions. In his book *Jazz in Black and White: Race, Culture, and Identity in the Jazz Community*, saxophonist, composer, and author Charley Gerard, a man of European heritage, notes that there was a huge gulf between himself and the Black musicians that he admired. "For them the music called jazz was more than a deeply satisfying aesthetic experience; it was an integral part of the African American identity. No matter how many lifetimes I spent in the jazz community, that music would never define me as it did them."⁴ Gerard is outlining an important point—for African Americans, jazz represents something very personal and significant to the larger Black cultural milieu. Jazz, for Black Americans, is an important cultural touchstone. In a 1989 radio interview, Albert Murray, the revered jazz historian and philosopher, spoke of Duke Ellington's feeling on jazz: "In fact, I remember very well a definition that he gave of jazz. Someone said, 'What is your definition of jazz?' And he said, 'It is Negro American feeling expressed in rhythm and tune.'"⁵

That jazz is an important cultural identifier for Black Americans has been noted by many. It is even woven into the US Congressional Record through H.Con.Res.57, which reads: "Jazz has achieved preeminence throughout the world as an indigenous American music and art form, bringing this country and the world a uniquely American musical synthesis and culture through the African American experience."⁶ For Black Americans, jazz has always been a source of pride—in the early years of the twentieth century, jazz musicians were the first Black artists widely recognized and accepted into white culture. In his book outlining the four-hundred-year history of Harlem, author Jonathan Gill recounts the 1919 return to Harlem of James Reese Europe, the most celebrated Black bandleader of his day. Europe and his band, the Hellfighters, had not only helped to secure victory in Europe during WWI, but simultaneously introduced the continent to jazz. "By the time [James Reese] Europe got back home and moved into an apartment at 67 West 133rd Street, American popular culture had undergone a sea change. Jazz was suddenly the dominant popular music of the United States, and Europe led eighty-five of his men on a wildly successful nationwide tour."⁷ Europe was killed not long after his return to the United States after the war, and his prominence afforded him a rare recognition, "a public funeral at St. Mark's Episcopal Methodist Church in midtown [Manhattan], the first such event for a Negro in the city's history.... Europe had made black music synonymous with American music."⁸

Jazz continued as the preferred popular music for Americans through the Swing Era of the 1930s and into the forties. However, as jazz changed and grew in the fifties and sixties, an interesting dichotomy can be seen with regard to the white critical perception of jazz of that era versus the practical consumption of jazz in Black communities at that time. Nowhere is this more obvious than in assessing the career of Nancy Wilson.

Let's begin with some basic facts—Nancy Wilson (1937–2018) had a performing career that began in the mid-1950s and lasted until her retirement in 2011. In her lifetime, Miss Wilson was the recipient of numerous awards and accolades: she won three Grammy Awards and an Emmy Award for her own television show; she was named a 2004 National Endowment of the Arts Jazz Master (the highest art honor bestowed by the US government); she won an NAACP Image Award—Hall of Fame recognition; and she was inducted into the Big Band and Jazz Hall of Fame. Nancy Wilson also has a star on the Hollywood Walk of Fame, and she is included in the International Civil Rights Walk of Fame at the Martin Luther King Jr. National Historic Site. She recorded over seventy albums, thirty-five of which were on Capitol Records, where in the 1960s, she was second in sales only to the Beatles. Miss Wilson recorded with jazz trios, with big bands, with orchestras, with pop musicians, with soul musicians, and with numerous jazz greats, such as Cannonball Adderley, Ramsey Lewis, George Shearing, Art Farmer, Hank Jones, Benny Golson, Oliver Nelson, and so many others [Nancy Wilson's website is called "Miss Nancy Wilson," and she seemed to prefer that title. She was also nicknamed "Fancy Miss Nancy." In recognition of her preference, she is referred to as "Miss" throughout this book]. Upon her passing, newspapers around the globe ran glowing remembrances. Nancy Wilson remains a revered name in the world of music in general, and to a segment of the American population, she is THE jazz singer of the 1960s.

There is one more fact to add to that list: Nancy Wilson is nonexistent in most of the books on the history of jazz. Not just slighted, not just marginalized—completely nonexistent.

In the book *Jazz: A History of America's Music*, published in 2000 in conjunction with the Ken Burns documentary of the same name, you can find index listings for Alice V. Wilson, Cassandra Wilson, Earl Wilson, Teddy Wilson, even President Woodrow Wilson, but not one entry for Nancy Wilson. There are similar omissions in most other commercial books about jazz as well as most textbooks devoted to jazz in academia. In books devoted to jazz singers, Nancy Wilson does appear, but usually in a passing remark or in an incorrect assessment of her appeal and style. In their 1997 book *Singing Jazz: The Singers and their Styles*, Bruce Crowther and Mike Pinfold mention Miss Wilson briefly four times; the longest passage that mentions her states, "The area loosely termed 'jazz-soul' covers a wide stylistic range. Among singers with close links to jazz are Nancy Wilson, who gained a large international following for her popular repertoire while straining her jazz connections."[9]

What makes this specific example more perplexing is that the last section of the 256-page Crowther/Pinfold book is an A-to-Z directory of important singers of various styles associated with the jazz world who were not featured in more detail in the main body of the book. This section lists singers alphabetically and gives a brief biography, including important solo recordings as well as recordings made in collaboration with others. It would be safe to assume that a singer with the credentials listed above in regard to Nancy Wilson would surely be listed there. But no, Nancy is not included in that section, either. She is listed on the very last page of the book in a space provided for the names of singers about whom the authors speculate that "perhaps at some future date these will form the basis of an expanded listing."[10] Here, as number 114 of only 118 names, you will find Nancy Wilson. (By contrast, Carol Sloane, a very fine singer born one month after Wilson, who started her career around the same time but who has nowhere near the list of recordings or accomplishments, is featured quite prominently throughout the book, as well as in the A to Z directory.)

The lack of acknowledgment of this major talent can be attributed to two factors. The first is the way that history of the 1960s in general, as well as jazz history in the sixties in particular, is retold; the second is the fact that popular jazz, marketed to and consumed by Black Americans in the sixties, is not represented in the historical record.

In regard to the first factor, when one reads general histories of the 1960s, there is much emphasis placed on the turmoil of the times. The sixties were indeed tumultuous—there were civil rights struggles across the country, most of which were spurred on by "Jim Crow" laws in the South and poverty in the North; there were numerous assassinations of high-profile leaders, including President John F. Kennedy, Malcolm X, Medgar Evers, Dr. Martin Luther King Jr., and Senator Robert F. Kennedy; there were riots and uprisings over poverty, inequity, police brutality, and the very unpopular Vietnam War; and the increased use of psychedelic drugs helped to fuel the generation gap between older and younger Americans. There was much upheaval, but in the retelling, these issues come to the forefront, and other equally pertinent events that might not fit into that narrative get shoved to the side.

The sixties in particular seem to be susceptible to grand historical revisionism and hyperbole. Part of this might just be a natural tendency to create a history that contemporary critics and historians wish had happened as opposed to telling the story of a history that actually happened. In his book *The Sixties: Years of Hope, Days of Rage*, activist-turned-sociologist Todd Gitlin observes:

> All times of upheaval begin as surprises and end as clichés . . . No sooner do we enter a year whose final digit is nine than the great machinery of the media is flooding us with phrases to sum up the previous ten years and characterize the next. The phrases are conveniences, of course, handles for unwieldy reality. They are also ideological code, a symbolic repertory for the perplexed. The prefabricated images are wheeled out to enshrine myths.[11]

Jazz history, throughout its century-plus existence, has been and continues to be susceptible to this very same phenomenon. This helps explain why the revolutionary musical stylings of avant-garde jazz musicians are represented very prominently in the story of jazz in the sixties. Music historian Howard Mandel writes that the avant-garde, "synonymous with 'new thing,' 'free jazz,' and 'black music,' typified the experiments . . . of musicians eager to challenge the habits and conventions of jazz past."[12] Mandel, in noting the innovations of saxophonists Albert Ayler, Ornette Coleman, John Coltrane, Miles Davis, and others, observes that "jazz commentators persuaded by sixties politics thought jazz's leaders were heading to the fore, advancing on musical frontiers which subsequent musicians would occupy, settle, perhaps civilize and refine."[13] In his textbook *Jazz: A History*, Frank Tirro writes, "The entire decade of the 1960s was a period of great turmoil throughout the world. . . . Jazz musicians were among the protesters. . . . They felt and expressed the tension of the era in their art, and the new jazz of the decade literally became a mirror of society."[14]

In this version of the sixties and the jazz that comes out of it, Nancy Wilson doesn't fit into the tension and turmoil narrative as well as the narrative, generally speaking, regarding jazz singers. History seems to love the tale of the tragic jazz singer (Billie Holiday, Dinah Washington, Anita O'Day), the singer who rose from poverty (Ella Fitzgerald), or the difficult diva (Dinah Washington, Nina Simone). Ashley Kahn observed in the notes to a Nina Simone box set, "From the outset, Simone was never one to mince words or suffer perceived fools gladly. And where some saw a difficult personality, many found a brutal integrity."[15] It is interesting to witness the resurgence of Simone's profile as a symbol of the sixties—her music is everywhere, it seems, in 2024; numerous commercials, television shows, and film soundtracks are using Nina Simone as a reference point, and there have been at least five documentaries made about her life, as well as a proposed feature film.

Not only did Nancy Wilson not fit into any of those jazz singer narratives, she seemed, from the beginning, to be the opposite of all of them. Barbara Gardner, in a November 1964 edition of *DownBeat* magazine, noted, "When Nancy Wilson first came to prominence, several qualities marked her immediately, and they all spelled 'passing sensation—she'll never last.' . . . To begin with, she shot out of nowhere on a hit record. She was physically attractive; she had both stage presence and personal appeal; she had not a single neurosis on display. She was friendly rather than withdrawn, co-operative rather than temperamental, poised but not blasé, confident but not arrogant."[16] And this seemed to be a consistent description of her personality throughout the years. Tim Owens, the producer of the NPR show *Jazz Profiles*, which was hosted by Miss Wilson for the entire seven years of its run from 1995 to 2002, said this upon her death: "She was the soul of *Jazz Profiles*. With an engaging, listenable, silky-smooth delivery, combined with a manner that evoked credibility and authority because she lived jazz and personally knew many of the artists featured.... I loved working with Nancy."[17] An honest assessment of her total recorded output shows that Nancy Wilson did record some music that does not fit under the banner of "jazz"; some rhythm-and-blues/soul and pop music and even some straight Broadway stylings can be found in her catalogue. She preferred to call herself a "song stylist."

But Black Americans of the 1960s not only thought of her as a jazz singer; for many, she was THE sixties jazz singer. The July 11, 1963, edition of *Jet* described her as "Nancy Wilson, the bright-eyed songstress from Chillicothe, Ohio, whose intimate, throaty style has earned her the title of 'No. 2 Woman Jazz Singer.'"[18] Forty-one years later, in a cover story commemorating her fiftieth year in music, *Jet* noted that Miss Wilson "released her first album on a major label [Capitol] in 1959.... during most of her twenty years with Capitol she was second in sales only to the Beatles, surpassing even Frank Sinatra and Peggy Lee."[19] Established in 1951, *Jet* was, during the fifties, sixties, and seventies, the leading chronicler of Black life, and the magazine could be found in the majority of Black households in America. Stories about Nancy Wilson appeared in *Jet* magazine at least sixteen times, with two of them being cover stories. Will Friedwald has dedicated a large amount of scholarship to jazz and popular music singers and has written numerous biographies and anthologies on the subject. Of Nancy Wilson, Friedwald observed that "what's amazing but not in the least surprising is the respect that Wilson commands in the black community. She has become a role model, and not only to singers, but to the entire community, and as a symbol of class and achievement second only to Lena Horne."[20] To many, Nancy Wilson *was* jazz. But it was not only Black America—in 1975, Bobby Shiffman, the son of Frank Schiffman, the cofounder of the Apollo Theater in Harlem, wrote a letter to Miss Wilson seeking assistance in keeping the legendary theater open after his father's passing, in which he wrote "you are a key show business personality to the Apollo, for you stand alone as the elegant Queen of Beauty and Love."[21]

This brings us to that second factor at play in regard to the lack of acknowledgment of Nancy Wilson's place in the jazz world. Jazz histories, jazz books, jazz movies, etc., rarely acknowledge the vitality of jazz in 1960s Black America. Put another way, those stories of jazz in the sixties fail to recognize that jazz was a very important part of Black life in that decade. The same index listings in the *Jazz* tabletop book released in conjunction with Ken Burns's PBS documentary that neglected to include Nancy Wilson also neglect to include Stanley Turrentine, Wes Montgomery, Eddie Harris, or Brother Jack McDuff, all of whom had high profiles and sold numerous records in Black communities in the sixties. The Ken Burns PBS book does have one listing for Ramsey Lewis and Jimmy Smith—both are remembered in a three-paragraph sidebar in the back of the book that mentions some jazz musicians who had big hits in the sixties until "an arsenal of other electric instruments took over—electric basses, electric keyboards, synthesizers . . . and Jimmy Smith . . . along with most other jazz musicians found themselves drowned out by rock and the new amalgam called fusion."[22]

Many of these books, including that book released in conjunction with the Ken Burns documentary, are, in other areas of jazz history, quite thorough and very attractive, with lots of great photos and extensive discographies. Included among those books is one by the British author and jazz critic John Fordham. Simply titled *Jazz*, the book is beautiful—numerous color photos, great timelines, sections spotlighting the instruments of jazz and the great players, as well as highlights of some of the important albums—and this tabletop jazz overview is one that gets much of the jazz story correct. And the discussion regarding the 1960s (one of the sections of the book is broken down by decades) starts off promisingly; " . . . the historical connection between jazz and dance music had not withered away in the 1950s. It just did not make the newspapers. . . . The modern descendants of boogie-woogie pianists arrived, Hammond organists like Jimmy Smith and Jimmy McGriff, halfway between jazz and rhythm and blues."[23] But instead of detailing the organ jazz movement, the danceable boogaloo grooves that began to dominate, and the great singers who were such a vital part of the sixties' jazz scene, Fordham uses that promising start as a set-up to the "fusion" movement that would grow to fruition in the 1970s. Roy Carr's book, *A Century of Jazz: A Hundred Years of the Greatest Music Ever Made*, actually has a short but relatively thorough chapter on organ jazz as well as a chapter titled "Soul to Soul," dealing with the style that came to be known as "soul jazz." The book quotes Cannonball Adderley: "We were pressured quite heavily by Riverside Records when they discovered there was a word called 'soul.' We became, from an image point of view, soul jazz artists. They kept promoting us that way and I kept deliberately fighting it, to the extent that it became a game."[24]

Carr's book is, comparatively speaking, much more thorough in portraying various styles of jazz in the sixties, but like almost all the histories of jazz, it frames everything in that decade around the stylistic movement that came to be known as the "New Thing." That moniker was attached to the free jazz/avant-garde music centered around saxophonists Ornette Coleman, John Coltrane, Eric Dolphy, and especially Albert Ayler, who has two full-page photographs that are featured at the beginning of the long chapter dedicated to that musical movement. Ayler, the tenor saxophonist who was one of the avant-garde's most visible representatives, is a frequent highlight in histories of sixties' jazz. He has become one of the most recognizable symbols of the

"New Thing," and despite his short life (he died at thirty-four) and modest recorded output, Ayler's life and music is well chronicled in the story of sixties' jazz. Highlighting Ayler's 1965 album *Spiritual Unity*, musician and critic Tom Moon notes, "Even the jazz faithful struggle with Ayler (1936–1970), one of the genre's most polarizing talents. On this wild ride of a record, his best studio work, the multi-instrumentalist scatters bleats and whinnies and lashing gales of sounds in all directions."[25] Ayler is a major focus in writings on sixties' jazz, and as such, his music must be examined in the teaching of jazz. But should that intense focus on free jazz and the avant-garde be at the expense of other jazz styles, especially if those other styles were very much embraced by the consumers at the time? This focus on the "New Thing" and the turbulent world of Black America as the dominant motif in the story of jazz in the sixties is representative of a larger issue seen throughout musicology.

Carl Dahlhaus, the West German music scholar who was considered by many to be the premier musicologist of the postwar era, wrote about "the twin pitfalls of music history: dissolving music into a general social history or stringing together critical/analytical assessments of particular works with no linking historical thread."[26] Dahlhaus warned that "music should not become absorbed into social history, especially one that understands the economic base to be the final, determining factor."[27] That statement seems to recognize that the need (or desire) to combine the narrative of specific times with the history of the music of the times (whenever those "times" happen to be) can be utilized to create a (sometimes) false sense of the reality of specific eras for the purposes of financial gain. And that seems to play out frequently—music can be used to create nostalgia for "better days" (for that, one can look at all of the repackaging of the music of the Beatles for the baby boom generation); music is often packaged to represent a sense of the righteousness of a certain time (think of the numerous compilations of protest anthems from the 1960s that feature Barry McGuire's "Eve of Destruction," Buffalo Springfield's "For What It's Worth," Sam Cooke's "A Change Is Gonna Come," and any number of Bob Dylan tunes); and music can be repackaged and manipulated to give certain eras the glow of significance (see all of the compilations released in the aftermath of Woodstock). This is true across styles and genres, and it is used in the service of promoting histories as well as promoting (and selling) music.

When that need or desire to create a narrative that fits within a general social history eliminates an entire era of music from the historical record, it also eliminates the culture and the people who created and lived that culture. The dominance of the "New Thing" theory of jazz in the sixties has created an entire new history, one that has been taken up entirely by the jazz history worldview. And it has eliminated, in total, the notion of popular jazz of the 1960s, as well as the culture that sustained it.

That historical view of jazz in the sixties belies the reality of the role that jazz played in African American culture of the era. There was a demand for jazz, not just from jazz aficionados, but from the general population—there were numerous jazz records on soul music radio station playlists, and there were evening and weekend slots at those stations dedicated to jazz. There were also many all-jazz radio stations as well as jazz record stores located throughout Black neighborhoods. There were bars, taverns, and nightclubs located throughout cities that featured both local and national jazz musicians, and many jazz players and bands released live albums recorded in those venues. Put another way, jazz was financially viable—there was an infrastructure that allowed jazz to thrive in the sixties because jazz, for many, was a moneymaker. Music journalist Jack Maher wrote in an April 1963 edition of *Billboard*, "Though the number of jazz singles has been at its highest point on the Hot 100 chart, it's not the quantity that's flipping record men, it's the regularity."[28]

Another indication of the viability and popularity of jazz in the sixties is the number of jazz record labels that were established in the late fifties and throughout the sixties. Argo, Cadet, Impulse, CTI, Sue, and Flying Dutchman are just a few of the labels that were established during that era for the purpose of releasing jazz records; they joined the earlier established, highly regarded jazz labels, such as Blue Note, Clef/Verve, Pacific Jazz, and Prestige Records. Atlantic Records, which was established as an independent rhythm and blues label in 1949 and jumped into the jazz fray in the mid-fifties, had become a jazz powerhouse in the sixties, and the major labels, such as Columbia, RCA Victor, Decca, Mercury, and Capitol, all beefed up their jazz rosters in the sixties. Thelonious Monk, Charles Mingus, Miles Davis, and Dave Brubeck were all part of the Columbia Records family, and all of them made money for the label. Columbia heavily promoted jazz and considered its jazz roster an important link in its quest for excellence. As noted in a book on the history of the label, "Anything Monk performed and recorded was superior jazz . . . and so the albums were prize additions to the Columbia catalogue."[29]

In regard to the viability of jazz, it is vital to return to a theme mentioned earlier: jazz as an important component in Black cultural identity. Noted philosopher and social critic Dr. Cornel West makes the point that jazz is a critical mode of Black self-expression: "Jazz is the middle road between invisibility and anger. It is where self-confident creativity resides. Black music is paradigmatic of how black persons have best dealt with their humanity, their complexity—their good and bad, negative and positive aspects, without being excessively preoccupied with whites."[30] That speaks to an understanding of the importance of connecting jazz as a symbol of the Black American experience. Jazz, as a Black signifier, is a natural extension of the roots that come directly from Black oral and musical traditions. Dr. Henry Louis Gates makes connections between Black writers, the oral traditions, and the Bible: "But even in these written works, we 'hear' the printed word striving to imitate the power of the spoken word, just as Zora Neale Hurston's fictions mimic secular Black vernacular forms and Langston Hughes's and Sterling A. Brown's poetry sought to make a formal poetic diction out of jazz and the blues."[31] Later on, Gates notes, "The vocals, the melodies, the repetition, the ring shout—all were as distinct from white American music as Black people were from white people. Musicians and singers used repetition as a basis for improvisation, like a jazz soloist breaking away from the beat. Call-and-response vocals reflected the African influence. Enslaved people sang 'blue notes.'"[32]

The recognition of jazz as a symbolic relationship was one of the important concepts that was central to the ideology of the Black Arts Movement, which began in the wake of the success of the LeRoi Jones's play *Dutchman*, a critical and commercial success written and performed in 1963. Jones, later known as Amiri Baraka, would helm the Black Arts Movement, which drew in other Black playwrights, visual artists, writers (including Maya Angelou and Nikki Giovanni), and musicians. It is Jones/Baraka who popularized the term "New Thing" to promote the avant-garde jazz musicians who seemed to signal the arrival of players who performed in a distinctly different and defiant way.

The Black Arts movement understood the importance of jazz as a quintessential Black form of expression. The preeminent Black music scholar Samuel A. Floyd Jr. noted that "jazz was the music of the Black Arts Movement. The literary figures of the 1960s wrote poetry that celebrated it, others theorized about its value, and most became conversant with the prowess and particular skills of the genre's most notable practitioners."[33] Jazz is, and always has been, an essential marker for all Black Americans—a source of pride even for people who are not jazz listeners or practitioners. The "New Thing" was, indeed, a show of freedom—the freedom that many musicians felt to express themselves in new, provocative, and sometimes radical ways. But New Thing avant-garde jazz was only one part of the larger jazz scene of the sixties, and it is safe to say that it wasn't the style that connected with most jazz listeners of the day.

For most, jazz in the 1960s wasn't just the music of protest; it wasn't just the music that spoke to feelings of rage, anger, and resentment. Jazz could be all of those things, but it was also much more. Jazz was the music of expressions of love, as in Etta Jones's "Don't Go to Strangers"; jazz was the music that expressed gratitude for one's upbringing, as in Horace Silver's "Song for My Father"; jazz was the music that made you want to dress up and head down to the nightclub, as in Ramsey Lewis's "The 'In' Crowd." Jazz could provide the background for get-togethers—Jimmy Smith's "Back at the Chicken Shack" or Brother Jack McDuff's "Rock Candy" provided the perfect musical accompaniment for Bid Whist or poker card parties, and Lee Morgan's "The Sidewinder" was perfect for listening at a backyard barbecue or for dancing The Jerk. Jazz was the music on the radio in the car on the ride from the South Side of Chicago to the West Side, as in Hugh Masekela's "Grazin' in the Grass" or Herbie Mann's "Memphis Underground." Jazz, for many Black Americans, was the musical soundtrack of everyday people.

Those are some of the facts regarding 1960s jazz that seem to have been forgotten. Those are some of the things that have been lost to history.

Part of the problem in regard to the historiography of jazz in the sixties has to do with labeling and description. This could be because the worldwide jazz community has always been concerned with what is and what is not jazz. Does the standard ride cymbal pattern (diiing, ding da, diiing, ding da . . .), the most identifiable rhythmic symbol in jazz, have to be present for something to be called jazz? Does it have to have a triplet subdivision of the basic beat (compound meter)? Does improvisation (soloing over prescribed chord changes) have to be present? Does the blues have to be somewhere within the harmonic or melodic framework (or both)? Does it have to have a walking bass line? These are all questions that jazz musicians, critics, academicians, and fans continue to debate and argue. And many of these issues fuel a lot of the questionable writings regarding sixties jazz.

It is important to remember that over the course of one hundred-plus years, the history of jazz has seen many stylistic variations, advancements, and changes due in large part to changes in technology, economics, and changing tastes and popular trends. It should also be noted that there was resistance every time a new style has come along. Much of the resistance is with musicians themselves, who, like all people, abhor change. But changes always happen, and eventually everyone comes around (or gets left behind). Bebop, which we now think of as standard jazz language, was met in the 1940s with resistance and derision by many, including Louis Armstrong (who could have easily mastered bebop, had he chosen to). Change is necessary in order for music to survive, and jazz is no exception.

Some of the issues concerning the labeling and description of jazz are about what the different stylistic changes are called. In jazz, style and name changes are common and frequent. One forgotten fact is that among Black musicians, jazz was not called jazz in its earliest iteration; they preferred the moniker "hot music." Writing on "genuine jazz," the musician/critic Richard M. Sudhalter commented, "When it had a name at all, its practitioners and acolytes called it 'hot music' or just plain 'hot.'... If the public drew any distinction at all between 'jazz' and 'hot,' it was casual, and usually racial based."[34] In fact, many forms of music come to be known by a specific term after the fact. To wit, "rhythm and blues," "doo-wop," "cool jazz," "hard bop," and many other commonly accepted style names came to be conferred after the style was already underway or had passed onto the next "thing." But the outlier in this regard seems to be the moniker applied to jazz in the sixties: "soul jazz."

As one looks at the larger world of nonclassical music, one can see that every decade brings about changes that weren't apparent when that decade began. It is only in looking back that one can see the big shifts in style, sound, lyrical content, etc. Music always changes, and despite early resistance, everyone eventually accepts change. But popular jazz in the 1960s seems to, even fifty to sixty years after the fact, face resistance to being accepted as "real jazz." There seems to be a "soul jazz" versus "real jazz" standoff among critics and writers on the music of that decade. John Fordham's *Jazz* book breaks down the chapters on 1960 classic jazz recordings as follows: "mainstream" (recordings by Duke Ellington, Oscar Peterson, Benny Carter, Erroll Garner, and others); "postwar vocals" (Ella Fitzgerald, Anita O'Day, Lambert, Hendricks & Ross, Sheila Jordan, etc.); "free jazz" (Albert Ayler, Ornette Coleman, John Coltrane, George Russell, etc.); "post-bop big bands" (Stan Kenton, Charles Mingus, Don Ellis, Gil Evans, etc.); "modal jazz" (Miles Davis, Bill Evans, McCoy Tyner, Pharoah Sanders, etc.); and "early funk." In the early funk we find the albums of Lee Morgan, Jimmy Smith, Cannonball Adderley, Donald Byrd, and Grant Green—the very music that fits into the category of sixties popular jazz as it is defined in this book. In his book on Black popular music and Black culture, Dr. Mark Anthony Neal has this to say about Lee Morgan, Cannonball Adderley, Grant Green, and others: "These artists would infuse jazz with the syncopated rhythms often associated with James Brown and introduce a new sub-genre of jazz, with an emphasis on catching the attention of a younger, politically motivated, culturally assured audiences [sic] raised on the music and production techniques of the Motown and Stax recording companies."[35] Scott Deveaux and Gary Giddings describe some of the players recording for Blue Note Records in the sixties this way: "The leaders of soul jazz attempted to cut out the middle man: rather than make records that generated pop versions, they made three-minute singles immediately suitable for pop radio."[36]

There seems to be a clear need to delineate the popular jazz of the sixties with big record sales from jazz that sounded like a continuation of styles from the past, such as bebop, cool, and hard bop. There is nothing wrong with funk whatsoever, but why call it "early funk," and why "soul jazz"? This popular sixties jazz seems to be put into the categories of "soul jazz" and "early funk" simply because the music was popular, danceable in many cases, and enjoyed radio airplay, and for many, that seems to be a mark of shame. For some, jazz that connects with a large number of people loses that veneer of respectability that many critics and writers seem to require for "authentic jazz." But then the question becomes this: if this was the predominant style of jazz performed during the era, if it was the preferred style of jazz for listeners at the time, if musicians made a good living selling albums and getting people out to hear the music, and if labels were signing acts to replicate successes based on record sales, wasn't that jazz? Shouldn't that music just be referred to as the sixties iteration of jazz? Wasn't it just the natural reflection of the progression of jazz in the 1960s?

There is another challenge to the moniker "soul jazz"—that name tends to lump all jazz with that designation into one kind of style. But consider the 1964 album *The Sidewinder*. Lee Morgan and his cohorts on the album run through a myriad of styles in forty minutes, from the funky, straight-eighths groove of the title cut to the Latinesque "Totem Pole" to two different tunes with two very different approaches to 3/4 time, "Gary's Notebook" and "Boy, What a Night." The last track on the album, "Hocus Pocus," would have fit right in on a Charlie Parker/Miles Davis bebop session in the early fifties. Many jazz musicians of the sixties continued in the bebop tradition, like saxophonists Johnny Griffin and Sonny Stitt, while others, like Art Blakey's Jazz Messengers, continued the hard bop style that became a mainstay in the fifties. And many other musicians in the sixties would, like John Coltrane, mix stylistic variants of jazz at will—Coltrane's *A Love Supreme* is of a very different mood than *John Coltrane and Johnny Hartman* despite only being separated by a year and a half. As he did throughout his career, in the sixties Miles Davis did whatever he wanted, whenever he felt like it! And lest we forget, many of the players focused on the blues: Jimmy Smith, Jack McDuff, Shirley Scott, and all the other masters of the Hammond B3 organ gave us endless variations on the blues. Have we forgotten the 1960s big bands? Oliver Nelson, Thad Jones, and Quincy Jones are just some of the names that one would miss.

In regard to community, culture, and lore, jazz is a very interesting style of music. There are people who have become beloved, larger-than-life figures who are more like legends than real people; there are stories that are etched in the cultural landscape (Fats Waller noting the presence of God as piano virtuoso Art Tatum walks into a club; Billie Holliday singing the anti-lynching anthem "Strange Fruit" at Café Society; Louis Armstrong's rebuke of President Eisenhower over the harassment of the "Little Rock Nine" in 1957); concerts that have become landmarks (Benny Goodman's Spirituals to Swing Carnegie Hall concerts in the late thirties; Ellington at the Newport Jazz Festival in 1956;

Mingus's disastrous Town Hall concert in 1962), and recordings that are must-haves for any serious fan (or want-to-be fan). And in regard to community, lore, and jazz recordings, no year looms larger in the jazz world than 1959.

Miles Davis's *Kind of Blue*; the Dave Brubeck Quartet's *Time Out*; Charles Mingus's *Mingus Ah Um*; John Coltrane's *Giant Steps*; Ella Fitzgerald's *Ella in Berlin*; Ornette Coleman's *The Shape of Jazz to Come*—all of these revered classic albums and so many others were released in that year, lending credence to the often-expressed idea that 1959 was the greatest year in recorded jazz. The year 2019 saw the creation of a blog called *The 1959 Project* with a subtitle that reads, "A snapshot of jazz sixty years ago, every day."[37] The blog exists to give the reader a sense of "how life might have looked among the bohemians in the Village, or walking along 125th Street next to Ralph Ellison and Langston Hughes. Where Thelonious Monk and Sonny Rollins and Dinah Washington went [*after*]the gig, and what music was playing in that now long-gone club."[38] Writer and critic Nate Chinen noted on an NPR segment that "1959 began with a very special issue of *Esquire* magazine called 'The Golden Age of Jazz,' a full issue devoted to this idea.... The year opens with this bold proclamation, and I think it was in some ways a self-fulfilling prophecy."[39]

The year 1959, as an idea of perfection in jazz, plays an important role in the story of jazz in the 1960s partly because it is the last year of a decade, leaving critics to look at it as a clean break with the whole decade (per the earlier-referenced Todd Gitlin quote) and partly because for some, the fascination with the 1959 jazz classics makes everything released after that year feel less-than-perfect (rock music has a similar fascination with the year 1967 because of the Beatles' *Sgt. Pepper's Lonely Hearts Club Band*, the Jimi Hendrix Experience's *Are You Experienced*, the Doors' self-titled debut album, Aretha Franklin's triumphant breakthrough, *I Never Loved a Man*, etc.). Considering 1959 jazz's greatest year may have much to do with the need to not only find a radical way to define jazz moving forward (which perfectly aligns with Ornette Coleman's *The Shape of Jazz to Come*, an album that totally shook up the jazz community in 1959), but perhaps also the need to totally reject music that might be deemed safe or non-earth-shattering.

It may be as simple as this: it's harder to write about certain subjects or topics when there isn't a lot of conflict to report on, especially when you have other topics where radical shifts are happening at the same time. That could explain the popular jazz/"New Thing" jazz imbalance. Or it could be that it is easy to assume that if the masses like it, it mustn't be worth remembering. Maybe Nancy Wilson made it look and sound so effortless and easy that critics were bored when they looked back. But Nancy Wilson wasn't boring—far from it! She was dynamic, she had impeccable pitch and phrasing, she could change and adapt her style to the song, and she could swing like mad. If there is any doubt about that last point, all one has to do is listen to her take on Duke Ellington's "I'm Beginning to See the Light" on the 1965 album *The Nancy Wilson Show!* That exclamation mark is actually in the title of the album, but it is well-deserved—Miss Wilson did, indeed, put on a show. It is well past time for a reassessment of Nancy Wilson's place in the world of jazz singers.

The original title of this book was *The Hustler, the Country Preacher, and the Watermelon Man: Popular Jazz in 1960s Black America*. The title was derived from three recordings: "The Hustler," a track from Stanley Turrentine's 1965 album *Hustlin'*; "Country Preacher" from the 1969 Cannonball Adderley Quintet album of the same name; and "Watermelon Man," Herbie Hancock's smash hit song from his first solo album, 1962's *Takin' Off*. Each of those tunes is an important stylistic touchstone for 1960s popular jazz. "The Hustler" represents sixties jazz that is firmly rooted in tradition; it is a mid-tempo, twelve-bar blues in C, which allows Turrentine and the rest of the ensemble on the record to blow—an easy tune to just sit back and snap on two and four (very reminiscent of John Coltrane's classic "Mr. P.C."). "Country Preacher," an ode to the Reverend Jesse Jackson and recorded at one of his weekly Operation Breadbasket meetings in Chicago, is popular jazz in 1969 as it is moving forward, signaled by the use of electric piano and electric bass as well as Cannonball's soprano saxophone, played in a very soulful style that paves the way for players like Grover Washington Jr. and Gary Bartz in the 1970s.

In many ways, the course for jazz in the 1960s was charted by "Watermelon Man," Herbie Hancock's 1962 hit record, because it proved, without a doubt, that jazz was alive and kicking and adapting to the world that was unfolding. Placing jazz within the context of the straight-eighths groove that was in vogue in the soul music world while remaining firmly rooted in the world of jazz harmonies, improvisation, phrasing, and ensemble interaction was a stroke of genius that, looking back in hindsight, probably saved a musical genre that could have become staid, stale, and unwanted by listeners of the time. Incorporating "Watermelon Man" into the title seemed to be a good way to reflect its importance to the topic at hand.

But just as this book was completed, Ramsey Lewis passed away, and it seemed obvious that his hit recording "The 'In' Crowd" (which was made possible by the path laid by "Watermelon Man") was the perfect tune to use to represent popular jazz in the 1960s. Without a doubt, Lewis's 1965 recording was the biggest jazz breakthrough of all. It is because of this and in memory of Mr. Lewis and his many years of popularity with Black audiences that this book is now titled *In with the In Crowd: Popular Jazz in 1960s Black America*.

Herbie Hancock's ongoing contributions, as well as the wonderful music left behind by Ramsey Lewis, Stanley Turrentine, Cannonball Adderley, and Miss Nancy Wilson, continue to inspire young musicians in the twenty-first century just as they did a certain young musician starting out in the 1960s. That musician, who wrote this book and is now in his sixties, is still in awe!

CHAPTER ONE

Who's Afraid of Eddie Harris?

Why the Story of Jazz in the Sixties Is Almost Always Misrepresented

Very few jazz musicians sell one million copies of a recording; even fewer sell one million copies of a jazz recording on a small, independent record label. Add to that the fact that it is virtually impossible to sell many copies of your first album in any genre, but especially in jazz. And the odds of any of those things becoming a reality shrink that much more if you are a twenty-seven-year-old Black man. But somehow, through sheer luck, a grand alignment of the stars, a quirk of fate, or perhaps all three, those things did happen, and they happened for Eddie Harris.

In 1961, Eddie Harris (1934–1996) released his debut album titled *Exodus to Jazz*. Harris was a multi-instrumentalist—as a small child, he learned to play piano by ear, and he later learned to read music. While in high school, under the tutelage of the legendary Chicago bandmaster Captain Walter Dyett, Harris added clarinet, vibraphone, and saxophone to his arsenal of instruments. After graduating, Harris's musical activities accelerated. According to the official Eddie Harris website,

> Eddie continued his musical studies at Illinois University and Roosevelt University. Eventually, he was drafted into the Army and placed in the area of electronics. He later went airborne and quickly grew disgusted with the realities of war. By this time, Eddie excelled at piano, saxophone, vibraphone, clarinet, trumpet, trombone, and bassoon and decided to audition for the Army band.... He was

recommended to play saxophone with the Seventh Army Symphony Orchestra in Germany. The symphony was unable to take on additional band members at that time, so Eddie was placed in the Army band in Fulda, Germany, for eight months. After that, Eddie joined the Seventh Army Symphony Orchestra and became a part of the jazz band that was formed from members of the orchestra. The jazz band toured France and Germany and brought Eddie international notoriety. During this period, Eddie also took classical saxophone lessons at the Paris Conservatory of Music.[1]

After his time in Europe, Harris went first to New York City and then returned back to Chicago, where he attracted the attention of Vee-Jay[2] Records, a Black-owned company based in the city, which released *Exodus to Jazz*. To everyone's surprise (including Harris's), the song "Exodus" (an adaptation of the main title song from the movie of the same name composed by Ernest Gold) became a huge hit, selling two million copies and landing on the *Billboard Magazine* Hot 100 charts at number thirty-six. But the fact that this happened to an album that was released on Vee-Jay Records made perfect sense. Author Robert Pruter notes that "the folks who ran the label...did not think of Vee Jay as a regional r&b [sic] company but as a company competitive in the same popular markets as the majors."[3]

Vee-Jay was, before the success of Motown in the sixties, the largest and most successful Black-owned record company in America. The label was founded in Gary, Indiana, in a record shop owned by Vivian Carter and Jimmy Bracken (hence the name Vee-Jay). Shortly after the label's launch in 1953, Carter and Bracken got married, then they set up shop in Chicago, which made sense because Chicago had a vast distribution network and Gary was close enough to Chicago to be considered a suburb. Vee-Jay was wildly successful right out of the gate—the first group that was signed to the label, The Spaniels, went to the top ten of the national rhythm and blues chart in 1954. Vee-Jay soon began releasing hit after hit—they recorded R&B, blues, gospel, and soon crossed over into the pop charts with Frankie Valli and the Four Seasons and other white acts. Author and historian Nelson George notes that "in the period before Motown blew its competitors out of the water, Vee-Jay was one of the most ambitious black labels operating; in terms of marketing white pop artists, it was the most effective ever."[4]

Carter and Bracken wisely hired people like Chris Carter (Vivian's brother) and Ewart Abner to learn the ins and outs of music business and production. Abner would later become president of Motown Records in the 1970s. During his time at Vee-Jay, he was the driving force behind the label's move to record and market jazz. Pruter writes that in 1959, "he established the company's jazz line with such artists as Wynton Kelly, Wayne Shorter, Eddie Harris, and Lee Morgan.... Put in as A&R [artists and repertoire] head of the jazz department was Sid McCoy, who by the mid-1950s had become one of [Chicago's] premier jazz deejays."[5] Wayne Shorter's signing with Vee-Jay was particularly noteworthy: it was the beginning of one of the most consequential musical careers in the history of jazz. Shorter biographer Michelle Mercer notes that "Wayne played as a sideman on Wynton Kelly's *Kelly Great* recording for Vee-Jay just after he joined [Art Blakey and] the Jazz Messengers, on August 12.... Wayne was signed to Vee-Jay himself after his Messengers enlistment and recorded his first record for the label on November 9 and 10 [1959]."[6] In 1963, Vee-Jay made history by releasing the first US recordings in 1963 by the Beatles, but by 1966, Vee-Jay Records filed for bankruptcy. The story of the label's thirteen-year rise and fall is fascinating, but in 1961, they were hot.

Exodus to Jazz, from a stylistic perspective, is very much an album of its time and fits neatly into the modal style similar to the celebrated Miles Davis album *Kind of Blue*, which was released two years earlier in 1959. The album established Harris as a tenor sax player with a unique but very smooth and personable sound, which would serve him well for the next thirty-six years. Harris's reputation as a fine composer is established on the album as well—four of the eight tunes are Harris originals, with two more composed by the pianist on the date, Chicago legend Willie Pickens. But it was the lead track, "Exodus," that took off—the song was everywhere on the radio at the time, and after that, Harris's career took off as well. After a few more albums for Vee-Jay, Harris recorded for Columbia, then he moved to Atlantic Records in 1965, where he would record prolifically for more than ten years. A number of his tunes have become modern standards: "Listen Here," "Cold Duck Time," "Freedom Jazz Dance" (which is one of the highlights of Miles Davis's 1965 album *Miles Smiles*), and many others. *Swiss Movement*, his 1969 album with Les McCann, became a million-seller as well. "Exodus," his first hit, lives on; it continues to be included on terrestrial, satellite, and internet jazz radio playlists.

That kind of success and popularity would seem to be a cause for celebration and commemoration. After the Swing Era, rare is the time that jazz has made inroads onto the pop charts. Sixty years after "Exodus" hit the charts, it is even more unusual for a jazz record to make a dent in the *Billboard* charts. But within the world of jazz, Harris's tremendous debut showing is all but forgotten—"Exodus" (as well as Eddie Harris) is almost universally ignored in jazz history texts and surveys of jazz in the 1960s.

When jazz in the sixties is discussed in textbooks, magazine articles, peer-reviewed journals, and other academic writings, as well as commercial tabletop tomes, emphasis is placed on the styles and movements that show the music in a progressive, forward-moving way. Free jazz and avant-garde styles prevail, and the fusing of jazz and rock in the latter part of the decade is presented as the style that will carry jazz into the future. The ways that jazz musicians interacted with the civil rights movement and Black Nationalism, both musically and on a personal basis, are among the main themes of writings on jazz in the 1960s. But jazz, as a popular style of music, consumed and utilized in Black communities across the country for purposes that address the social nature of music (a function that has been of paramount importance for all music types at one time or another), is almost never addressed when surveying the music of the sixties. A look at index entries in numerous textbooks and other histories of jazz reveals almost no listings for Eddie Harris (except those that occasionally make the statement that he was influenced by John Coltrane), whereas index listings for the highly regarded but little-known avant-garde tenor saxophonist Albert Ayler are numerous. This is not to compare the worth or importance of Ayler and Harris—both are very fine musicians—but to note that Harris, who recorded prolifically through the nineties (he died in 1996) sold very well and was very popular in the sixties and seventies, while Ayler (who died at thirty-four years old in 1970) was considered by most listeners in the sixties to be a very obscure, very uncompromising musician, and to a large degree that is Albert Ayler's popular legacy today. Ironically, Albert Ayler's story is enshrined in the historical record of jazz in the sixties and Eddie Harris almost never rates a mention. The concept of jazz as popular music in the sixties is nowhere to be found in the historical discourse.

Jazz in the 1960s did what jazz had, since its inception, always done: it changed and grew to reflect the times. And throughout its history, most of the changes in jazz reflected changes in society—from a technological standpoint, from the standpoint of popular tastes and trends, and from the standpoint of economic concerns. Most of the musicians who were involved in the jazz scene of the early sixties weren't necessarily trying to change jazz; they were just doing what musicians always do, adapting to the times. Recalling that Chicago was at the forefront of jazz activity, Ramsey Lewis has this to say: "It was during the early sixties that musicians such as Eddie Harris, Ahmad Jamal, and a group called the Ramsey Lewis Trio were unknowingly setting the stage for things to come.... They also were not hesitant to use ideas not traditionally associated with jazz."[7]

That there was plenty of new and exciting activity happening at the time was obvious but scarcely recalled. The textbook *Jazz: A History* by Frank Tirro has no index listings for Ramsey Lewis, Eddie Harris, or Ahmad Jamal, who had a big breakthrough in 1958 with the success of his jazz trio version of "Poinciana." In the section of the book devoted to the 1960s, Tirro highlights Ornette Coleman, John Coltrane, Charles Mingus, and Miles Davis (who is also featured prominently in the section on the fifties). There is a section dedicated to the "new groups," but it is mainly focused on composer-theorist George Russell and Chicago's AACM, who, as their website notes, are a "collective of dynamic and visionary artists formed . . . to meet their emergent needs to expose and showcase their original compositions and to create an outlet for the development and performance of their music."[8] Curiously, there is a small paragraph dedicated to musicians who played with Miles Davis in the sixties that ends with this observation: "Modern jazz of the sixties and seventies was exciting and intellectual, and the younger musicians, who were not schooled in the swing era or postwar bebop combos, were beginning to take their place as artistic leaders."[9] What makes that observation curious is that it fails to detail the music that those younger musicians were making, which happened to be some of the most important and best-selling music of the era.

In the book *Jazz: A History of America's Music*, published in conjunction with the ten-part PBS documentary *Jazz* released in 2000, Geoffrey C. Ward and Ken Burns address jazz as popular music in the 1960s not by referring to Eddie Harris, or Ahmad Jamal, or Ramsey Lewis, but by referring to Louis Armstrong, the legendary musician who first made his mark in the early 1920s. In 1964, Armstrong had a surprise hit with "Hello Dolly," a song from the Broadway musical of the same name, and Ward and Burns wrote that "two months after the Beatles landed, 'Hello Dolly' became the number one song in America. . . . It was a sweet victory, but short-lived. Within a few weeks, rock had recaptured the airwaves."[10] What makes this a curious choice to point out as an example of popular jazz in the sixties is that the recording, while featuring perhaps the single most important person in the history of jazz, is not really a jazz record. Armstrong's performance of "Hello Dolly" is best described as an example of sixties easy-listening pop music with slight Dixieland overtones. It is also curious because in the same year that Armstrong's "Hello Dolly" was released, Lee Morgan's "The Sidewinder" had made inroads onto the *Billboard* chart, as did Stan Getz's "The Girl from Ipanema" and, one year later, Ramsey Lewis would have a Top Five jazz hit with "The 'In' Crowd" (all three of those tunes are discussed in detail elsewhere in this book).

In the jazz world, there is a stigma regarding jazz and popularity. One of the invectives used against jazz musicians who make hit records is "sellout." Stanley Crouch, the celebrated (and sometimes despised) jazz writer/social critic/intellectual, was constantly on the prowl against sellouts, no matter how big or small, and one of his frequent targets was Miles Davis. A chapter of Crouch's book *The All-American Skin Game, or, the Decoy of Race* is devoted to Miles Davis; in it, he writes, "Davis made much fine music for the first half of his life . . . but he has fallen from grace—and been celebrated for it. As usual, that fall from grace has been a form of success.... Davis turned butt to the beautiful in order to genuflect before the commercial."[11] There is reluctance to even recognize jazz albums with big record sales as jazz albums. Jazz journalist Gene Seymour, in an essay about hard bop, makes a reference to Wes Montgomery's "1966 album *Tequila* (Verve), one of the heavily orchestrated albums produced late in the guitarist's life that have drawn fire from critics and historians for being too commercial. In spite (or because?) of the pop luster of such covers as 'Goin' Out of My Head,' 'California Dreamin',' or 'A Day in the Life,' Montgomery ... remains the most influential guitarist in jazz after Charlie Christian."[12]

One could infer that the jazz world is afraid to acknowledge the popularity of jazz in the sixties because it would interfere with the effort to equate jazz with European classical music. As noted by jazz critic Richard B. Woodward in 2001, "For two decades now, the high-minded phrase 'Jazz is America's Classical Music' has served as a kind of marketing jingle for the music during the culture wars. As popularized by Billy Taylor, Grover Sales, and others, the slogan became a patriotic rallying cry in the eighties . . . by those seeking to bring intellectual respect and institutional focus to jazz."[13] Grover Sales, who was a writer and jazz history lecturer at Stanford, San Francisco State, and other universities, even wrote a book titled *Jazz: America's Classical Music*, in which he makes a valiant attempt to both separate jazz from and equate jazz with European classical music. In one section, Sales talks about the discipline of listening to jazz: "The finest jazz is not the mindless distraction of elevator or supermarket musak [sic]. Charlie Parker, Duke Ellington, and John Coltrane demand the same single-minded concentration and repeated hearings as Beethoven quartets and Bach's *Goldberg Variations*."[14]

This idea of elevating jazz to the level of European classical music for the purpose of celebrating "America's Classical Music" has deep roots in this country. The expansionist activities that began with the Louisiana Purchase in 1803 necessitated an inward look for an identity or character that binds and unites us as Americans. In the post-Civil War era, the need to identify and define an American type of music aligned with the nationalism sweeping the country. Interestingly, it was a highly regarded musical outsider who, at the time, identified a truly unique American musical style. Czech composer Antonín Dvořák was invited to America in 1892 to become the director of the National Conservatory of Music in New York. The NCM was founded by Jeanette Thurber, a wealthy patron of the arts, who was interested in establishing the Conservatory in order to cultivate an American classical music culture. At her behest, Dvořák set about in his attempt to identify a uniquely American musical spirit that might also have led to the creation of an American school of composition.

Distinguished American music historian Richard Crawford notes that Dvořák "did become a strong public advocate for musical nationalism in America . . . [Dvořák] was quoted in the *New York Herald* as saying that after eight months in America, he was 'now satisfied . . . that the future music of this country must be founded upon what are called negro melodies. . . . There is nothing in the whole range of composition that cannot be supplied with themes from this source.'"[15] This was an important moment because it is the first time that the music of African Americans was noted for its artistic qualities. Dvořák also encouraged more Black Americans to become conservatory-trained musicians; among his students was Will Marion Cook, a Black violinist and composer, who became, in addition to many other accomplishments, Duke Ellington's mentor in composition. Around the same time of Dvořák's arrival in America, the World's Columbian Exposition (aka the World's Fair) was taking place in Chicago. Among the many things that people from all over the world experienced for the first time at that fair was music created by Black Americans. Writing about the World's Fair of 1893, ragtime scholar Terry Waldo states, "This massive technological-artistic-commercial display demonstrated for the first time what the 'New America' was all about. . . . And for the first time, many of the Negroes who would shape a nationalistic movement toward a legitimacy of black folk music were collected in one location . . . and somewhere among all the activities of the fair wandered a young Scott Joplin, who would establish his prominence in the ragtime field."[16]

Ragtime music would soon capture the imagination of people around the world, including many of Europe's great composers. Igor Stravinsky, in his 1918 work *L'Histoire du soldat* (*A Soldier's Tale*), included a section in part two titled "Ragtime." After finishing *Soldat*, Stravinsky wrote of another piece that he began to work on—

> Its dimensions are modest, but it is indicative of the passion I felt at the time for jazz, which burst into life so suddenly when the war ended. At my request, a whole new pile of this music was sent to me, enchanting me by its truly popular appeal, its freshness, and the novel rhythm which so distinctly revealed its Negro origin. These impressions suggested the idea of creating a composite portrait of this new dance music. . . . So I composed my *Ragtime* for eleven instruments.[17]

Dmitri Shostakovich was another Russian composer who was inspired by jazz—he composed two different *Jazz Suites*; pioneering French impressionist Claude Debussy, too, was moved by jazz—*Golliwog's Cakewalk*, a combination rag/cakewalk, is one of his most well-known works—and another French composer, Darius Milhaud, was captivated by jazz on a trip to Harlem. His 1923 ballet suite, *La Création du monde*, uses jazz idioms throughout.

During World War I, James Reese Europe, the most prominent black musician in America at the time (whose story is highlighted in the introduction), earned the respect of Europeans both as a soldier and a musician—he and his band would set off the jazz craze in Europe by performing, among other works, W. C. Handy's *Memphis Blues* and *St. Louis Blues*.

These activities, as well as the success of the Original Dixieland Jazz Band, the white combo whose recording of *Livery Stable Blues* set off the jazz craze here in America, caused many people in this country to panic. Richard Crawford notes that "in the years after World War I, jazz was seen in some circles as a symptom of civilization's decline. Many community leaders had opposed ragtime, and now they made jazz a target, though with no agreement about whether the music should be suppressed or just ignored."[18] This kind of attack on jazz led to a defensiveness and a need to seek legitimacy that continued into the twenty-first century.

The need to elevate jazz to the level of classical music in the early twentieth century was also an important way to fend off the naysayers in the "legitimate" music world, who, for many reasons (some obvious and some more subtle), feared that jazz would corrupt the many young musicians who were now attempting to learn to play it as well as anyone attempting to listen to it. The August 1924 edition of *Etude* (an early twentieth-century magazine aimed at piano and vocal teachers as well as music enthusiasts at all levels) has become legendary in the jazz world. The cover of the magazine boldly announces what a large portion of this edition is devoted to—"The Jazz Problem: Opinions of Prominent Men and Musicians." A number of composers and musicians gave opinions on the problem of "modern jazz" that has "invaded countless millions of homes in all parts of the world"[19] As one can imagine, there were some opinions that were, to put it mildly, not on board with this music: "If jazz originated in the dance rhythms of the negro, it was at least interesting as the self-expression of a primitive race. When jazz was adopted by the 'highly civilized' white race, it tended to degenerate it towards primitivity."[20] This was the reply by Frank Damrosch, director of the Institute of Musical Arts. There were a few, like conductor Leopold Stokowski, who expressed a fondness for the new form, and there were some, like American march king John Philip Sousa, who accepted the fact that jazz was here to stay. Sousa's views on jazz can, at best, be termed patronizing; he was quoted in the *Etude* article as saying, "Jazz, like the poor, are ever with us,"[21] adding a bit later, "There is no reason, with its exhilarating rhythm, its melodic ingenuities, why it should not become one of the accepted forms of composition."[22]

Etude Magazine, "The Jazz Problem," August 1924. *Etude Magazine* graphic accessed from https://www.schubertiademusic.com/items/details/7571.

Make no mistake, Sousa was no fan of ragtime or jazz, but he was a smart showman. He realized that there was a hunger for jazz among the masses, so despite his distaste, he would mix it in his concerts; however, he was convinced that his performances elevated the music to a different status. "We play common street melody with just as much care as if it were the best thing ever put on our program . . . I have washed its face, put a clean dress on it, put a frill around its neck, pretty stockings. . . . It is now an attractive thing, entirely different from the frowzly-headed thing of the gutter."[23]

That patronizing attitude toward jazz was also evident in Paul Whiteman, the man known in the 1920s as the "King of Jazz." Whiteman had the most popular jazz orchestra in the twenties, and he had more than a few admirers in the Black press and among the general Black population, including both Louis Armstrong and Duke Ellington. Whiteman understood exactly where the music that he became known for originated, and he would say so when asked. But Whiteman was a skillful self-promoter, and he understood the value of associating his music with jazz. Author Edward Jablonski wrote that Whiteman was aware of the value of capitalizing on the music that was capturing the imagination of Americans who weren't discriminating in regard to stylistic differences: "As the self-proclaimed 'King of Jazz,' Whiteman applied the term warily but loosely. He was not referring to jazz at all. . . . The band leader referred to popular song and dance music and the manner in which it was performed by his virtuoso orchestra."[24] It has been written that Whiteman wanted to integrate his band, but of course the conventions and laws of the twenties and thirties would not allow that.

In 1924, Whiteman was at his peak, both nationally and internationally. After a 1923 appearance before the king of England, Whiteman set about putting together a grand experiment that aligned with the continuing effort and desire to define an American musical character. Jablonski's biography of George Gershwin sets up Whiteman's role in the events that led to the first performance of *Rhapsody in Blue*. "'I intend,' he stated, 'to sketch, musically, from the beginning of American history, the development of our emotional resources which have led us to the characteristic American music of today'"[25] In reality, this was, once again, an example of Whiteman's self-promotional instincts kicking in. The so-called *Experiment in Modern Music* was, according to Jablonski, "in fact a promotional event to further Whiteman's fortunes, then at a monetary peak."[26] But Whiteman's promotion of his *Experiment in Modern Music*, which included his orchestra's 1924 debut performance of Gershwin's *Rhapsody in Blue*, had the ring of snobbery bordering on racism: "Mr. Whiteman intends to point out, with the assistance of his orchestra and associates, the tremendous strides which have been made in popular music from the day of the discordant Jazz, which sprang into existence about ten years ago from nowhere in particular, to the really melodious music of today, which—for no good reason—is still called Jazz."[27]

This consistent questioning of the worth and usefulness of jazz by the American musical elite as well as the moral panics that accompanied the music's popularity in "the Jazz Age" led to an inescapable and long-lasting feeling of defensiveness in the world of jazz. Unsurprisingly, that jazz world has developed an inferiority complex, magnified through the years by arguments regarding whether jazz belongs in academia or in the halls of American public schools (one of the reasons that, in many public schools, jazz band is still called "stage band" is the stigma that many school administrators associated with the word "jazz"). The desire that all Americans recognize jazz as "America's classical music" is a well-meaning goal that is technically correct in many ways. But that slogan has had the unintended effect of removing jazz from the realm of popular music much to the detriment of the music. And it has left no room for jazz musicians who make recordings that are popular with "the folks." "High art" is not that which is danced to or listened to on popular radio stations or played in nightclubs. That is the realm of "pop art" or, worse still, "low art." If Eddie Harris sells one million copies of the album *Exodus to Jazz*, is it art? Or put another way, if jazz is America's classical music, can an album that sells one million copies be called jazz?

One could also infer that because of the monumental changes that were a part of life in the 1960s the jazz world is embarrassed to acknowledge the success of *Exodus* and the numerous other popular jazz recordings that found their way to the upper reaches of the Billboard 100 charts (which charted the bestselling songs for each week throughout the year) and Top 40 radio (the top 40 songs on that Billboard chart, played in an endless rotation on radio stations to maximize listeners and, hopefully, advertising dollars). It seems that when it comes to jazz produced in the 1960s, the more popular the music became, the more the jazz guardians denied its worth. Mark Gridley notes in his textbook *Jazz Styles* that in the sixties "the highest record sales went to the organ-guitar-drums and piano-bass-drums groups of Jimmy Smith and Ramsey Lewis, respectively. These are players who musicians and critics do not ordinarily consider to be within the main stream of jazz developments, though their music helps define funky jazz, and they fit the hard bop designation more closely than they fit any other."[28] British author and critic John Fordham makes a similar observation: "Other musicians closer to pop music have made creative use of hard bop styles—such as the orchestras of Ray Charles, the organists Jimmy Smith and Richard 'Groove' Holmes, and pianists Ramsey Lewis and Les McCann."[29]

But with all those records being sold as well as all of the folks going out to hear live jazz, one has to ask why does the jazz world refuse to acknowledge all this success? Who's afraid of Eddie Harris?

The New Sounds of the 1960s

The sense that jazz should be much more than popular and successful took on added significance during the sixties. This was the era of Black pride, Black Power, and the artistic movements that were an outgrowth of the civil rights challenges that began in earnest with Rosa Parks and the Montgomery Bus Boycott in 1955. The sociological and political changes of the times began to mirror the increasing unease that many Black Americans not only felt, but also became more comfortable expressing publicly. Music, as well as other arts, began to reflect a sense of awareness on the part of Black Americans that their contributions to the world could (and perhaps should) reflect that unease with the status quo as well as expressing a newfound sense of pride in the differences brought about by being Black AND American (what W. E. B. Du Bois refers to as "double consciousness"). Jazz musicians like Charles Mingus and Sonny Rollins began to address the concept of discrimination that was rampant throughout America much more directly in their recordings, both thematically and sonically. Sonny Rollins's 1958 album *Freedom Suite* set a template that a young alto saxophonist from Fort Worth, Texas, would utilize one year later to shock the jazz world.

Ornette Coleman (1930–2015) began experimenting with new scales, modes, harmonies, and timbres as early as 1954 during a stay in Los Angeles. After two albums in 1958 that hinted at his new way of thinking, Coleman released the album *The Shape of Jazz to Come* on Atlantic Records in 1959. The album title could be considered a manifesto both for Ornette Coleman as well as for jazz. In his book *1,000 Recordings to Hear Before You Die*, Tom Moon begins his segment on *The Shape of Jazz to Come* this way: "Cue this up whenever you want to be transported back to a time when radicalism was on the loose in America."[30] Jazz historian Geoffrey C. Ward noted that Rollins, pianist Cecil Taylor, and others began earlier explorations into the avant-garde, "but it was Ornette Coleman's untrammeled, richly melodic improvisations that upset the world of jazz . . . it signaled to everyone that the transformation of jazz into an art music that began with the birth of bebop was nearing its completion."[31] This new style of jazz performance, which de-emphasized tonality, traditional harmonic progressions, and the usual melodic and rhythmic concepts that were standard in jazz, would be called many things—"avant-garde," "action jazz," "rhythm-sound-energy," "free jazz" (after the title of Coleman's 1961 double quartet album)—and a name that seemed to perfectly capture this new jazz aesthetic, the "New Thing."

The "New Thing" would, as bebop had done twenty years before it, polarize jazz musicians and critics alike. This musical movement that took off in the wake of Coleman's national breakthrough included musicians on all instruments but seemed particularly suited to be applied to saxophonists, as well as being perfectly suited for the intensifying civil rights struggles that became even more urgent with the Greensboro, North Carolina, Black college student lunch counter sit-ins in 1960. In his book detailing the history of John Coltrane's

A Love Supreme, Ashley Kahn writes this about the nascent avant-garde movement: "To many, their fierce, tradition-defying music blew with the politically charged anger of the time. The fraternity of the 'New Thing'—Albert and Donald Ayler, Archie Shepp, Bill Dixon, and others—claimed a leader, a saxophonist whose aggressive style informed their own sound and exploratory spirit: John Coltrane."[32] Kahn goes on to explain the derivation of the term itself: "Such was the collective force of this youthful vanguard that critics who had comfortably employed terms like 'avant-garde' for Mingus and 'free' for [Ornette] Coleman threw up their hands, abandoned old vocabulary, and chose a catch-all name for the controversial sounds that flooded in after Coltrane: the 'New Thing.'"[33]

The New Thing musicians and the sounds that they made were, by virtue of the pro-Black agenda that was an aesthetic and philosophical part of the process, very polarizing, to say the least. America was, in 1960, a powder keg with a very short fuse, and Black musicians, playwrights, visual artists, poets, etc., began to use their platforms to express their extreme dissatisfaction with the status quo. Black pride would become not only a goal but also a rallying cry, as would Black Power. Eventually, a new term would be coined—the Black Arts Movement—for a group of creative people who would become a kind of modern equivalent to the Harlem Renaissance that had begun almost a half-century prior. The Black Arts Movement and the New Thing jazz that followed the reception to Ornette Coleman's free jazz sonics on *The Shape of Jazz to Come* would signal a new and vitally Afrocentric approach to jazz composition and performance. The jazz avant-garde was very much aligned with the values of the leaders of this new artistic mode of expression. One can sense that in the writings of LeRoi Jones (aka Amiri Baraka[34]), one of the leading jazz intellectuals and critics of the day, who also led the Black Arts Movement. In the intro to the book *Black Music*, a collection of his essays from the sixties, Jones/Baraka wrote of his championing of the jazz avant-garde: "The specific revolution these musicians were making was against the Tin Pan Alley prison of American commercial mediocrity. Down with the popular song! Down with regular chord changes! Down with the tempered scale! . . . They would play free! Free? You bet, it has been our philosophy, our ideology, our aesthetic since slavery began. And at this point in our history, we shouted it again. Free Jazz! Freedom suite! Freedom Now!"[35]

This new demand for musical freedom would not be well received by many in the jazz press, and the uncompromising sounds and Afrocentric focus were seen by many white jazz fans as threatening as well as detrimental to a music style they loved. Dr. Kwami Coleman, in an essay on free jazz, refers to a 1965 *DownBeat* magazine article written by Jones/Baraka. Dr. Coleman notes that "Baraka's article provoked swift and scathing responses from *DownBeat*'s readership. Reader Jerry Guild . . . refers to Baraka's article as a 'venom-filled thrust from his dagger of hate.' It has become apparent that the small success that Jones received for his plays makes him feel that whatever field he treads, he must hate the white man."[36] It was that natural discord present in the political nature of progressive avant-garde jazz musicians in the sixties, as well as the dense textures, accent on percussive timbres, and acceptance of dissonant harmonies, that easily allowed their music to be put forward as the future of jazz, the new wave of musical interaction that aligned with the story of the changing world of the sixties. As record labels like Atlantic, Blue Note, and Impulse began to record more avant-garde jazz players (in search of the next Ornette Coleman or John Coltrane, both of whom recorded for all three labels), the New Thing began to become begrudgingly accepted in jazz criticism. Ashley Kahn references a *DownBeat* article that, in 1966, noted that major labels also began to take notice: "There were stirrings from the two giants, Columbia and RCA Victor. All this makes a promising picture. The jazz avant-garde has not yet 'arrived,' but its breakthrough in 1966 has confirmed its growing eminence as the jazz of the decade."[37] This new movement helped to seal the deal—the fear of popularity and embarrassment of success that one could note in the wake of Eddie Harris's success had become woven into the jazz psyche of the sixties, and it has become entrenched in the histories and writings on jazz that are now used in teaching jazz in academia and in commercial film documentaries that are released every few years.

To be fair, free jazz and the New Thing was an exciting and original style of jazz composition and performance that opened up possibilities for future endeavors in both jazz and rock music. That it should be noted in the histories of jazz is unquestionable. But to ignore the music that was popular; the music that captured the sense of the times as well, or perhaps better, than the avant-garde; the music that was preferred by the listeners of the time seems dishonest at best. Fear and embarrassment of popular jazz is an unacceptable excuse for an incorrect assessment of the music of this specific period. Such fear and embarrassment might be somewhat understandable, if not for one factor—most of these popular jazz tunes are not only the best representations of jazz in the sixties but also the best representations of jazz from any era.

As it does in every decade, music of all styles and genres in the 1960s underwent some drastic changes based on technological advances in recording and changing tastes in American society. The creation of the 33 1/3, 12-inch LP (long-playing record) in 1948, the seven-inch 45 RPM single in 1949, affordable high fidelity (HI-FI) home systems, and stereophonic records (albums and 45s recorded to be played through a multi-directional sound system as opposed to monaural, or monophonic, which is one basic sound direction) led to an explosion in sales of singles, albums, and for some, reel-to-reel tape systems. By the fifties, jazz albums had become a cohesive, creative outlet for musicians to deliver their newest sounds, culminating in the great jazz classics of 1959. In addition to Ornette Coleman's *The Shape of Jazz to Come*, that year also saw the release of Miles Davis's *Kind of Blue*, Dave Brubeck's *Time Out*, Ella Fitzgerald's *Ella In Berlin*, and Charles Mingus's *Mingus Ah Um*, which were just a few of the recordings released that year (or just after, as in the case of John Coltrane's *Giant Steps*, released in early 1960) that resulted in 1959 becoming known as "jazz's greatest year." Jazz record labels also figured out that album graphics were an effective way to attract buyers, and labels like Blue Note, Verve, Atlantic, and Prestige would create a paradigm that would be copied to sell records by pop, soul, and rock musicians. But musically, within the general Black population, one of the most important cultural factors at the turn of the decade was a new aesthetic sensibility that were desired by Black listeners. What folks wanted in their music was a quality that took from the blues as well as the church, a quality that made you want to dance, or at the very least groove, wherever you happened to be. Black folks wanted their music to have soul. And that quality became known as "soul music."

Interestingly, jazz musicians sensed the need for soul before the general public because the music considered hard bop began to exhibit those qualities in the 1950s. Musicians named tunes after this quality, such as Horace Silver's "Soulville" and Mal Waldron's "Soul Eyes" in 1957 (the chapter of this book dedicated to jazz and Black cultural identity details how jazz musicians were on the forefront of the "soul" revolution). Around that same time, the jazz-infused rhythm and blues music created by a blind multi-instrumentalist from Georgia named Ray Charles also began to be associated with soul. Even though Black popular music of the 1950s still contained the dominant rhythm and blues characteristics that had created rock 'n' roll (and propelled Elvis and others to superstardom), performers such as Charles and fellow Georgian James Brown began to imbue more elements from the jazz world and the Black church into their music, creating a loop and inspiring jazz musicians to add some of the elements of Black popular music of the mid-fifties and early sixties into *their* recordings. It is worth noting here that Ray Charles recorded a few purely jazz albums for Atlantic Records in the fifties, on which he proved himself to be a splendid bebop piano player as well as a more-than-adequate alto saxophonist. And if there is any doubt of James Brown's love of jazz, try to imagine his 1967 hit "Cold Sweat" without the influence of Miles Davis's "So What" from the album *Kind of Blue*. As will be noted throughout this book, the soul music aesthetic will have a tremendous impact on popular jazz throughout the 1960s.

But those soulful sounds that became an important characteristic of hard bop in the fifties weren't appreciated by all. One of those who was unimpressed by this new direction was the aforementioned LeRoi Jones/Amiri Baraka. In *Blues People*, his enduring tome on Black music published in 1963, Jones/Baraka wrote, "The hard boppers finally were left with a music as cultureless in its emotional propensities as mad Mantovani[38]—a mood music for Negro colleges."[39]

Much of the jazz that made up the sixties' popular jazz renaissance was inspired by soul music, but it is undoubtedly jazz in its performance style, its use of improvisation, and its underlying harmonic structures. And it is here where distinctions must be drawn—in the 1960s, there were many very popular performers who recorded instrumental music that was, in performance practice as well as song structure and presentation, soul or pop music. Some of these bands are well remembered and highly regarded; names like Booker T. and the M.G.'s, King Curtis and the Kingpins, and Herb Alpert & the Tijuana Brass made some of the most enduring tunes in the history of soul and pop music (Herb Alpert and M.G.'s leader Booker T. Jones are still active in 2024, as is M.G.'s guitarist Steve Cropper). These bands were absolutely splendid, but they weren't jazz bands. A simple way to distinguish those bands is this: if you added a vocal and some lyrics to the melody of their tunes, it would sound like a pop or a soul song, whereas the lyrics and melodies added to the tunes outlined here as popular jazz songs would still present as jazz. It is also very important to remember that jazz in the 1960s also included bebop, big band recordings and performances, a continuation of fifties hard bop, bossa nova, mambo, Afro-Latin music grooves, and the blues, which was always somewhere close to the surface.

To be certain, popular jazz in the sixties started off a lot like the jazz in the fifties, but it would sound drastically different by the end of the decade. This is, more than anything, a reflection of the radical changes brought to bear by the technological changes (electric keyboards and synthesizers, larger amps and drums, and numerous changes in studio technology), changes in popular tastes (different dance styles and more funky grooves), trends (psychedelia and the influence of drug culture) and societal changes (protest movements based around civil rights and race, the Black Power movement, environmental issues, and an unpopular war in Vietnam), and, like every decade before (as well as every decade that followed), there was no way to predict the changes that one would see as the sixties began. And as we will see in this survey of popular jazz in the sixties, the beginnings sounded very conventional.

It seems to come down to this: is it possible for a music form to be both high art and popular? Put another way, does it automatically cease to be high art if it is widely accepted? The various different styles that were present in the jazz of the

1960s suggest that the answer to the first question is yes and the answer to the second is no. There needn't be a divide between jazz as artistic expression versus jazz as a form of popular entertainment. Black musical expression has always run the gamut of functions and emotions. Eubie Blake's Broadway show tunes and James P. Johnson's stride piano styles existed in the same era as Jelly Roll Morton's blues stomps and Cow Cow Davenport's variations on boogie-woogie; Duke Ellington's extended jazz orchestral concepts happened simultaneously with Count Basie's Kansas City big band roadhouse blues; Charlie Parker used his alto to redefine what saxophonists could do on "Koko" in the same year that Louis Jordan was growling the blues into his alto after asking "Caledonia, Caledonia, what makes your big head so hard?"; Louis Armstrong was leading a traditional jazz resurgence in 1949, the same year Miles Davis was leading a modern jazz explosion with the sessions that would come to be known as *The Birth of the Cool*; and in the fifties, when Ella Fitzgerald began exploring the Great American Songbook, Sun Ra and His Arkestra began exploring "Saturn."

In the sixties, Eddie Harris's contributions were as vital to the jazz scene as those of Ornette Coleman, John Coltrane, and Albert Ayler, and they should be recognized as such. Jazz has always been able to accommodate all levels of communication for all levels of listeners. Jazz can, and quite often does, represent the cutting edge of American creativity both as a composed art form and a means of expressing intense vocal and instrumental brilliance in live performance. But sometimes at its best moments, jazz can connect with Americans on a very personal level, as a means of consolation and catharsis in dark moments or as vehicle for joyous celebration and happiness or just sublime solitude. Jazz can make you think and it can make you chill; jazz can make you dance and jazz can make you just sit in amazement at what you're hearing. Jazz can make you laugh and it can make you cry, sometimes at the same moment. Jazz is best when it moves the masses. Remarkably, twenty-seven-year-old Eddie Harris seemed to have figured that out on his first record in 1961.

CHAPTER TWO

Serenade to a Soul Sister

Nancy Wilson and the Popular Jazz Divas

In a 1970 interview that was included in his groundbreaking book *Notes and Tones*, Arthur Taylor asked Nina Simone if she had ever been categorized as a jazz singer, to which she replied, "They can't seem to decide. Some critics say I'm a jazz singer, others say I'm not. Still others will say I'm a jazz singer plus another kind of singer. The truth is that they don't know what I am, and I'm glad."[1] That statement may strike readers in the twenty-first century as odd—most people who are not familiar with jazz in the 1960s would likely, if asked to name a sixties jazz singer, cite Nina Simone. In the sixties, however, Simone was, indeed, hard to categorize—legendary jazz critic Leonard Feather had this to say in 1965: "Despite their occasional association with jazz settings, such artists as Billy Eckstine, Al Hibbler, Nina Simone, and Della Reese should not be classified as jazz singers."[2] The idea that attitudes and opinions change over time for various reasons is one of the main themes of this book, and Nina Simone is a perfect example of this. In 2024, Simone is having a moment—her music is used as background in several commercials, both on television and online, her music is included in compilation soundtracks for numerous films, and there are at least five documentaries about her life and works. And almost all of her recorded output is available to purchase and to stream. Not bad for a woman who passed away in 2003. That statement about Nina Simone in Feather's book also reflects the reality that many in the world of jazz in the sixties did not necessarily think of her as a jazz singer, and she probably would not have been the first one cited by those who did consider her a jazz singer. This does not reflect negatively on Nina Simone as much as it illustrates the wealth of great jazz singers of the time.

The main focus in this survey of the popularity of jazz music within 1960s Black culture is instrumental music; however, it was with songs by (mainly) female singers that the trend initially became evident. There was a number of singers who either started their recording career in the late fifties and the early sixties or hit their stride during that time who ushered in this new popular jazz movement. That this is the case is not surprising; from the earliest days of jazz, singers have always had an easier time connecting with the public. There are a couple of obvious reasons for this, one musical and the other aesthetic. In regard to music, singers outline the melody and use words to connect through song. For Black audiences in the early sixties, that was of prime importance, even in places like the legendary Apollo Theater in Harlem. A history of that venerable theater notes that, according to Bobby Shiffman, who managed the Apollo in the sixties, "no jazz show was successful unless it had a major female artist headlining.... If you had Sarah Vaughan, you had a successful jazz show. You had Nancy Wilson, then you could have Cannonball Adderley, and any number of major attractions there. But you better have that vocalist, who is gonna express what they had to say in words—rather than on the horn—as the main attraction of the show."[3]

In regard to aesthetics, there is nothing like a beautiful, well-dressed singer who can mesmerize and capture the jazz fan's imagination, and in the jazz world, the female singer was expected to be the face of the band. This was certainly the case for the great Sarah Vaughan in the numerous big bands she was in before becoming a sensation as a solo act. Vaughan biographer Elaine M. Hayes notes that the guys in Earl "Fatha" Hines's band in the early forties had an easy job when it came to dressing up for a gig, but "Vaughan, the sole woman in the band, had a harder time. She was expected to wear fancy gowns and exude an effortless glamour and beauty, an extreme femininity, complete with immaculate hair and makeup."[4] And Vaughan realized that, as the face and the voice of the band, she could bridge worlds: "Early on, Vaughan realized the power of her voice to unite and bring people together. She was able to get southern whites to see and hear her as an individual rather than a racial stereotype—an impressive feat at the time."[5]

That early 1940s time when Sarah Vaughan was with the Hines band was a heady time for the record business—the American population was buying big band records in droves. But WWII and a musicians' strike put the record industry in jeopardy. Shellac was needed for the war effort, and for a time, the record labels were prevented from making records. But the musicians' strike of 1942 was the major factor that led to drastic changes in the music world.

The strike had many unexpected and far-reaching consequences, and one of them was the rise of popular singers. Officially known as the American Federation of Musicians recording ban, the strike was called because James Petrillo, president of the AFM, realized that recordings that were played on the radio and on jukeboxes were cutting into the earnings of the members of the union (records played on radio were replacing the live performances that were the standard practice in the thirties and forties).

The ban, which began in August 1942, called for a halt to studio recordings. Interestingly, since they were not classified as musicians in the AFM, the ban did not apply to singers. Singers were free to record, and many, like Frank Sinatra, would go into the studio and record with voices taking the place of instrumental backgrounds. Author Sean Wilentz notes that "due to the Petrillo ban, however, never again would the big bands like Goodman's and Basie's enjoy the kind of adulation they had known before 1942; instead, public fascination began to focus on the vocalists instead of the musicians, an important further step in the history of celebrity moving forward toward the single charismatic star."[6] Suddenly, singers like Ella Fitzgerald, Billie Holiday, Doris Day, Frank Sinatra, Bing Crosby, Louis Jordan, and Carmen McRae, who were featured singers with big bands and orchestras (or, like Jordan and McRae, instrumentalists who also sang), were now stars in their own right. Many of the white singers like Day, Crosby, and Sinatra were now being categorized as pop singers, whereas Black singers were being grouped into the jazz, pop, and rhythm and blues categories.

Rhythm and blues, the music style that combined big band jazz arrangements pared down for small combos with jump blues, became the preferred popular music style in Black America in the mid-1940s. Louis Jordan, who had been an alto saxophonist and singer in Chick Webb's Orchestra, became a sensation, even crossing over to sell numerous records to white listeners, and in the wake of his success, many independent record labels began promoting other singers of a similar ilk: Roy Brown, Wynonie Harris, Joe Liggins, Roy Milton, and numerous other male singers would have big hits in the mid- to late 1940s. Female R&B singers didn't initially have as easy a go on the charts. Sister Rosetta Tharpe, Nellie Lutcher, Julia Lee, Ella Johnson, and Ella Mae Morse were some of the first female singers to make an impact in the world of R&B (Morse both benefited with Black listeners and suffered with white listeners, because most people could not tell that she was a white woman). It would not be until the 1950s that women such as Ruth Brown, Laverne Baker, and Big Maybelle began to have a major impact in R&B.

But the 1940s saw female singers begin to dominate on the jazz charts. Ella Fitzgerald, Billie Holiday, Sarah Vaughan, Carmen McRae, and Dinah Washington were all able to transition from the role of singer and/or pianist with a big band to stars in their own right, recording with small combos and large, lush orchestras. There were many notable white jazz singers as well, including Anita O'Day, June Christy, and Chris Connor, and some of those singers received airplay on Black radio. But among the Black population, the female jazz singers that ruled supreme were provided with titles worthy of their reputations. Billie Holiday became Lady Day, Ella Fitzgerald was the First Lady of Song, Sarah Vaughan was alternately the Queen of Bebop and the Divine Sarah (also Sassy), Carmen McRae was Miss Jazz, and Dinah Washington was Queen of the Blues. Radio disc jockeys understood the popularity of these singers, and they recognized the devotion that these singers seemed to engender. Elaine Hayes speaks of the very popular radio and television personality Dave Garroway (who would later go on to become the first host of *The Today Show*), and the role he played in hyping Vaughan in Chicago in the late forties: "And Garroway was but one in a quartet of Chicago disc jockeys advocating for Vaughan. Ernie Simon of WJJD, Eddie Hubbard of WIND, and freelancer Linn Burton ... all embraced their roles as taste makers and all used their platforms to voice their enthusiasm.... And they played her records all of the time, often at the expense of other artists."[7]

Fitzgerald, Vaughan, Holiday, and the rest continued to sell numerous records, get lots of radio airtime, and attract crowds at performances into the fifties. With the rise of the twelve-inch, 33 1/3 album, as well as high fidelity and stereo recordings, the record companies were able to expand their offerings for a record-hungry public. But as stated above, Ruth Brown and other female R&B singers began to make their presence known, and as the fifties began to draw to a close, a new category of recordings, termed "rock 'n' roll," started to compete with jazz for the attention of Black listeners. What jazz needed was a younger crop of jazz singers who might be able to keep the ear of the Black public.

One of the first to break through was Dakota Staton (1930–2007), a Pittsburgh native who, in the late fifties, was considered to be the heir apparent to Ella, Sarah, and Dinah. Staton got her start singing on the nightclub circuit in places like Detroit, Chicago, and Cincinnati, and eventually, she made her way to New York, where Dave Cavanaugh caught her act. Cavanaugh, a producer for Capitol Records, liked what he heard. As a label co-founded in the mid-forties by the great lyricist and singer Johnny Mercer, Capitol had a reputation for being very friendly to vocalists. Nat King Cole, Jo Stafford, Peggy Lee, Billie Holiday, June Christy, Mary Ford, and even Mercer himself had hit records as vocalists on Capitol Records. Cavanaugh heard in Dakota Staton's voice a distinctive, bright, and brassy sound that he thought the label could find success with.

And he was right—Staton's first album, 1957's *The Late, Late Show*, connected with listeners. In the book *100 Best Selling Albums of the 50s*, Staton's debut album ranks #88, an impressive feat for a jazz singer, especially for a new artist. Author Charlotte Greig notes that *"The Late, Late Show* became a staple not just of jazz and R&B stations, but also of pop radio.... Backed by a top-notch small combo, she had the bluesiness of Dinah Washington allied to a youthful freshness."[8] The album made it to number four on the *Billboard* album chart, making Staton a big star, albeit for a short time. She was not able to parlay her initial success into long-term sales stardom, but Staton continued performing until 1996, when ill health curtailed her career.

The above reference to Dinah Washington (1924–1963) carried a lot of weight in the late fifties. Washington was, in the fifties and early sixties, a superstar in the world of Black entertainment. Starting her career in the forties with Lionel Hampton's band, Washington began to distinguish herself as a vocalist who was comfortable singing jazz, blues, R&B, and pop. Washington's signature was her big, brassy attack and her perfect diction, and despite her gospel roots, she was not at all averse to singing some lowdown dirty blues. Washington's blues skirted close to the edge of the acceptable conventions of the fifties. On the song "Long John Blues," Washington sings of Long John, her seven-foot-tall dentist: "Well, I went to Long John's office, and told him the pain was killin', Yes, I went to Long John's office, and told him the pain was killin', He told me not to worry, that my cavity just needed fillin'." Washington could do it all—she sang standards and ballad, she was as comfortable with strings as she was with a small trio, and she could overpower even the biggest band. Washington was the most popular act on Mercury Records during the fifties, and as noted by Billy Vera, "As the label's all-time best-selling black star in her time, her recordings were released on both the pop and R&B series—often simultaneously, so broad was her appeal."[9]

Because of her versatility, it was hard to categorize Dinah Washington, but blues musicologist Jim O'Neal noted that "regardless of whether musicologists, critics, and present-day fans might consider her a jazz, rhythm & blues, or a pop singer, Dinah Washington was indisputably the Queen of the Blues to audiences of her day."[10] But anyone who might question Washington's jazz cred should consider this: she performed with the orchestras of Lionel Hampton and Cootie Williams; some of the greatest jazz legends performed on her records, including saxophonists Paul Quinichette and Lester Young, pianists Wynton Kelly and Joe Zawinul, guitarist Kenny Burrell, and drummer Jimmy Cobb; and her songs were covered by some of the greatest jazz singers, including her idol Billie Holiday. Quincy Jones's career was aided by his association with Washington in the late fifties and early sixties, when he worked as an arranger and producer for many of her Mercury Records albums.

Washington's musical life was on solid footing as the sixties rolled in. She had her biggest popular success in 1959 with the song "What a Difference a

Day Makes," which rose to number eight on *Billboard*'s popular music chart. Washington continued with more success, including duet singles with R&B singer Brook Benton, as well as other solo hits. Her personal life, however, was in a shambles. She has been described as unpredictable and volatile. Herman Roberts, owner of Roberts Show Club in Chicago, which was Washington's hometown, booked her in his club at least three times a year. Roberts remembered that "Dinah Washington was a very complex person.... I remember times when people would come into the club and order a drink and she would walk over to the end of the stage and say to them, 'Dammit, don't order no goddamn drinks while I'm singing.' You never knew what bag Dinah was coming out of."[11] Washington had an extensive, expensive wardrobe, including numerous mink coats, and Nadine Cohodas, who wrote a biography of Washington, noted that "Dinah liked a man on her arm, and she liked that man to look good, and she would make sure that that happened, buying suits and all kinds of things. But when that was over, she was not above saying 'Okay, I want 'em back.'"[12] The wardrobe and the numerous marriages (seven in her short life) were all a part of the battles she had with her self-image. Sadly, those image problems led her to take various different diet pills that kept her amped-up, requiring tranquilizers to help her to sleep. An accidental overdose caused her death in December 1963. She was thirty-nine years old.

Despite the numerous successes that she had from the late forties until 1963, Dinah Washington was just coming into her own as a musician and a star. She was at the top of her game, and there were no signs that she was fading in popularity or in vocal quality. Sadly, Washington died just as the concept of pride in Black identity was beginning to formulate. Unlike Nina Simone, Dinah Washington wasn't able to record deep into the sixties and reflect the changes in attitude that accompanied the Black pride movement. Unlike Ella Fitzgerald and Billie Holiday (who died in 1959), she wasn't as closely associated to the glorious big band past. Dinah Washington seems to be a victim of her time—not quite old enough to be considered one of the greats, yet she didn't live long enough to capitalize on the technological and sociological changes that were just beginning. Hers is a classic case of what could have been.

As the sixties began, there was no shortage of female singers who, like Dakota Staton and Dinah Washington, were prepared to assume the mantle of jazz star within Black popular culture. One was a singer from Harlem named Etta Jones (1928–2001, not to be confused with another, more well-known rhythm and blues singer from the same time period named Etta James), who had been recording since 1944 and who, in 1960, had great success with a song titled "Don't Go to Strangers." The single, taken from an album of the same name, was released by Prestige Records, an independent jazz label that in the 1950s counted Miles Davis, John Coltrane, and Stan Getz among its roster of stars. "Don't Go to Strangers" is sung as a ballad, and Jones is backed by a jazz quartet that provides a simple, basic accompaniment that supports her beautiful, soaring alto voice. Jones sings with much control and warmth, and she exhibits a very wide vocal range that conveys emotions and passion, which obviously connected with many listeners. The album was certified gold (over 1 million in sales), and it reached number thirty-six on the *Billboard* pop chart as well as number five on the R&B chart. It was considered a big jukebox hit, and in 2008, the song was inducted into the Grammy Hall of Fame. But "Don't Go to Strangers" is, in its execution, a jazz song, and in 1960, it was the first of many jazz songs that would feature great jazz singers, or as is the case of singers like Aretha Franklin (in her early days as a recording artist), great soul or pop singers performing songs in a jazz style.

In fact, it is interesting to consider the numerous jazz singers, like Etta Jones, who were appearing in the *Billboard* charts in the early sixties. Unlike many of their instrumental counterparts, most of these singers were not able to maintain a high profile despite their success. But Etta Jones was able to quietly have a long and distinguished career, collaborating with tenor saxophonist Houston Person, and continuing to record numerous albums in every decade up to 2001, when she released her final album in July, four months before her death from cancer at the age of seventy-two.

Nancy Wilson (1937–2018) is the focus of the introduction in this book, and in some ways, she is the poster woman for the need to chronicle this somewhat-forgotten musical world. Wilson was unique. In her very long career (she performed through 2011 and passed away in 2018), she had great success in varied styles with Black and white audiences. Nancy Wilson recorded for Capitol Records throughout the sixties and seventies, and quite a lot of her material in that time fit within pop and soul music styles, but initially, she recorded jazz songs and standards with the legendary arranger Billy May. Nancy Wilson went to New York from her native Ohio at the urging of Julian "Cannonball" Adderley, who had become a sensation as an alto saxophonist in Miles Davis's sextet in the fifties. Adderley, who is profiled extensively in chapter five, actually began recording with his own band before he joined Miles, but after his stint in the sextet that recorded *Kind of Blue* in 1959, Cannonball and his band became a very popular live draw. He would be very successful as a recording artist until his death in 1975.

In 1962, Wilson and Adderley teamed up to record *Nancy Wilson/Cannonball Adderley*, and the album was a hit, reaching number thirty on the Billboard chart and spawning two singles, "Saving My Love for You" and "A Sleeping Bee." The album remains one of the most popular by both artists, and critic

Tom Moon had this to say: "(Adderley's) collaboration with singer Nancy Wilson stands as one of the breeziest jazz vocal documents of all time."[13] Nancy Wilson had even more success in 1964 with the song "How Glad I Am," which reached number eleven on the *Billboard* charts (the album of the same name reached number four), but this song is much more stylistically associated with R&B/soul music. Most of her output from the later sixties forward fits more neatly in the soul/pop category, which might help to explain why references to Nancy Wilson as a jazz singer are all but nonexistent in jazz histories and texts. Will Friedwald is perhaps the most highly regarded scholar in regard to jazz and popular singers; he notes that "Wilson may be the first postmodernist of jazz-pop singing, the most important vocalist to come along after these genres were codified and move freely among them."[14] Nancy Wilson would continue to record with jazz combos, big bands, and jazz orchestras throughout her life, and her popularity with audiences never waned. In 2004, Wilson was the recipient of a National Endowment of the Arts Jazz Master award, one of numerous awards bestowed upon her during her lifetime. That this popular musician is not mentioned as an integral part of the jazz world of the sixties can be viewed, at best, as a shameful oversight.

The popularity of *Nancy Wilson/Cannonball Adderley* and other albums by Wilson led other record companies to groom female singers to be the next Nancy Wilson, including a young singer from Detroit who was signed to Columbia Records in 1960. It would be preposterous to describe Aretha Franklin (1942–2018) as an overlooked star in the 1960s. On the day of her death in August 2018, Franklin's passing was the lead story on newscasts around the world, and her eight-plus hour funeral was broadcast on CNN. Millions of people worldwide mourned her death, and tributes came from all corners of the globe. Aretha was "The Queen of Soul," and she remains a revered American icon. But what has been forgotten is that, in the earliest days of her career, Franklin was a struggling jazz and pop singer.

In her autobiography, Aretha wrote about her early days at Columbia Records and her work with the pioneering talent scout and producer John Hammond. "Hammond saw me as a blues-jazz artist . . . he didn't seem interested in pop hits. . . . As a nightclub performer I was mindful of the pioneering women who preceded me, like Dinah Washington, Sarah Vaughan, Lena Horne, Ella Fitzgerald. . . . Of my generation, Nancy Wilson and others became stars in that same classy mode, opening major doors and leaving the buyers and promoters with the unmistakable impression that the African American chanteuse was responsible, qualified, and fabulous."[15]

Aretha recorded for Columbia from 1960 through 1966, the year she signed with Atlantic Records, and the rest is legend. Because of that success at Atlantic, her Columbia recordings were considered by some to be inferior. But those recordings are interesting and quite often brilliant representations of Franklin's artistry. The challenge when listening to these albums is that, stylistically, they are all over the map. This is partly due to John Hammond—the legendary music impresario was credited with discovering, among others, Billie Holiday and Bob Dylan, but he didn't know what to do with Franklin. The book written about the history of Columbia Records notes that "Hammond, along with everyone else at Columbia, was unsure about where her talents lay, so they tried a bit of everything, shifting from jazz stylings along the lines of one of her idols, Dinah Washington (whom Hammond favored), to girl-group tunes."[16] And it was obvious that before her Atlantic Records years the plan was for Franklin to become the heir to Washington; in the 1965 edition of Leonard Feather's *The Book of Jazz: From Then till Now*, written before Franklin became a legend, he wrote, "Dinah Washington's counterpart in the 1960s was a young Detroit girl, the church-trained Aretha Franklin, discovered by John Hammond."[17] And while it could be said that Columbia wasn't quite successful in crafting Aretha into the new "African American chanteuse," their attempt to do so proves that this goal was considered important for the label in order to provide music for a vital market.

There was no shortage of female jazz singers or "African American chanteuses" or "Queens of the Blues" who were on the *Billboard* charts in the early sixties. There was Gloria Lynne (1929–2013), a Harlem-born singer, who was nurtured by both the AME church and the Apollo Theater, where, as a teen in the 1940s, she won first prize at the Amateur Night contest. From there, Lynne proceeded to build a reputation for herself playing the nightclub circuit in places like New Orleans, Detroit, Chicago, and Las Vegas, where she recorded the very popular 1963 album *Gloria Lynne at the Las Vegas Thunderbird*. In 1964, Lynne scored a huge *Billboard* hit with her version of the song "I Wish You Love," a song recorded by many but most closely associated with her. She recorded prolifically from the late fifties until 2007, but due to unscrupulous management, Lynne never saw much money from those recordings. She continued to be a popular draw in live performances up to August 2013, two months before her death at eighty-three. Upon her passing, Lynne was remembered fondly by many including B. B. King, who said that "Gloria Lynne was one of the great female jazz vocalists [and] lyricists of our time.... She left the world with her beautiful music and will be missed by all the people whose lives she touched. Gloria was truly a jazz legend."[18]

And then there is the story of Lorez Alexandria (1929–2001), a singer who, in the estimation of many, is the most underappreciated singer in the history of jazz. In a 2019 article for *Jazz Scene* magazine, Scott Yanow wrote "[Sixty] years later, it seems strange that Lorez Alexandria not only did not make it big but is somewhat forgotten today. Her vocal talents were on the level of Ella Fitzgerald and Sarah Vaughan."[19] Taking her cues from the vibrant jazz scene in her native Chicago, Alexandria began her recording career in the late fifties by releasing albums for King Records, an independent label out of Cincinnati not known for releasing jazz records (their big hitmaker was James Brown) and Argo Records, which was Chess Records' jazz imprint. Despite the fact that those records were recorded quickly and without much of a budget, Alexandria made the best of the situation—she swings (as on 1962's "Almost Like Being in Love"), she sings the blues (check out her rendition of "Early in the Morning" with the Ramsey Lewis Trio), she's comfortable scatting ("It Could Happen to You"), she caresses gently on ballads (listen to "But Beautiful" from 1960), and she can belt with the best of them on a Broadway-styled showstopper (as she does on Cole Porter's "Just One of Those Things").

But those early, indie gems were just the prelude to her move to Impulse Records, the jazz label that, by 1964, was quickly becoming one of the most important labels in jazz. With John Coltrane as the face of the label, Impulse had become a name that signified excellence in jazz. In 1964, the label was the home of singers Johnny Hartman and Freda Payne, and with the addition of Lorez Alexandria, they were poised to become the place for vocal jazz excellence. Jazz writer Ashley Kahn noted that "it was Lorez Alexandria who carried [label founder Bob] Thiele's crossover hope into 1964.... On *Alexandria the Great*, she covered it all with ease and style.... And what support: the Wynton Kelly Trio (pianist Kelly, bassist Paul Chambers, and drummer Jimmy Cobb, formerly Miles Davis's rhythm section) . . . and a big band on 'I've Grown Accustomed to His Face,' 'Get Me to the Church on Time,' and 'Show Me.'"[20] That album and her follow-up, *More of the Great Lorez Alexandria*, showed her to indeed be one of the great jazz stylists of her time. Sadly, Impulse pulled the plug on recordings by jazz singers, instead deciding to concentrate on pop vocalists on its big sister label, ABC Records.

Of all of the singers who came to prominence in the late fifties and sixties highlighted here, Lorez Alexandria may be the purest jazz stylist. She had a brilliant clarity of tone, a wonderfully instinctive rhythmic jazz sense that showcased her great phrasing, and she sounded at home in all the stylistic variations within jazz. It speaks to the lack of recognition that all jazz musicians of the sixties have received, as well as the lack of respect for jazz singers in particular that Lorez Alexandria is not more highly regarded. The 1997 book *Singing Jazz: The Singers and Their Styles* barely acknowledges her accomplishments, and most of her recordings are not available on streaming services. In a more equitable jazz landscape, Alexandria would be remembered not only as well as fellow singers Betty Carter and Abbey Lincoln, but also as well as instrumentalists Cannonball Adderley, Lee Morgan, and Wes Montgomery.

In regard to Betty Carter and Abbey Lincoln, their stories are in many ways similar—they would both become highly acclaimed jazz stylists, but it took years for both of them to enjoy that acclaim. Betty Carter (1930–1998) began to get noticed in the forties in her native Detroit. She sang with Dizzy Gillespie, Charlie Parker, and others when they appeared in town. Soon, she caught the ear of Lionel Hampton. Carter became the vocalist with his band, and the vibraphonist and bandleader began calling the singer, born Lillie Mae Jones, "Betty Bebop" because of her vocal facility in that music style. Her time with Hampton was said to be quite contentious, and the independent streak that was a part of her nature clashed with the notoriously controlling bandleader. She left the band in the early fifties, and Carter began her recording career in 1955 with the pianist Ray Bryant.

In 1960, Betty Carter began recording with ABC-Paramount Records, which in the same year signed Ray Charles to a recording contract. Miles Davis had performed with Carter while he was a member of Charlie Parker's band, and he recommended that Carter and Ray Charles perform together. In 1960, the album *The Modern Sounds of Betty Carter* was released, followed by *Ray Charles and Betty Carter* in 1961. Both albums present a singer who is not the least bit interested in singing anything that has to do with pop or soul music, as well as a singer with a total command of jazz style and scat vocal improvisation. Regarding her independent streak referenced above, Carter refused to bow to pressure to adapt her musical vision for financial gain. Carter told an interviewer in *New Republic* that "she had resisted the temptations of commercialism. . . . At the end of the sixties, Carter had decided that making records for others was no way to progress her career along the lines that she wanted. . . . After that she was determined to be her own record producer, and in 1971 set up her own label, Bet-Car."[21]

Slowly but surely, Carter began to build on her reputation as a jazz singer of the highest order. She had control of her output and became a big draw at jazz festivals. Recalling Carter's performance at the first Kansas City Women's Jazz Festival, writer Carolyn Glenn Brewer notes that "Betty was a horn player's singer. . . . She felt that jazz and spontaneity [were] synonymous. . . . Her soulful version of 'Can't We Talk It Over' proved her versatility, and a medley of Charlie Parker tunes gave more insight into the familiar."[22] In reviewing that concert, Leonard Feather wrote a less-than-glowing account, but Brewer notes that "the crowd, in the mood for something different, contradicted that with a standing ovation."[23] In 1987, Carter signed with Verve Records, and a year later, won a

Grammy Award for "Best Vocal Jazz Performance, Female" for her album *Look What I Got* (beating out, among others, one of her idols, Carmen McRae).

By 1997, the year that she released her last album, *I'm Yours, You're Mine* (and one year before her passing), Betty Carter had, herself, become an idol to two generations of singers, and her influence continues into the twenty-first century.

Abbey Lincoln, who, like Betty Carter, was born in 1930 (some sources claim Carter was born in 1929), released her first album, *Abbey Lincoln's Affair . . . The Story of a Girl in Love*, in 1957, two years after Carter's debut. Lincoln, as a stylist, showed herself to be a fan of Billie Holiday's freer style of phrasing. Lincoln's second 1957 album, *That's Him!* was released on Riverside Records, which was beginning to gain notice as an important independent jazz label. Backed by some of the finest young jazz players including tenor saxophonist Sonny Rollins, pianist Wynton Kelly, and drummer Max Roach, *That's Him!* shows a twenty-seven-year-old singer with an abundance of vocal talent and confidence. Lincoln is so confident she sees no reason not to include "Don't Explain," a song written and made famous by her idol, Billie Holiday. But perhaps the most stunning song on the album is "Tender as a Rose," a song which Lincoln tackles a cappella and in which she exhibits tenderness, power, and pathos, often within the same phrase (Lincoln returned to "Tender as a Rose" on her 2000 album, and on this recording, that same tenderness, power, and pathos have only deepened with age). *That's Him!* is the work of a young singer who is on her way to becoming a legend.

But a couple of factors altered Lincoln's path along the road to jazz fame. One, unexpectedly, was Hollywood. Lincoln was cast as a nightclub singer in the movie *The Girl Can't Help It*, the film that rocketed actress Jayne Mansfield to fame. Performing the quasi-gospel/swing song "Spread the Word" in the film, Lincoln's vocal ability and stunning beauty must have caught the eye of many Hollywood producers. Soon, she would be cast in numerous movie and television roles, including a star turn with acting legend Sidney Poitier in the film *For The Love of Ivy* as well as a role in Spike Lee's 1990 tribute to jazz, *Mo' Better Blues*.

The other factor that altered Lincoln's path was the civil rights movement. In the year 1960, in a collaboration with Max Roach (who would become her husband in 1962), Lincoln recorded the album *We Insist!* that is chronicled in the chapter of this book devoted to civil rights. This was a turning point for Lincoln—she began to envision herself as a Black woman who could express herself in her own terms. Lincoln told an interviewer that "I saw myself as beautiful, [but] I didn't see myself as an imitation of anybody, but an original, and I found songs that would express what was in my heart."[24] According to her friend, musician and booking agent Jacey Falk, Lincoln totally changed her approach: "She was a chanteuse.... She was a pretty face—she more or less ran from that image. And she ran to the role of a truth teller."[25]

That new approach was evident in her 1961 album *Straight Ahead*, released on the independent Candid Record label, the same label that issued *We Insist!* a year earlier. Pictured on the cover with an Afro hairdo at a time when that act itself was considered provocative, the album features both the tenor sax great Coleman Hawkins and the new alto sax sensation Eric Dolphy. Saxophonist and writer Kenny Berger, in a retrospective piece on Hawkins, calls *Straight Ahead* "one of the most emotionally intense jazz vocal albums ever recorded."[26]

But that review of *Straight Ahead* was years after its release. In a 1961 *DownBeat* review, Ira Gitler could not handle what he saw as her militant approach; he gave the album two stars (out of a possible five) and accused Lincoln of becoming "a professional Negro." That review led to a *DownBeat* roundtable with Gitler, Lincoln, Roach, and others. At the roundtable, Gitler accused Lincoln of exploiting her blackness for her career, to which Lincoln replied, "It is impossible for me to be a 'professional Negro,' because I am a black woman.... Exploit a career? How can I sing as a black woman, as a Negro, if I don't exploit the fact that I am a Negro?"[27] Gitler's response also points to an issue that would crop up numerous times in the jazz critical establishment during the sixties. In an article devoted to free jazz, Dr. Kwami Coleman, music professor at NYU, notes that "the expectation among white critics and fans that black musicians appeal to 'universal' tastes and divest their work of radical politics blatantly ignored the lapses in citizenship and legal protections that Black Americans faced."[28] But Gitler's two-star review has not hurt the reputation of *Straight Ahead*; as noted in Kenny Berger's assessment above, it has widely become recognized as one of the great jazz albums of the sixties.

Straight Ahead also signaled the arrival of Abbey Lincoln the songwriter. She began to find songs that expressed what was in her heart, and quite often she found them by writing them herself. Her lyrical output is extremely evocative and introspective; consider the title song from the album *Straight* Ahead— "Straight ahead the road keeps winding, narrow, wet, and dimly lit; vainly looking for a crossroad, where a weary soul can sit."[29] In the seventies and eighties, her recorded output slowed down, but in 1990, Lincoln signed a contract with Verve Records (three years after Betty Carter), and that began a renaissance of her music career. Lincoln recorded prolifically in the nineties through 2007, three years before her death in 2010, and her highly original albums sold very well, often topping the *Billboard* jazz charts.

Both Betty Carter and Abbey Lincoln benefited from their associations with a revitalized Verve Records in the late 1980s and early nineties. Another singer whose career got a reboot at Verve Records in the late eighties was

Shirley Horn (1934–2005). Horn, an accomplished pianist who was awarded a scholarship to Juilliard (but instead chose to go to Howard in her hometown of Washington, DC) recorded her first album, *Embers and Ashes*, in 1960. That recording gained her a very important booster—Miles Davis loved her sound, and when he heard her singing and playing in a live performance, he insisted that Horn open for his band at the Village Vanguard. Interestingly, she did not play piano on that debut album, nor did Horn play piano on her next two albums, recorded for Mercury Records. After her 1965 album, *Travelin' Light* (on which she finally got to utilize her considerable piano skills), Horn's output was sparse; she took time to raise her daughter, as well as record the occasional album for the independent label SteepleChase.

When she began recording for Verve in 1987, Horn found wide acclaim from critics and audiences, something that eluded her early in her career. Her unique, intimate singing and piano style connected deeply with jazz fans and critics, including Tom Moon, who noted that "[Horn's] voice seems to float along, an illusion she creates by the way she accompanies herself on the piano. . . . She carves out a cozy space where her voice goes and makes sure that space remains completely uncluttered."[30] Upon her return to active recording, Horn was rewarded with brisk record sales and Grammy awards. She also managed to accomplish something rare in the jazz world—she convinced Miles Davis to record as a sideman on her album *You Won't Forget Me*. Horn would record a tribute album in 1998 dedicated to her friend and booster titled *I Remember Miles*.

The vibrant world of jazz singing in the year 1960 included male singers such as Oscar Brown Jr. (who is chronicled elsewhere), Ray Charles (also highlighted elsewhere; in the sixties, Charles checked off boxes in many styles and genres, including country), Joe Williams, and Nat King Cole. Cole was one of the most celebrated entertainers of the era (as well as one of the finest jazz pianists ever), but in 1960, he was almost exclusively releasing albums as a pop singer. The great ladies of jazz, which included Ella Fitzgerald, Sarah Vaughan, and Carmen McRae, were at the height of their powers, and a British-born singer named Annie Ross (1930–2020) saw big success with her vocalese version of tenor saxophonist Wardell Gray's tune "Twisted." Ross, who first recorded that tune in 1952 was, in 1960, a member of the vocal group Lambert, Hendricks & Ross. The trio, which included Dave Lambert and Jon Hendricks,[31] became popular in the fifties singing with Count Basie's band, and by the time of their 1960 recording *The Hottest New Group in Jazz*, they were able to live up to that lofty title, winning the *DownBeat* award for Best Vocal Group five years in a row.

Although the focus of this book is instrumental jazz, it should not be implied that jazz singing was of lesser importance as a cultural force in 1960s

Black America. It should also not be inferred that jazz singing ceased after the early successes outlined here. Even though hit records by jazz singers became fewer and farther between as the sixties wore on, the singers themselves persisted—in some cases, they recorded more soul and pop-oriented material, but many continued in jazz mode. And most singers could still draw crowds in performances at nightclubs and jazz festivals.

Many of the vocalists who began to explore other styles returned to jazz. Nancy Wilson was a continuous presence on the *Billboard* Rhythm and Blues charts well into the nineties, but she recorded big band albums and small combo jazz all the way up to her last recordings. Wilson released her final album, *Turned to Blue*, in 2006, that featured some of the giants of the jazz world including Dr. Billy Taylor on piano, John Clayton on bass, Hubert Laws on flute, and both Jimmy Heath and James Moody on saxophone. On the website *All About Jazz*, reviewer Dr. Judith Schlessinger wrote, "This recording is like heirloom silver: finely etched and gleaming with a rich and mellow sheen.... At age 69, [Wilson] remains the musical definition of class, using her lovely, flexible, still-powerful voice to caress and swing, whisper and wail.... This release will surely delight the legions of long-term Wilson fans, even as it gains her new ones."[32]

Another singer who first came to prominence as a jazz vocalist only to explore other styles is Marlena Shaw (b. 1942). After her initial success with a vocal version of Cannonball Adderley's "Mercy, Mercy, Mercy," Shaw recorded her first album in 1968. Her initial albums were recorded for Cadet Records, which, in 1965, replaced Argo as Chess Records' jazz subsidiary. Those early albums brought her to the attention of Count Basie with whom she performed for four years. In 1972, Shaw became one of the rare jazz vocalists to record for Blue Note Records during its classic period. The Blue Note Records website has this to say about Shaw: "Shaw was the first female vocalist signed to Blue Note Records . . . critics likened her singing style to Dinah Washington and Sarah Vaughan. At her club shows, Shaw dazzled audiences with her intoxicating blend of straight-ahead jazz, soul, pop, and classic R&B, but her recordings will also satisfy fans of traditional jazz who have no prejudices about blues and R&B."[33] As of summer 2024, Shaw is still performing.

Jazz singing is, in the twenty-first century, alive and well, thanks in part to two factors: a renewed focus on recording "standards" by both jazz and non-jazz popular singers, as well as the popularity of "duets" albums. The "New Standards" movement has been a way for singers to dig into the Great American Songbook, that collection of songs by the Gershwins, Cole Porter, Rodgers and Hart, Ellington and Strayhorn, Waller and Razaf, and others that Ella Fitzgerald, Nancy Wilson, and so many other vocalists mined for musical gold in the fifties and sixties (even Bob Dylan couldn't resist the call of the Songbook; he released three albums of standards from 2015 to 2017). The obvious benefit of these standards for contemporary singers is a renewed sense that words and melodies, which are the natural domain of vocalists, are paramount in music and are a way to appeal to an audience ripe for a return to lush, romantic music. And the "Duets" format has also been a way for a younger generations of music fans to hear some of their favorite vocalists like Lady Gaga, John Mayer, and John Legend tackle music closely associated with jazz legends of the past alongside the likes of Tony Bennett, Frank Sinatra, Ray Charles, and others.

There is, however, something else adding to the vibrance of jazz singing in the twenty-first century: a long roster of singers who are making the vocal jazz world buzz with excitement. Cécile McLorin Salvant, Samara Joy, Jazzmeia Horn, Esperanza Spaulding, Camille Thurman, Lizz Wright, and Cyrille Aimée represent a group of younger women. There is a group of fine singers in the middle, too, represented by Norah Jones, Roberta Gambarini, and Gretchen Parlato; and there are the elder stateswomen—Cassandra Wilson, Carmen Bradford, Catherine Russell, Diana Krall, Roseanna Vitro, Stacey Kent, Dee Dee Bridgewater, and Dianne Reeves, whom Will Friedwald describes this way: "From her resplendent costumerie to her equally resplendent intonation . . . everything about Reeves establishes her as the most expressively communicative of contemporary performers. . . . Reeves is a perfect voice for a twenty-first century that likes big voices."[34] There are many more, but these singers are, as of this writing, all actively performing live and on recordings. And they all are continuing to build upon a foundation laid down in the fifties and sixties by Nancy Wilson, Dakota Staton, Lorez Alexandria, and all the other popular jazz divas who left a rich recorded legacy that continues to amaze and inspire.

Upon Nancy Wilson's death on December 13, 2018, Dianne Reeves posted on Twitter a photo of Wilson's 1967 album *Lush Life*. Reeves also wrote, "My favorite Nancy Wilson album eternally beautiful [*sic*]. Rest in Peace and Grace."[35]

CHAPTER THREE

"The Sidewinder"

The Groove That Launched a Thousand Clones

When it comes to the record business, there is one certainty: if an artist or a band has a big hit, their record label will try to recreate it over and over again, as will other labels, until it is sufficiently played out. This is true across all styles of music, whether jazz, country, R&B, or rock 'n' roll. This explains how Pat Boone, a young white singer from Nashville who knew nothing about rhythm and blues music, came to be known as a rock 'n' roll teen idol by covering the records of Little Richard and Fats Domino in the fifties. White acts rerecording or covering R&B songs originally recorded by Black singers was a very common occurrence in the fifties. Boone's label realized that white parents would not allow their kids to bring home Little Richard's records, but they also understood that Little Richard was the hottest act in rhythm and blues, so the obvious solution, to them at least, was to have the white singer (who was, in many ways, the polar opposite of Little Richard) cover the songs. Despite the fact that Boone sounded nothing at all like Little Richard, the plan worked like a charm. Pat Boone's label was able to copy the essence of the song with an inferior singer and still have success. Although it is easy to take the cynical (and perhaps correct) view that this was a racist practice, the reality is that most of the label heads saw only one color—green. And in the fifties and sixties, the record labels raked in a lot of it. New stereo recordings and hi-fi (high fidelity) systems meant that the record companies were making a ton of cash and the disc jockeys were becoming stars in their own right by playing those in-demand records on the radio. It was in the best interests of the record labels to recreate hits any way they could.[1]

As will be covered later, jazz, much like rock 'n' roll, benefited from the phenomenon of superstar disc jockeys, but the matter at hand is the desire by record labels to capitalize on successful records. One of the most influential popular jazz recordings of the sixties was "The Sidewinder," the title track from a 1964 album by trumpeter Lee Morgan. The popularity of this tune caught everyone by surprise, and it led just about every jazz label to try to recreate the "Sidewinder" groove to their advantage (including Blue Note, which was Morgan's label). From 1964 through 1969, there were countless tunes that had that groove. Some were very successful in emulating the style, and some were pretty forgettable. For a time, you couldn't put on an album without hearing at least one "Sidewinder" tune. But as influential as this song was, it probably couldn't have happened without an arguably even more influential tune, Herbie Hancock's "Watermelon Man."

Herbie Hancock (born in 1940) was a child piano prodigy who made his debut with his hometown orchestra, the Chicago Symphony, at the age of eleven. According to his website, "He began playing jazz in high school, initially influenced by Oscar Peterson and Bill Evans. He also developed a passion for electronics and science, and double-majored in music and electrical engineering at Grinnell College."[2] Like most Black youth in the fifties and sixties, Hancock's musical tastes were formed by the popular disc jockeys who ruled Black radio. "My earliest exposure to jazz was on WGES deejay Al Benson's radio show. Known as the Godfather of Chicago Black Radio, Benson spun records all day, mostly blues and R&B, but with the occasional jazz cut thrown in."[3] After being inspired by a classmate at Hyde Park High School, Hancock became enamored with playing jazz and, in particular, improvising. Once Hancock landed in Iowa to begin studies at Grinnell College, he immediately set about organizing that college's first jazz concert. That experience clarified Herbie's path to the future—jazz, not engineering, was where his heart was.

After college, Hancock moved back to Chicago and began gigging around town. Fairly soon he became known as one of the best players in the area, which is where he caught the ear of the up-and-coming trumpet star Donald Byrd. In 1962, at the recommendation of Byrd, Hancock moved to New York. After playing gigs as a sideman, Hancock went into the studio and recorded an album for Blue Note Records, which at the time was the leading label for the style that would come to be known as "soul jazz." Blue Note, which in 2019 celebrated its eightieth anniversary, had a roster in the sixties that included Art Blakey, Lee Morgan, Wayne Shorter, Horace Silver, and numerous others that we now think of as some of the finest musicians of the twentieth century, and Hancock was one of the young lions whom the label counted on to keep them on the cutting edge.

In the spring of '62, Hancock, along with Freddie Hubbard on trumpet, Dexter Gordon on tenor sax, Butch Warren on bass, and Billy Higgins on drums, recorded his debut album *Takin' Off*, which was comprised of six original Hancock compositions including the song "Watermelon Man." As Hancock recalled, "*Takin' Off* was released in May of 1962, and it climbed to number 84 on the *Billboard* 100. At the time, *Billboard* didn't have different charts for different genres, like pop, jazz, and R&B. There was just one chart for all of the records released, so for a jazz record to reach the top 100 was considered pretty good. 'Watermelon Man' was the single that propelled the record, and when I started hearing it on the radio, it was really cool."[4]

A showing on the *Billboard* chart was quite an accomplishment for the debut album of a relatively unknown pianist, but the song "Watermelon Man" really clicked with listeners. Interestingly, it was an even bigger hit in a new version that was recorded a year later by the Latin jazz bandleader Mongo Santamaria. Hancock remembered that "Mongo Santamaria released his version of 'Watermelon Man' in early 1963, and it became a huge hit, eventually reaching number 10 in *Cash Box* and number 11 on the *Billboard* chart. I could walk down the street and hear it blasting out of people's windows, hear it coming out of people's cars as they drove by. I was twenty-two years old, almost twenty-three, and I had a big hit record!"[5] Since then, Hancock has been consistently popular as a jazz musician and in crossover styles, and in 2008, he became only the second jazz musician to win the Grammy Award for Album of the Year for his record *River: The Joni Letters* (the first jazz musician to win that award was Stan Getz for *Getz/Gilberto*, discussed later in this book).

The key to the success of Hancock's recording of "Watermelon Man" is its groove. Despite the fact that, from the standpoint of form, it is simply a twelve-bar blues with measures nine and ten repeated twice, the recording was groundbreaking in its time for one simple reason—its use of a straight-eighths groove.

Perhaps the strongest identifier of jazz is the beat that is described by most as a "swing" beat. The place where this is most clearly outlined is in the standard ride cymbal pattern (diiing, ding da, diiing, ding da), and everyone in the band uses that to create a triplet subdivision of the basic beat (compound meter). If one thinks of many of the classic jazz tunes—Cab Calloway's *Minnie the Moocher*, Benny Goodman's *Sing, Sing, Sing*, Duke Ellington's *Take the A Train*, Ella Fitzgerald's *A-Tisket, A-Tasket*, tunes that are known even to non-jazz listeners—the swung triplet rhythmic subdivision style of jazz performance is the most obvious jazz identifier.

But "Watermelon Man" is different. Instead of the swung triplet subdivision of the beat, known in technical terms as compound meter, "Watermelon Man" uses a simple meter, a "straight-eighths" groove. In a four-beat measure, instead of each beat divided into three (think *el-e-phant, el-e-phant, el-e-phant, el-e-phant*), "Watermelon Man" has four beats divided into two even "straight" beats (think *don-key, don-key, don-key, don-key*). In present-day 2024 jazz performance, it's easy to forget that before Herbie Hancock and his recording of "Watermelon Man," no one in jazz played that way. But Hancock, bassist Butch Warren, and one of the MVPs of sixties jazz, drummer Billy Higgins, establish, from the first eighth-note pickup on Higgins's snare drum, a whole new paradigm. On a 4/4 time signature (four beats per measure and each quarter note gets one beat), they laid down a pattern that they repeated over and over—Hancock plays chords in the right hand on beats two, three, and the "and" of three. That is matched by Higgins playing his snare on beats two and the "and" of three while playing straight eighth notes on his ride cymbal (one *and* two *and* three *and* four *and*, or *don-key* from above). While all of that is happening, Warren is playing a half-note on beats one and two, then playing a figure on three *and* four, which is echoed in Hancock's left hand and lightly in Higgins's bass drum.

This was a new thing for jazz, but it was reflective of the pop, soul, and Latin styles of the day. There were numerous tunes that were recorded with a quasi-cha-cha feel in the early sixties. Cha-cha had come out of the mambo craze of the forties; cha-cha was mambo's easier 1950s dance music cousin, and there were numerous cha-cha hits. But what Hancock did was to remove the strict cha-cha clave ("clave" translates into key, or code, meaning rhythmic pattern) and to emphasize the backbeat that was, after Little Richard and his drummer Earl Palmer, prevalent in rhythm and blues and soul music (if you listen to "Lucille" by Little Richard, you hear the point in 1957 where Earl Palmer and the other musicians at J&M Studio in New Orleans make that straight-eighths groove standard in R&B). It is interesting to note the similarity of the groove on "Watermelon Man" and some of the music coming out of Motown in that same year of 1962, notably two tunes by Marvin Gaye, "Stubborn Kind of Fellow" and "Hitch Hike." Music and dancing were important components of the socializing ritual in Black culture.

Social dancing serves many functions—it is a way to get a large group to have a good time together, it can be a great mode of personal artistic expression, and it is a way to attract a potential mate. Dance historian and scholar Dr. Julie Malnig notes that "a particularly underexplored relationship has been that between social dance and music, both of which historically have been inextricably linked."[6] This is especially true within Black culture. Whether we are talking about the ring shout, the cakewalk, the animal dances of the early twentieth century (foxtrot, camel walk, etc.), the jitterbugs doing the Lindy Hop, or any modern wedding reception where the Electric Slide or the Wobble will happen before the night is over, social dancing is a critical part of the Black American experience.

Eileen Southern and Samuel Floyd Jr. researched and chronicled Black music and left a rich legacy of scholarship that is unmatched. They note that one of many the themes that runs throughout Black music across the diaspora is the connection between music and dance. Southern observes that this connection has always been imbedded in Black folks' DNA; in a section of *The Music of Black Americans: A History* subtitled "African Retentions in the New World," she writes, "But though they could bring no material objects with them, they retained memories of the rich cultural traditions they had left behind in the motherland and passed these traditions down to their children. The importance given to music and dance in Africa was reflected among black men in the colonies . . . in the songs they sang, in their dancing and folk festivals."[7] Making the case for the importance of "cultural memory" in the lives of Black Americans, Floyd, in *The Power of Black Music*, discusses the African practices that have been retained in American music and dance: "The manifestations of these elements in Dance, Drum, and Song . . . created an African American ethos, a common consciousness, a cultural unity, that is reflected also in 'our language . . . our thought patterns, our laughter, our walk' (Richards 1980, 14), and other aspects of African American's being."[8] Dance scholars articulate the importance social dancing and African American culture as well; Dr. Nadine George-Graves, in her writings on ragtime dance, cites Professor Katrina Hazzard-Gordon (aka Hazzard-Donald), who says, "Social dancing links African Americans to their African past more strongly than any other aspect of their culture."[9]

That music made by, and for, Black Americans should place much value on danceability is natural. And until the 1950s, this was paramount in jazz, even in the bebop era. In the book *Murray Talks Music*, Wynton Marsalis asked the preeminent Black music scholar Albert Murray, "When did jazz music change? When people stopped dancing to the music, let's say around the mid-1950s. . . . What type of effect did that have on the performances of musicians who didn't grow up playing in dances?"[10] Murray replied, "I think it distorted the view of a number of them. It's like, the intrusion of politics and sociology into something. . . . It became something else. They wanted to be part of something else."[11]

The reality is that not only did records like both versions of "Watermelon Man" retain dance grooves that were in vogue at the time, but people actually danced to them! Mongo Santamaria would turn "Watermelon Man" into an unmistakable cha-cha, and in the process, change sixties Latin music history by igniting the boogaloo music movement. That Hancock's and Santamaria's recordings were easy to dance to was not only an important factor in their massive sales numbers, but it would also change the direction of jazz in the sixties from that point forward.

Herbie Hancock is, at this writing, unquestionably a living legend. He is one of the most celebrated and (because of numerous crossover hits) one of the most well-known jazz musicians ever. For most of the sixties, Hancock was one of the most in-demand session musicians in jazz, even during his time as the pianist in the celebrated Miles Davis sixties quintet (he joined Miles's band within a year of the release of *Takin' Off*). He would play on numerous sessions for Blue Note Records, his label, as well as sessions on Verve, Atlantic, Argo, Prestige, and just about every other label that released jazz records at the time. Hancock's reputation as a player and a composer led everyone from young up-and-comers like Freddie Hubbard and Roy Ayers to established greats like Davis and Sonny Rollins to request his magic. And "Watermelon Man" made everyone want what Herbie had—a big jazz crossover hit!

One of the musicians whom Hancock frequently interacted with was Lee Morgan. Morgan, who was two years older than Hancock, released his first album at eighteen years old, and by the time of his untimely death at thirty-three, he had recorded at least thirty solo albums and played on numerous others as a sideman. Morgan, who began playing trumpet at fourteen, was from North Philadelphia, a very fertile area in regard to musicians who would have a big impact on jazz in the sixties. Reggie Workman, the bassist who is known for his association with John Coltrane, grew up with Morgan in North Philadelphia, and he recalled that "Lee was a child prodigy, but there were many of them in Philadelphia at the time. . . . Lee was very well-disciplined. Very jovial, with a great sense of humor—an almost exaggerated sense of humor. He was from a very close-knit family."[12] Philadelphia's thriving jazz club scene in the fifties allowed the young musicians to use the bars and taverns as a kind of workshop where they could have jam sessions and play gigs while they were still school age. Morgan's discipline, his family support, and the scene that nurtured him were all that he needed to craft a very personal sound, and in 1956, at eighteen years old, he recorded his first album for Blue Note.

Blue Note Records was run by Alfred Lion and Francis Wolf, a couple of German immigrant jazz fans who came to America to escape Nazi persecution. At Blue Note, they hit on a winning strategy by hiring the best young musicians on the New York scene and allowing them the time to rehearse and fine-tune their own original compositions as opposed to rehashing the same standards that many of the other labels relied on to keep their rosters afloat. Music journalist Michelle Mercer, in her biography of Wayne Shorter, makes note of this fact: "'Blue Note was like going to the bank for us,' Wayne said. Musicians were paid $500 for a recording and additionally for each day of rehearsal. The label typically allowed one week per record date: three or four days of rehearsal, and a final day for the actual recording."[13] Lion and Wolf also kept an ear on what was selling in Black neighborhoods. Shorter relayed to Mercer how that came to play in a Jazz Messengers session: "The Messengers had done several takes of a tune, and producer Alfred Lion asked them to play it one more time with a stronger backbeat. 'You're looking for somethin' more down home?' Lee Morgan asked. 'Yes, can you give it a little more grease, a little more gravy'... 'He means commercial,' Alfred's partner, Frank Wolf, translated."[14] In a compilation CD that accompanied the documentary film *Blue Note: A Study of Modern Jazz*, producer Michael Cuscuna notes that "with the sixties came more changes and greater variety in the way people played and listen to jazz. While Blue Note always had strong sales with Jimmy Smith, Horace Silver, and others, Donald Byrd's *A New Perspective*, a unique 1963 album for jazz group and choir, began crossing over to more general audiences. The next year and a half brought two blockbusters albums that each had a long run on the pop charts, Horace Silver's *Song for My Father* and Lee Morgan's *The Sidewinder*."[15]

Song for My Father was, in early 1965, just the latest in a string of albums by Horace Silver that would, in time, come to be known as jazz classics. Silver was a fine pianist (in the art of comping, or playing figures behind soloists, he is unrivaled), and he surrounded himself with some of the finest musicians in jazz, including tenor saxophonist Joe Henderson, trumpet player Blue Mitchell, and one of the most underrated drummers in all of jazz history, Roger Humphries. But it was his gift as a composer and arranger that made his albums sparkle. Silver's memorable melodies continue to amaze and inspire. The title track, "Song For My Father," remains his most recorded work, with versions by George Benson, Dee Dee Bridgewater, Leon Thomas, Victor Wooten, Gregory Porter, and even the pop duo the Captain and Tenille, recorded in every decade since its first appearance on the album in 1965. Horace Silver once mused, "I've always wanted to write the kind of music that would stand the test of time. Always, in the back of my mind, I would be thinking, 'Will this stand up twenty, thirty years from now?'"[16] Jazz writer and film critic Gene Seymour notes that "*Song for My Father* . . . is considered Silver's peak achievement and, perhaps, his most popular, given the title track's commercial success."[17] Cultural studies professor Mark Anthony Neal, in a discussion of Lou Donaldson's *Alligator Boogaloo* (released in 1967 and discussed below), notes, "Accordingly, *Alligator Boogaloo* which Donaldson said 'brought them back,' meaning the black audience, was one of Blue Note label's all-time top sellers during the era, along with Lee Morgan's *Sidewinder* and Horace Silver's *Song for My Father*."[18] With *Song for My Father* and so many other albums and songs, Silver, without question, succeeded in his goal of music that has withstood the test of time.

But *Song for My Father*, for all its melodic beauty and fiery ensemble interplay, wasn't the album that would chart the course forward for jazz in 1964/65—that path would be laid by Lee Morgan. *The Sidewinder* was just the latest album by the extremely prolific trumpet star. In the year 1964, when the album was released, the twenty-six-year-old Morgan already had twelve albums under his own name (with three different labels) as well as countless appearances on other recordings, including his time as a member of Art Blakey's Jazz Messengers (this speaks to the mind-boggling number of recordings generated by jazz musicians in the sixties. That Morgan recorded twelve albums as a leader in seven years was the norm). *The Sidewinder*, as an album, was, from a musical standpoint, a standard jazz outing. There was "Totem Pole," a Latin groove AABA tune in a minor key that went into a swing groove in the "B" section—it's the type of tune that Horace Silver perfected in the fifties that became a style that was emulated by a number of players. "Gary's Notebook" and "Boy, What a Night" were both tunes in 3/4 time, and both, like Miles Davis's classic "All Blues," were variations on blues form, with "Boy, What a Night" being the faster of the two. "Hocus-Pocus" is pretty standard post-bop jazz. What all those tunes have in common is Lee Morgan's gift of melodic invention. He wrote each of the songs on the album. It would be easy to just lump this into the category of great jazz albums recorded in the sixties for Blue Note records without considering how well-written the tunes are and how well-played the album is. *The Sidewinder* would be a classic album even without the title tune.

But in fact, the title tune is something else entirely! "The Sidewinder," as the opening track on the album, is a twenty-four-bar blues (actually a twelve-bar blues with each chord extended for one extra measure) with a funky pseudo straight-eighths groove that actually owes quite a debt to Hancock's *Watermelon Man*. The tune is fairly melodic, scalar in construction, and very diatonic—the key of E-flat is easy to hear throughout. The range is comfortable, and the melody is mostly played in unison between Morgan on trumpet and Joe Henderson on tenor sax. Rounding out the ensemble are Barry Harris on piano, Bob Cranshaw on bass, and Billy Higgins on drums. Higgins was one of the go-to drummers of the day, and it is somewhat staggering to think of the recordings on which he supplied his unique drumming approach: Hancock's *Takin' Off* (which included "Watermelon Man"); Ornette Coleman's *The Shape of Jazz to Come*; Eddie Harris's *Mean Greens*; and Sonny Rollins's *Our Man In Jazz*. There were so many recordings from the sixties into the twenty-first century that featured Billy Higgins's percussive artistry.

Higgins was the favorite of many of the players that he performed with. Dexter Gordon "regarded 'Smilin' Billy' as the 'swingingest' drummer in the world,"[19] and, in the notes to John Scofield's 2000 album *Works for Me* (which was one of Higgins's last recorded performances), Scofield writes, "Billy Higgins is a jazz legend and some of the songs on this disc were inspired by his classic recordings.... His beat and creativity make the music come alive."[20] When he died in 2001, his *New York Times* obituary noted that "his style did not draw attention to itself and could not be described by mannerisms; his musicianship simply raised the standard of every band he played in."[21]

Billy's playing was one of the key factors in the allure of "The Sidewinder." He does something interesting and unusual: over the rest of the band's straight-eighths groove, Higgins plays a straight-eighths groove on all of his drum set except for his ride cymbal, which is playing a swing groove. It's the kind of nuanced playing that you don't really notice until you listen for it, and then it's kind of astounding. The best way to describe the groove is relentless; it never lets up. Morgan, Henderson, and Harris all sound terrific, as they always do, but it's the combination of Bob Cranshaw's bass and Higgins's drums that pulls you in and keeps you in.

In his book on Hard Bop, David Rosenthal notes that "The Sidewinder" was simultaneously a unique and typical groovin' tune, well played by fantastic young musicians—what you'd expect for tunes released on Blue Note, Prestige, Atlantic, and all of the other labels actively releasing jazz records—except for the fact that it became a massive hit. Jazz disc jockeys pushed the tune over the top, and it crossed over when pop and soul music deejays began playing it as well. "'The Sidewinder'... took his disc of the same name to number twenty-five on *Billboard*'s LP charts, and the song made an appearance on *Billboard*'s Hot 100 (pop song) chart, peaking at number eighty-one.... The song was widely played on the radio, and in 1965 even cropped up (with strings) as background music for a Chrysler television commercial."[22] That last fact deserves some explanation. In 1965, it was highly unusual that a car company, or any other company, would use jazz in the background. It bears repeating that in 1965, Jim Crow still ruled in the South, segregation was the rule in schools across the country, and miscegenation (mixed race dating and marriage) was not deemed unconstitutional (that occurred in 1967). The fact that Chrysler would take a chance on using a jazz song like "The Sidewinder" in a commercial (against Blue Note and Lee Morgan's wishes) was quite a bold move, but one that illustrates the appeal of the tune. Critic Gene Seymour says of "The Sidewinder": "The hip-shaking title tune was exactly the kind of soul jazz standard that could hold its own with any pop tune making its way up the charts."[23]

The success of "The Sidewinder" made the jazz labels of the day eager to replicate that feat, including Blue Note. In August 1964, Morgan recorded two albums, *Search for the New Land* and *Tom Cat*. Work on both albums began before the massive chart success of *The Sidewinder*, so there was no financial incentive to try to recreate its success on those releases. However, following massive record sales, Alfred Lion at Blue Note decided to shelve the two new Morgan albums in favor of him recording albums that replicated the "Sidewinder" groove and attempted to replicate the sales that it brought in (*Search for the New Land* would be released two years after it was recorded; *Tom Cat* would not see its release until 1980).

And Lion wasn't alone. In the wake of "The Sidewinder," there were dozens of tunes that tried to use the basic formula to try to capture lightning in a bottle (or perhaps lightning within the grooves). Big John Patton used his Hammond organ to power up "Fat Judy" on his Blue Note album *Oh Baby!* in 1965. Morgan (aided by Billy Higgins) recorded "The Rumproller" in 1966, which was the same year that Brother Jack McDuff used his organ skills to cook up some "Hot Barbeque." The year 1967 saw a number of "Sidewinder" clones: tenor saxophonist Hank Mobley contributed "A Caddy for Daddy" (featuring Lee Morgan), while drummer Chico Hamilton threw his hat into the ring by recording Archie Shepp's "For Mods Only." Cannonball Adderley's Quintet recorded Jimmy Heath's "Heads Up, Feet Down," Lou Donaldson contributed the aforementioned "Alligator Boogaloo," while Morgan returned again to the groove (with Billy Higgins in tow) with "Cornbread." Then, 1968 saw Donaldson, once again, hitting that "Sidewinder" groove with "The Humpback" while Blue Mitchell recorded his version of Jimmy Heath's "Heads Up, Feet Down," and Morgan and Higgins did the "Sidewinder" thing they created, this time on the tune "Yes I Can, No You Can't."

That "Sidewinder groove" proved irresistible to jazz musicians; these tunes are just a few of the many that took their inspiration from Lee Morgan's big jazz hit. But it must be noted that not everyone appreciated the fact that there were so many "Sidewinder"-type tunes. Critic Tom Moon noted that "The Sidewinder" "became one of the first crossover records of the 1960s, showing countless jazz musicians a (soon to be worn-out) path toward commercial viability marked 'soul jazz' or some such."[24] In his book *Hard Bop*, David Rosenthal acknowledges the success of "The Sidewinder," but his assessment of the aftermath is not positive. He says that many of Morgan's generation of players "had to abandon their music or water it down in a quest for commercial success or, in some cases, mere survival. While remaining true to jazz, Morgan's own records deteriorated in the late sixties and early seventies."[25] Rosenthal also opines of Morgan. "He seems to be turning into a mannerist of his own style, repeating his clichés.... In short, he was in a rut, while the milieu that had buoyed him up—ghetto life with jazz at its center—had vanished."[26]

Rosenthal's statements assume that Morgan and his generation of players were recording a kind of music that went against their sensibilities by making music that he deems commercial. Because Rosenthal doesn't like it (or at least it seems that he doesn't), he assumes that they didn't like it either (and the statement "ghetto life with jazz at its center" comes across as condescending, at best). But all indications point to the fact that these musicians recorded this type of jazz because they wanted to. This popular jazz music was a way for jazz musicians to play music that could connect with the people. As will be seen in chapter seven, organist Jimmy Smith was always about playing to the masses. In his book on Black popular music and Black popular culture, Professor Mark Anthony Neal writes this about Lou Donaldson: "Donaldson's 1967 release *Alligator Boogaloo* is perhaps the best example of his efforts to remain connected to his core black audience."[27] Many of the players were like Brother Jack McDuff; they recorded for many different record labels at the same time (McDuff recorded for Prestige, Atlantic, and Cadet Records in the mid-1960s). These jazz musicians had the choice to record all types of music, which they all did. A cursory listen would reveal lots of different styles over the course of a record, including music that might, as Herbie Hancock noted, sound good coming out of car radios. Morgan, McDuff, Mobley, Patton, and the rest recorded the music that they did because it sounded like the music of their time. The music that Moon derides as "soul jazz or some such" was what spoke to those musicians and listeners in that moment in time. That it sounded like the music of its time is only natural, and to make a contemporary observation devoid of the view from the culture that grabbed it up (that so-called "ghetto life") does a disservice to music that meant a lot to a lot of people.

"The Sidewinder" has now attained "classic" status, a fact that might have amused Lee Morgan. The tune created by that twenty-six-year-old trumpet player from Philadelphia has, without question, stood the test of time. But he would only have eight more years to live following its release." There has been plenty of documentation regarding the tragic ending of Lee Morgan's life. That part of his story won't be retold here because the sensational nature of his demise tends to obscure discussion of his tremendous contributions. Suffice it to say that although Morgan didn't live a long life, he did leave quite a recorded legacy, and by all indications, he intended to leave a lot more. It is easy to forget that most musicians, even the ones deemed great by society, will never contribute a song into the canon that has the impact of Lee Morgan's "The Sidewinder."

CHAPTER FOUR

33s and 45s

The Record Labels That Put the Sound in the Grooves

In 1960, Ray Charles (1930–2004) was a man in transition. He was transitioning from a career as a rhythm and blues star with tunes like "I Got a Woman" and "Drown in My Own Tears" into a crossover soul/rock 'n' roll superstar with "What'd I Say," he was transitioning from 'Brother Ray' into "The Genius," and, more importantly, he was transitioning from Atlantic Records to ABC-Paramount Records. At Atlantic, Charles was allowed to do what he wanted: "They had every right to tell me what to sing and how to sing it. But they didn't. They said, 'Ray, if you feel it, do it,'"[1] Charles remembered in 2002. But ABC-Paramount had financial resources that Atlantic couldn't match. "ABC-Paramount offered him a significantly higher royalty rate plus ownership of his masters, an unprecedented consideration."[2] In terms of his music, Ray Charles was also about to transition at ABC-Paramount into a country music star as well. But before that would happen, Charles did something else that was different—he released big band jazz albums on both his old and new labels.[3]

Ray Charles recorded quite a lot of jazz on Atlantic in the fifties with smaller-sized groups, but he had longed to front a big band. Fortunately, he had a childhood buddy who was more than willing to supply arrangements, a buddy named Quincy Jones. Jones, who was born in Chicago, suddenly, at the age of eleven, found himself transported to Seattle (according to Jones, his dad found himself on the wrong side of gangster Al Capone). A few years later, Jones met Charles, who had just arrived in Washington and secured a gig for himself in Seattle at an Elks Club. Though he was only two years older, Ray Charles quickly

Ray Charles, *The Genius of Ray Charles*: Atlantic Records, SD-1312, 1959.

became Jones's mentor. Jones would go to Charles's apartment and soak up all he could. "We'd eat, and he'd sit at the piano and show me what he knew, and I ate it all up, everything, his fried chicken, his knowledge, his friendship.... He understood the world in ways that I didn't."[4]

Those early interactions were important for both men's future endeavors. "Ray opened my eyes to orchestration.... I was trying to unlock that magic door to what orchestration was all about.... I had such a thirsty mind. I wanted to learn everything."[5] Not long after those initial encounters, both Jones and Charles would make their ways in the world of popular music. When the opportunity arose to finally do a big band album, Charles knew exactly whom to call.

With his old friend Quincy Jones handling the arrangements, Ray Charles seized his opportunity in 1959. But Charles also loved the Great American Songbook and slow ballads, and he was a fan of Ralph Burns's work as an arranger with Woody Herman's band. To fulfill his desire for both, Nesuhi Ertegun and Jerry Wexler at Atlantic Records would produce an album with one side devoted to the big band and the other side with Charles supported by lush string arrangements. The album was aptly titled *The Genius of Ray Charles*. One year later, ABC-Paramount, Ray Charles's new label, created a

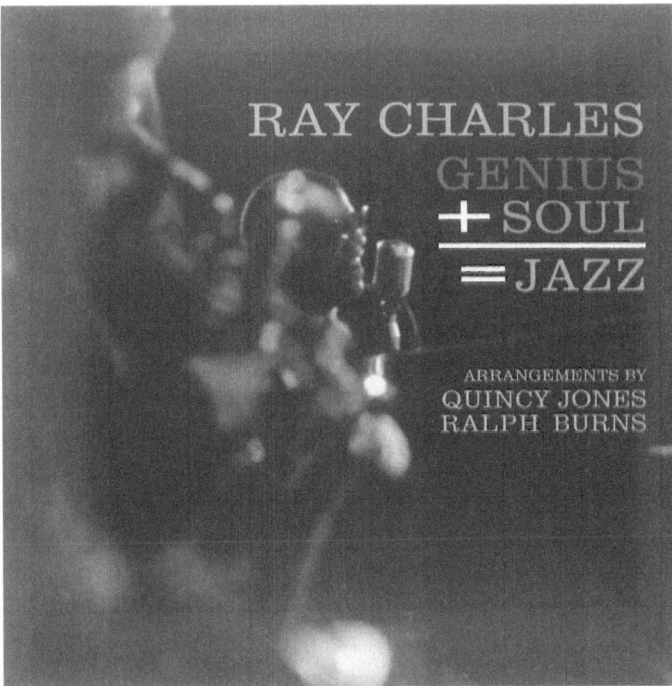

Ray Charles, *Genius + Soul = Jazz*: Impulse Records, A-2, 1961.

jazz subsidiary that they branded Impulse. The new label put a young man named Creed Taylor (1929–2022) in charge, and although his time at Impulse was short-lived, he would go on to have a major impact on the sound of jazz with other labels for two decades. Taylor's first success at Impulse was with ABC's newest acquisition, Ray Charles.

The album, released in 1961, would, just as the album recorded for Atlantic that preceded it, put Ray Charles's musical honorific to good use: it was titled *Genius + Soul = Jazz*. This album was like its predecessor in another way; it also utilized the arranging talents of Quincy Jones and Ralph Burns, but this album was different in the sense that it was entirely comprised of big band arrangements, and only two of the ten tracks featured Charles on vocals. The other eight tunes were arranged to show Charles as a soloist on the newly fashionable jazz instrument, the Hammond organ. *Genius + Soul = Jazz* has the catalogue listing A-2, meaning that it is the second album ever produced on the Impulse label (the first was a reuniting of trombonists J. J. Johnson and Kai Winding), and the album established Impulse right out of the gate as a leading player in the jazz world of the sixties. In his book on the history of Impulse, Ashley Kahn notes the importance of the single "One Mint Julep" to the success of the album and the label: "In fact, the single from the album—an instrumental version of 'One Mint Julep' with Charles's memorable aside 'Just a little bit of soul, yeah,'—was a Top Ten hit on the pop chart and stands alone as Impulse's lone charting single."[6] And although they never scored any more Top Ten singles, after Ray Charles's success, Impulse became a giant in the world of jazz.

The story of Impulse Records' beginnings is an interesting tale, but it is not at all unique. Jazz was doing good business in the late fifties, and it would do even better business in the sixties. Because of this, there were numerous labels recording jazz, some new, like Impulse and Reprise, and some well established, like Blue Note, Verve, and Prestige; some were independent with a slim budget like Vee-Jay, Sue, and Riverside, and some jazz musicians had the backing of major label giants like Columbia, Capitol, and Mercury. Some labels were exclusively dedicated to jazz, like Argo (later to become Cadet) and Pacific Jazz, and there were some, like Atlantic and King, where jazz was but one of many different genres produced. But the labels all benefited from the fact that the sixties was the decade that had more recording activity by many of the people that we now consider to be the greatest musicians of all time than any other era. In the 1960s, Duke Ellington, Louis Armstrong, Count Basie, Dizzy Gillespie, Thelonious Monk, and Coleman Hawkins were all still actively recording; Miles Davis, John Coltrane, Dave Brubeck, Gerry Mulligan, and Art Blakey were at their creative peak; and a crop of new players, like Wayne Shorter, Herbie Hancock, Bill Evans, Wes Montgomery, and Eddie Harris began to make their mark.

To that you can add the New Thing musicians. Ornette Coleman, Archie Shepp, Albert Ayler, Pharoah Sanders, Cecil Taylor, Andrew Hill, and Grachan Moncur III were recording new, different, and vital music. Then there were those who wrote and recorded music that blurred the lines of many different styles—Coltrane, Charles Mingus, Eric Dolphy, Sam Rivers, and Tony Williams had their feet firmly planted in numerous camps. Consider John Coltrane. In 1963, Coltrane recorded an album with Duke Ellington comprised mostly of Ellington tunes that was a relaxed, easy-going affair, as well as the album *John Coltrane and Johnny Hartman*, one of the most sublimely beautiful and lush ballad albums ever recorded. In 1964, Coltrane began his big shift to a freer, more spiritual approach on the album *Crescent*, followed up by his four-movement masterwork, *A Love Supreme*. Coltrane was clearly interested in many directions at once. Or consider Charles Mingus. In the first three years of the sixties, Mingus recorded large ensemble music, and he recorded with his small group; he recorded blues tunes as well as jazz/classical crossover music, known at the time as "Third Stream"; and he recorded for Atlantic, Columbia, Impulse, Candid, and Mercury Records!

The record business has always been much more interested in the money part of the business than the music part. Throughout the history of the record business, recorded music was often just a byproduct of some other money-maker (one can think of Warner Brothers as a movie studio, as a record label, as a sheet music publisher, and as a book publisher. This is not to imply that the leaders at Warner Brothers Records are not interested in the music that they release, just an acknowledgment that many of the major labels are a part of a multi-national conglomerate that makes money in many different areas). Gennett Records, one of the first labels to record jazz, blues, country, and gospel musicians, was an outgrowth of the Starr Piano Company, located in Richmond, Indiana. In 1916, the company realized that the phonograph was beginning to rival the parlor piano in the home entertainment market, so Starr Piano was able to utilize its mechanical and woodworking resources in the service of making phonograph records and phonograph record players. After winning a court challenge by Columbia, Victor, and Edison (the companies that held the patent on the recording process), Starr Records came into being. Realizing that other recording companies were wary of selling their records in Starr Piano stores, they changed the name from Starr Records to Gennett Records, which was the last name of the company's president.

An important component to Gennett Records' success was that the Starr Piano Company had piano stores throughout the country, which created a wide distribution network. Distribution was, in the days before the internet and streaming, the most important component in selling records. In his book about the record business titled *Hit Men*, Fredric Dannen makes the point: "Distribution is no small matter. It is one of two essentials to landing a national pop star, the other being radio play.... The most effective national advertising is worthless if you cannot get shelf space for your product in stores across the country."[7] In the case of Gennett Records, since they owned the Starr piano stores, they had no problems in that regard. It's important to note that in the early twenties, there were not many options for Black musicians (or rural white musicians, then known as "hillbillies") looking for places to record. Gennett Records had no problem recording those artists, so by process of elimination, Richmond, Indiana, the home of Gennett Records, became "the birthplace of recorded jazz."

Gennett created the model for later independent record labels across genres. In locales across America, some furniture company stockroom or dance hall that had microphones or back room of a record shop could be converted into a makeshift recording space by a shrewd businessman with access to a portable recorder; or in the case of people like Ralph Peer, Moses Asch, or John and Alan Lomax (all early recording pioneers), they would bring the recording machine to you. In most cases, unlike Peer, Asch, or the Lomaxes, these businessmen were not interested in the music that they recorded. They saw this recording technology as a way to make a quick buck.

But that was not the case with the jazz record men of the fifties and sixties. Those jazz labels were run, in most cases, by men who loved jazz. Ahmet Ertegun, founder of Atlantic Records, Alfred Lion and Francis Wolff, founders of Blue Note, Bob Weinstock, founder of Prestige, Norman Granz, founder of Verve, and Orrin Keepnews, founder of Riverside, were all nonmusicians who converted their love of jazz into a record label, initially (in many cases) by promoting concerts or setting up jam sessions that ended up being recorded. Others had a different path to the record business. Creed Taylor, who was first put in charge of Impulse (and later at Verve and A&M), was a jazz trumpet player. After a stint in radio, Vivian Carter, founder of Vee-Jay Records with her husband James Bracken, got into the record business through their ownership of a record store. Leonard and Phil Chess, founders of Chess Records (which distributed Argo), got in the record business through owning jazz clubs in Chicago. Many of them were immigrants who realized that there was money to be made from their love of music. And although, with the exception of Carter and Bracken (who were Black) and Ahmet Ertegun (who was Turkish), they were all white, all of them forged a close working and personal relationship with the Black musicians who recorded with them.

Looking back at all this recording activity in the sixties, one thing stands out. All the independent jazz labels that thrived were successful in defining a distinctive look, a distinctive sound, and a centralized core of great musicians and producers. The major labels didn't necessarily have to worry about those concerns. Columbia had deep pockets, so artists like Miles Davis, Thelonious Monk, and Dave Brubeck had a bit more leeway in regard to the use of producers, places to record, etc. But the smaller, jazz-exclusive labels had to develop a listener base that could be counted on to keep coming back for their product. They had to be creative in cultivating an audience, and they were able to accomplish this in numerous ways. One of the easiest ways to capture people's attention is with visuals, and many of the labels used distinctive photos and album graphics to catch the buyer's eye.

Blue Note became one of the leaders in utilizing state-of-the-art graphic design, and many of their album covers now hang on the walls of art galleries. As it pertains to visuals, Blue Note had an edge—Francis Wolff, one of the label's founders, was an avid photographer, and many of the photographs that he took at different recording sessions for the label found their way onto the album covers. Blue Note also benefited from the services of Reid Miles, a young graphic designer who came to the label from the magazine world. Miles

Herbie Hancock, *Takin' Off*: Blue Note Records, BLP 4109, 1962.

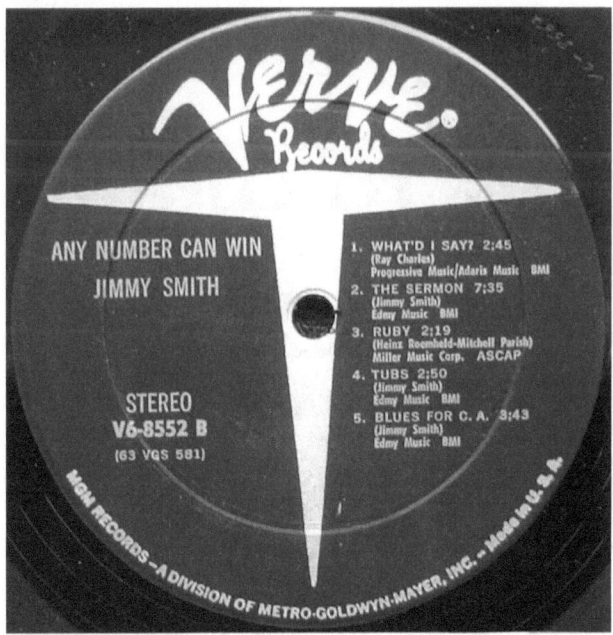

Jimmy Smith, *Any Number Can Win*: Verve Records, V-8255, 1963.

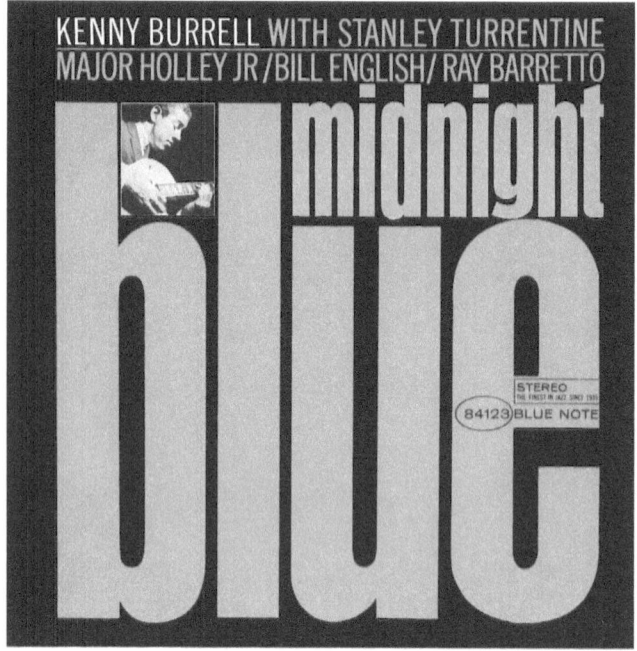

Kenny Burrell, *Midnight Blue*: Blue Note Records, BLP 4132, 1963.

Eric Dolphy, *Out to Lunch*: Blue Note Records, BLP 4163, 1964.

Freddie Hubbard, *Hub Tones*: Blue Note Records, BLP 4115, 1963.

began using very stylized graphics, different font styles, different-sized letters, and photos cropped in ways that borrowed heavily from the world of advertising. *Uncompromising Expression*, a book chronicling the history of Blue Note Records, notes that "[Reid] Miles was not a jazz fan.... Yet perhaps it was his distance from the music that was also his strength.... And of course, he had Francis Wolff's brilliant photographs."[8] Another young artist would gain from his experience working on album graphics for Blue Note. Andy Warhol, who became a major figure in the American art world, worked for Blue Note, as well as other labels, at the same time that he began creating his distinctive pop art.

Both Verve and Impulse would also employ a distinctive look for their album jackets, but in a different style from Blue Note. Impulse used big, glossy color photos of the artist on the cover, usually on the front and back, with a gatefold design that allowed for more photos on the inside. Verve used the gatefold design as well, and their covers were glossy, if not quite as colorful as Impulse. Verve covers usually featured a specific color scheme that framed the photo and dominated on the back and front. Atlantic Records didn't seem to stick to one specific style in the sixties, but there was much care put into their cover art. The highly regarded and very influential American photographer Lee Friedlander found work in the late fifties and sixties capturing jazz musicians for Atlantic Records, and many of Friedlander's jazz photographs now grace

Jimmy Smith, *Any Number Can Win* (back cover): Verve Records, V-8255, 1963

Chico Hamilton, *El Chico*: Impulse Records, AS 9102, 1966.

The Record Labels That Put the Sounds in the Grooves

John Coltrane, *Giant Steps*: Atlantic Records, SD-1311, 1959.

Eddie Harris, *Mean Greens*: Atlantic Records, SD-1453, 1966.

the walls of art galleries worldwide (Atlantic's album covers would become more specifically stylized in the seventies).

Prestige and Argo/Cadet didn't appear to be as distinctive as the others, possibly because of a smaller budget, but both labels were capable of coming up with striking visuals. Of note is the Ramsey Lewis Trio's album on Argo, *The "In" Crowd*. The cover features a large photo of two limousines pulling up to the front of a theater with a blurred crowd of people standing in a line. The photo creates the impression of a major event, and the blur gives the sense of motion and excitement. It's the kind of photo that would make one want to own the album, so as to feel like they were a part of the hip "in" crowd! Prestige jazz albums could similarly give you the sense of being there, as is the case with *At the Five Spot* from 1961 by Eric Dolphy. The black and white cover photo shows the quintet of saxophonist Dolphy, trumpet man Booker Little, pianist Mal Waldron, bassist Richard Davis, and drummer Ed Blackwell crammed onto the cluttered stage of the small New York club in an almost claustrophobic way. The somewhat no-frills photo gives a sense of intimacy and closeness that is matched by the sounds on the album. Compared to the Blue Note graphic style, the Prestige albums either didn't have the budget or the inclination to feature a fancy stylistic approach. As a consequence, we can now define the "Blue Note graphic art style" as distinct from the albums released on Verve and Prestige.

As it pertains to the sounds within, the sonic differences were, quite often, as drastic as the visual differences at the various labels. Musically speaking, a great example of the differences between jazz labels is the recorded output of Wes Montgomery (1923–1968) as a leader. Between 1959, the year of his solo debut, and 1968, the year of his death, Montgomery recorded for three labels: Riverside (nine albums between 1959 and 1963); Verve (six albums between 1964 and 1966 plus two collaborations with Jimmy Smith, who was also a Verve recording artist); and A&M (three albums, one in '67, and two in '68). Riverside Records, Montgomery's first label home, was a New York City label founded by Orrin Keepnews, who produced all Montgomery's Riverside albums (as well as producing most of the Riverside albums by Cannonball Adderley, Bill Evans, and others). Until the label went bankrupt in '63, Riverside was a leader in straight-ahead jazz, and Montgomery's output for the label usually featured the guitarist in a trio or quartet format, occasionally joined by a horn player, vibraphonist, or percussionist. The style is post-bebop with some tasty blues for added measure. Song selections are a mixture of jazz standards, tunes from the Great American songbook, and Montgomery originals.

Of note is the album *Fusion! Wes Montgomery with Strings*, a Riverside album that puts Montgomery's guitar on top of string orchestra accompaniment (much like Charlie Parker and Clifford Brown's albums of the late forties

The Record Labels That Put the Sounds in the Grooves

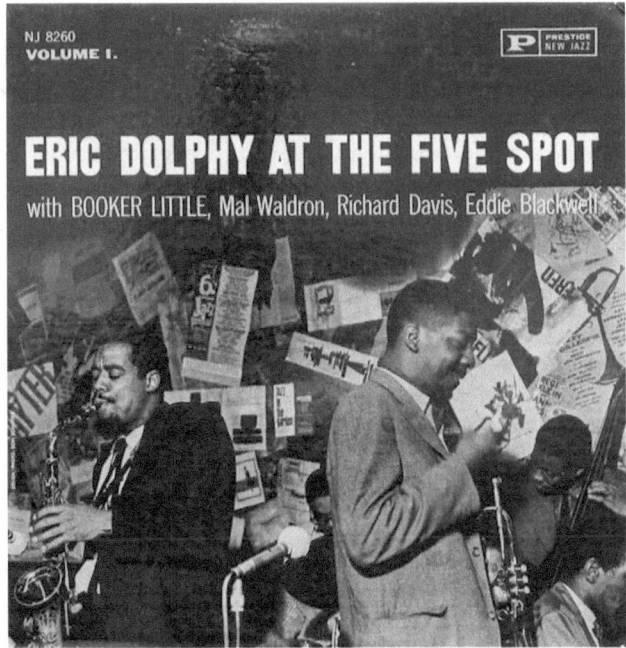

Eric Dolphy, *Eric Dolphy at the Five Spot*: Prestige Records, NJ 8260, 1961.

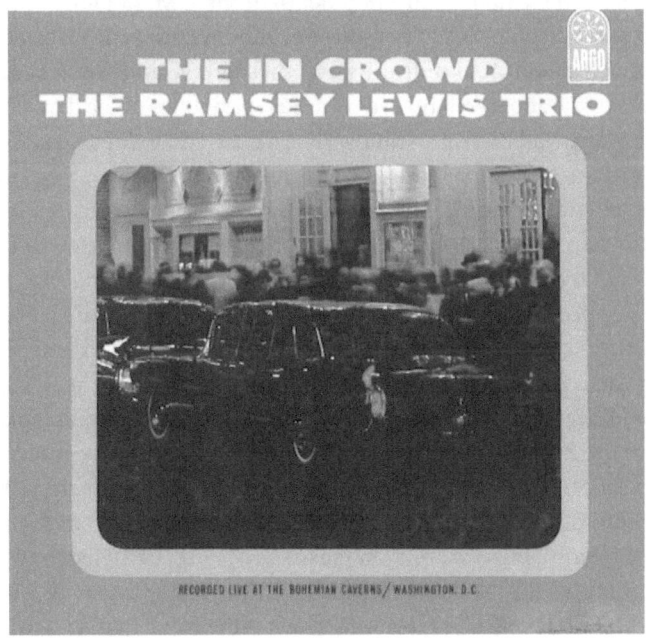

Ramsey Lewis, *The "In" Crowd*: Argo Records, LP-757, 1965.

and fifties). The album would be a harbinger of things to come because this heavily orchestrated style would be on display for much of Montgomery's output on Verve Records as well as his last three albums, released on A&M. Montgomery's entire Verve and A&M output was produced by Creed Taylor, who became the main force behind Verve recordings after leaving Impulse in 1961, and who would, after leaving Verve, establish the A&M subsidiary CTI (Creed Taylor Incorporated) that would become a highly influential label in the seventies. As mentioned, Verve was a Los Angeles–based organization and much of their output in the sixties was, sonically speaking, glossy and glitzy like their Hollywood surroundings. Taylor's sound production on Montgomery's Verve recordings is very bright with much in the way of added instrumentation. Oboes, French horns, soaring string scoring, and big band accompaniments (courtesy of arrangements by Oliver Nelson, Don Sebesky, and Claus Ogerman) were the norm on these albums, and Taylor included arrangements of pop tunes that were on the charts that were created for many of these albums.

The Verve and A&M albums sold very well, and they would generate plenty of radio airplay for some of the Montgomery tunes that were released as singles. These albums featured a wide variety of styles, numerous bossa novas and cha-chas, some blues, show tunes such as "Matchmaker, Matchmaker" (from *Fiddler on the Roof*), and a number of original Montgomery pieces that included rearrangements of tunes he recorded for Riverside. In retrospect, there is much criticism and dismissal of these Verve and A&M albums primarily due to the above-referenced reworked pop tunes of the day. "California Dreamin'" (originally a Top 10 hit by The Mamas and The Papas), "Goin' Out of My Head" (a Top 10 for Little Anthony and the Imperials), "Tequila" (a big instrumental hit for The Champs), and "A Day in the Life" (the last song on the Beatles' album *Sgt. Pepper's Lonely Hearts Club Band*) are just a few of the many pop and soul tunes recorded by Montgomery for these albums. Jazz journalist Gene Seymour notes that Montgomery's 1966 album *Tequila* is "one of the heavily orchestrated albums that have drawn fire from critics and historians for being too commercial."[9]

It should be noted that Montgomery's Verve and A&M output looks as distinct from the Riverside albums as they sound. As noted, Verve utilized a very glossy sheen on their albums, almost all of which had a gatefold jacket with a large photo of the artists on the inside as well as photos from the sessions. The A&M album graphics are even glossier, copying the style that was set in place by Impulse, the label established by Taylor. That glossy style would also become the hallmark for CTI Records, which is the name that A&M's jazz label morphed into. The visual presentation, as well as the sound production and the

Wes Montgomery, *Fusion!*: Riverside Records, RM 472, 1963.

Wes Montgomery, *California Dreaming*: Verve Records, V6-8672, 1966.

size of the ensembles performing on the recordings, was big and brassy, and Verve Records in particular seemed to hit on a successful strategy.

So what should one make of the criticism of Montgomery's Verve and A&M output? These albums featured arrangements by Oliver Nelson and Don Sebesky, two of the finest arrangers in jazz in the sixties and beyond; they featured great players like Clark Terry, Herbie Hancock, Snooky Young, and Grady Tate; and they featured Montgomery, who is arguably the second-most influential guitarist in jazz (just behind Charlie Christian). They are well-produced and engineered, and although they were not on the cutting edge, they are very listenable for many different jazz tastes. Each album has at least a couple of tunes that swing hard. There is never a time when you get the sense that Montgomery (or any other player) is coasting or phoning it in. That there was a distinctly recognizable approach to the Verve output in the sixties is one of the reasons the label not only survived but thrived.

One of the more amazing facts regarding jazz albums recorded in the sixties is the number of them that were recorded by a studio engineer named Rudy Van Gelder. Van Gelder (1924–2016) was actually a practicing optometrist who, in 1946, set up recording equipment in his parents' home in Hackensack, New Jersey. In 1959, it became obvious that the recording studio was much more than a side hustle, so Van Gelder had a state-of-the-art studio built in Englewood Cliffs, New Jersey, and his recording style became the industry standard. Van Gelder was meticulous in regard to the sound of the recordings made in his studio, and he understood that much of the magic was in the quality of his equipment. His Blue Note recordings in particular reflect that meticulous approach; so much so that the label began reissuing many of its classics under the subheading *The RVG Edition*. In her biography of Wayne Shorter, author Michelle Mercer notes that "Van Gelder engineered all of the label's recordings there [in his Englewood Cliffs studio], manning the console with such remote and precise professionalism that he came off as a little robotic.... Wearing white gloves, he would greet musicians with a warning to keep their hands off everything."[10]

The thing that made Van Gelder different from almost everyone else recording music at the time was his willingness to get a big, loud, live sound. Richard Havers, author of the earlier cited *Blue Note* book, writes that "Van Gelder was inspired by the sounds he heard in the concert halls and gigs he attended.... He wanted recordings to sound live, and he never deviated from that notion over his decades of working."[11] In particular, Van Gelder was able to capture the sound of drums at a volume that was, until that point, thought to be bad for the recording equipment. That specific aspect of his engineering work was especially appreciated at Blue Note Records. Haven notes that "Van Gelder was also a master at recording drums (a notoriously difficult instrument to record,

Stanley Turrentine, *Hustlin'*: Blue Note Records, BLP 4162, 1965.

as any modern-day producer will tell you), another significant factor in the distinctive Blue Note Sound."[12]

A prime example of the RVG approach is *Hustlin'*,[13] the 1965 offering by Stanley Turrentine (1934–2000), which is a kind of prototypical Blue Note release from that era. Side one of the album begins with "Trouble (No. 2)" (so named because it is the second version of the Lloyd Price song that was recorded by Turrentine), a bluesy, mid-tempo shuffle. The thing that one hears right away is the clarity of the sound of Otis "Candy" Finch's ride cymbal and snare drum; one would be hard-pressed to find a clearer percussion sound in 2024. In fact, everyone in the band benefits from Van Gelder's mastery—the call and response between organist Shirley Scott and guitarist Kenny Burrell as well as Bob Cranshaw's bass—the entire ensemble is heard perfectly in the mix. And perhaps a part of Stanley Turrentine's reputation for his big, bold tenor sax sound can be attributed to how well it is captured by RVG. That same beautiful clarity can be found on all of the tracks on the album. A relaxed, hushed lushness is apparent on "Love Letters," on which you can easily hear Finch's brushwork and Cranshaw's very mellow pizzicato attack; the straight-ahead blues feel on "The Hustler" (a Turrentine original, and one of the tunes that inspired the original title of this book), on which Burrell, Scott, and Turrentine capture fire in their solos.

Side two begins with a Candy Finch four-bar set-up to "Ladyfingers," and the lady in question is Shirley Scott, who composed the tune (Scott is featured in the section of this book dedicated to organ jazz). This song illustrates a point that was made in the introduction: so many of the great sixties' jazz band leaders focused on the blues. Distinguished jazz scholar and Ohio State Professor Emeritus Dr. Ted McDaniel refers to the blues as "the mother tongue of Black music," and in the sixties, the blues was very much on display on jazz albums. "Ladyfingers" presents the blues within the context of a 3/4 time signature, which was a favored groove for many fifties and sixties tunes (Miles Davis's "All Blues," Lee Morgan's "Boy, What a Night," Big John Patton's "One to Twelve," etc.), and Turrentine, Scott, and Burrell use the tune to demonstrate their mastery of the blues (with superb support from Cranshaw and Finch). "Something Happens to Me" is a fifties pop song that was recorded by Nat King Cole, Nancy Wilson, Blossom Dearie, and many others, and Turrentine and the band play it very straight forward, an easy two-feel on the melody, which makes way for a mid-tempo 4/4 with no surprises, on which the band plays swingingly. Once again, RVG's pristine audio mix allows the sound of Finch's cymbals to create another timbre that, sonically, enhances everything else. But the final track is a surprise—a relaxed, bluesy read of Dvořák's "Goin' Home," the main melody from the Largo movement of *Symphony No. 9 (From the New World)*. Interestingly, if you were not aware that this is from the most well-known movement of Dvořák's most well-known symphony, it wouldn't have mattered; Turrentine's band makes it sound like the most natural tune with which to end the album.

What is also surprising is that this album is only one of at least four albums that Turrentine recorded as a leader within the span of a year (this doesn't even include his role as a sideman on albums by his wife, Shirley Scott). Turrentine, as well as Lion and Wolff at Blue Note, understood that when you allowed terrific musicians to record with an audio engineering genius like Rudy Van Gelder, magic was likely to happen. But it wasn't just Blue Note that understood Van Gelder's genius; his August 2016 *New York Times* obituary notes "the many albums he engineered for Blue Note, Prestige, Impulse and other labels in the 1950s and sixties included acknowledged classics like Coltrane's 'Love Supreme,' Davis's 'Walkin',' Herbie Hancock's 'Maiden Voyage,' Sonny Rollins's 'Saxophone Colossus,' and Horace Silver's 'Song for My Father.'"[14] It is difficult to find to find a jazz musician from the 1950s to the 2010s who did not record with Rudy Van Gelder.

The only rival to Van Gelder insofar as his skills as a recording engineer was Tom Dowd. Unlike Van Gelder, who was likely to be heard on recordings on Blue Note, Prestige, Verve, and many others, in the sixties Dowd recorded exclusively for Atlantic. Another difference was that Tom Dowd was a musician, who could, if needed, fill in on just about any instrument that might be desired in the studio. Like Van Gelder, Dowd was not afraid to let the drum sounds come through loud and clear, which was unusual when he began recording at Atlantic in the early fifties. Dowd differed from Van Gelder in a couple of other ways. Van Gelder only served as a recording engineer, but Dowd would evolve into a producer. Van Gelder stayed within the world of jazz; along with the many jazz greats with whom he worked, Dowd branched out into the worlds of soul and rock 'n' roll, producing Aretha Franklin, Lynyrd Skynyrd, Eric Clapton, Rod Stewart, and so many others.

The years 1964 and 1965 would be very good in regard to popular jazz consumed by large parts of the American population, both Black and white, who didn't necessarily count themselves as regular jazz listeners, due in large part to the success of two musicians—saxophonist Stan Getz and pianist Ramsey Lewis.

Stan Getz (1927–1991) had, by the mid-sixties, been on the jazz scene for twenty years, first gaining notice during the big band era as a member of the celebrated "Four Brothers" sax section in Woody Herman's *Thundering Herd*. Getz's "cool" sound on the tenor sax grew from his love of Lester Young. Historian Frank Tirro noted that Young "has been deemed the founding father of a new school of jazz that was eventually dubbed 'cool,' and he was certainly the most decisive influence on the tenor saxophonists of the late forties and fifties, especially Stan Getz."[15] Perhaps because of his love of "Prez" Young, Getz became one of the first white jazz musicians who regularly played in Black bands, and he, in turn, hired Black musicians to play in his bands, most notably providing Horace Silver his first recording sessions in 1950. It is interesting to note, however, that during some of his recordings made during the bebop era, Getz played with a drive and sound more akin to the hotter Coleman Hawkins-Ben Webster school of saxophone than the Lester Young "cool" school. While playing as a sideman in the bands of Stan Kenton, Benny Goodman, and Jack Teagarden, Getz began his solo recording career in 1946, at first recording for a number of different labels (including Prestige) before beginning a twenty-year association with Verve Records through his connection with label founder Norman Granz.

Granz started out as a record promoter/producer in Los Angeles in the 1940s. The Verve Records website notes that "he had already founded the pioneering Jazz at the Philharmonic concerts and recordings series (1944–1983) that were, in essence, jam sessions that melded swing with bebop. In the midst of that, he founded Clef Records in 1946 and Norgran Records in 1953. But when he began to manage Ella Fitzgerald (known today as the First Lady of Song), he folded the catalogs of those labels into Verve Records."[16] Granz's association with Ella would pay big dividends; her recordings of the Great American Songbook were wildly successful, which gave the Verve imprint instant credibility.

Bossa nova has become such a ubiquitous style within the world of jazz that it's easy to forget it sprang out of nowhere in 1958 with João Gilberto's song "Desafinado." In their book *The Brazilian Sound*, authors Chris McGowan and Ricardo Pessanha note the reception of "Desafinado" was, initially, unfavorable: "The negative reaction had been occasioned by Gilberto's previous record, a landmark 78 RPM single with 'Chega de Saudade' (written by Antonio Carlos 'Tom' Jobim and Vinícius de Moraes) and 'Bim Bom' (by Gilberto himself), released in July 1958. Much of the Brazilian public was intrigued by the two songs, but others were offended by their unconventional harmonies, the apparent strong influence of American jazz, and Gilberto's unusual vocals."[17] That jazz influence would flow both ways; Stan Getz became, like many other jazz musicians at the time, enamored of the music of Brazil. McGowan and Pessanha noted that "bossa would explode in popularity in 1959—in Brazil with the success of Gilberto's album *Chega de Saudade* and internationally with the release of Marcel Camus's award-winning film *Orfeu Negro (Black Orpheus)*, the soundtrack of which featured songs by Tom Jobim, Vinícius de Moraes, and Luis Bonfá."[18] *Black Orpheus* would go on to win the Academy Award in 1960 for Best Foreign Language Film, and the soundtrack, composed by Luis Bonfá, Antonio Carlos Jobim, and Vinícius de Moraes introduced the music of Brazil to the world.

The allure of the melodies, the rich harmonic sense that supported bossa nova (McGowan and Pessanha describe "a harmonic richness previously heard only in classical music and modern jazz"[19]), and the natural rhythmic propulsion of bossa nova and samba grooves was immediately incorporated into the language that jazz musicians like Miles Davis and Cannonball Adderley used for improvisation. Numerous other Brazilian musicians, in addition to Jobim and João Gilberto, became a part of the jazz landscape in America. Stan Getz first recorded bossa nova on the 1962 album *Jazz Samba*, a duet album with guitarist Charlie Byrd (who himself was an early bossa nova devotee), and he would record numerous albums combining jazz and Brazilian music, the most successful being *Getz/Gilberto* with the aforementioned João Gilberto. Released in 1964, the album was a major hit due in large part to "The Girl from Ipanema," the Jobim song that was sung in Portuguese on the record by João and in English on the same recording by João's wife, Astrud. "The Girl from Ipanema" as well as the album *Getz/Gilberto* won top honors at the Grammy

Awards and paved the way for bossa nova to not only become popular with audiences, but also a style with which all jazz musicians needed to acquaint themselves. The sudden success of this song is still recalled, but in the retelling, we find, once again, an inaccuracy of the story of jazz in the sixties. Tom Moon accurately calls it one of the most successful jazz releases of all times, but also notes "'Ipanema' became a worldwide smash and the rare jazz song to turn up on jukeboxes."[20] In 1964, jazz was on jukeboxes all across the country.

"The Girl from Ipanema" was a big seller across the board. It sold well as a jazz tune, it sold well as a pop song, and it was played on Black radio stations. The success of the album *Getz/Gilberto* and "The Girl from Ipanema" led a whole host of jazz, pop, and soul musicians to release bossa nova-style records, and Verve Records became synonymous with jazz recording inspired by the music of Brazil. Cal Tjader, Bob Brookmeyer, Gary McFarland, and Stan Getz recorded entire albums on Verve comprised of bossa nova and samba tunes; Wes Montgomery and Jimmy Smith, both Verve artists, recorded individual Brazilian-styled tracks; and all of the originators of the bossa nova craze recorded albums for Verve Records, including Jobim, Luis Bonfá, and Astrud Gilberto, the voice of "The Girl from Ipanema."

Columbia Records and RCA Victor, perhaps the two most venerable of all imprints in the twentieth century, were still, even in the era of Beatlemania, invested in jazz. In 1962, Columbia added Thelonious Monk to their catalogue of jazz musicians. Monk, who had previously recorded for the jazz specialty labels Blue Note, Prestige, and Riverside, was now a labelmate with, among others, fellow pianist Vladimir Horowitz and the new folk phenomenon Bob Dylan, and he immediately began work on his first Columbia album, *Monk's Dream*. "Columbia heavily promoted *Monk's Dream* upon its release in 1963, and it became an instant bestseller. *Criss-Cross* came along the same year, followed by eleven more albums, including several recorded in concert."[21] RCA was, like Columbia, an early player in the jazz record world. In fact, the first recording of W. C. Handy's "The Memphis Blues" and the recording that has been given credit as the first "jazz" record, The Original Dixieland Jazz Band's "Livery Stable Blues," were both released on the Victor Records label in 1914 and 1917, respectively (the Radio Corporation of America acquired the Victor Talking Machine company in 1929, which was the year that RCA Victor Records was born). In the sixties, RCA Victor counted Duke Ellington, Sonny Rollins, and Nina Simone among its roster of artists.

The major labels, in the 1960s, continued to cultivate the jazz market, which was still a very vital part of the bottom line. This is reflected in the fact that all of the major labels had jazz subsidiaries. But an even better gauge of the viability of jazz in the sixties is the number of jazz labels that were established in the late fifties and the sixties. Sue Records (established 1957), Argo/Cadet (1956), Impulse (1960), CTI (1967), and Flying Dutchman (1969) are just a few of the many jazz labels that found major success in the sixties along with Blue Note, Prestige, Verve, and Atlantic.

As mentioned, many of the jazz labels began to see their records make inroads into the *Billboard* charts by releasing singles, but appearances on the *Billboard* charts weren't necessary. "While Main Street retail outlets were the primary source for weekly sales figures, many jazz records achieved impressive sales without ever gracing the charts. Art Blakey's 'The Preacher' sold well in excess of 100,000 copies, as did numerous singles on the Blue Note, Riverside, Prestige, Chess, and Pacific Jazz labels by Horace Silver, Bobby Timmons, Gene Ammons, Brother Jack McDuff, Les McCann, Stanley Turrentine, and others."[22] (A note here about sixties recordings. "Singles" refers to seven-inch 45 RPM records, and albums are twelve-inch 33 1/3 RPM records. Albums feature multiple selections, whereas singles focus on one song from an album plus a B side, which the record companies hoped would sell well enough on their own and simultaneously create interest in the album from which the single was extracted. In the 1940s and before, jazz, R&B, and pop music were released on ten-inch 78 RPM records, but in 1949, the 45 RPM single and 33 1/3 album were developed. Singles were considered the primary delivery system for music geared toward younger listeners, whereas albums were marketed initially to listeners of more serious, less popular recordings.) It is important to reiterate that when we speak of singles, we are talking about seven-inch 45 RPM recordings, which were primarily created for marketing to teenagers and their tastes. It's scarcely remembered that numerous jazz recordings were released as 45s that generated sales and radio airplay.

It was, in fact, one of the newer, independent jazz labels that would have perhaps the biggest hit in jazz. Chess Records, the Chicago label that became a leader in blues and rhythm and blues in the fifties, created a jazz subsidiary called Argo (there was already an Argo record label in Britain; Chess changed the name from Argo to Cadet in 1965). One of the first groups signed to the label was the Ramsey Lewis Trio. Led by pianist Ramsey Lewis, the trio would, in the early days, record at least two albums per year, many of which were live albums. In 1965, the trio recorded a live performance at Bohemian Caverns, at the time the most popular jazz venue in Washington, DC. The album featured a cover of the song "The 'In' Crowd" that was a hit for singer Dobie Gray in 1964. The story of that song, which went to number four on the *Billboard* Hot 100 chart, is detailed in the chapter about live jazz.

For fans in all eras, the labels are an important part of jazz lore. There are numerous books dedicated to the specific labels and the moguls who ran

The Record Labels That Put the Sounds in the Grooves 87

Brother Jack McDuff, "Can't Get Satisfied": Atlantic Records, 45-2402, 1967.

Jimmy McGriff, "I've Got a Woman": Sue Records, 770, 1962.

Ramsey Lewis, "The 'In' Crowd": Argo Records, 5506, 1965.

them. There are documentary movies focused on the glory days and hallmark albums (in fact, there are two documentaries about Blue Note, *Blue Note: A Story of Modern Jazz*, released in 1997, and *Blue Note Records: Beyond the Notes*, released in 2018). There are books dedicated solely to album cover graphics as well as websites where the albums can be seen in all their glory. And there is a beautiful documentary titled *Tom Dowd and the Language of Music* that gives a fascinating glimpse into the life of the legendary Atlantic producer/engineer. More than any other genre, jazz recordings are usually synonymous with the labels that released them because the labels were able to engender brand loyalty by creating a total aesthetic experience that was recognizable and desirable to music fans.

Of the many labels spotlighted here, it is interesting to note that some of them still survive in the third decade of the twenty-first century. Blue Note, Prestige, Impulse, and Verve are all still in the jazz business, although not as actively as they were in the sixties. Blue Note and Verve have added many non-jazz musicians to their rosters, but they still sign new jazz artists. Atlantic is now a major label, part of the of the Warner Music Group, but their jazz output is restricted to rereleases of their back catalogue (listed on their website as "Legacy"). The same is true for Columbia—all of their jazz recordings

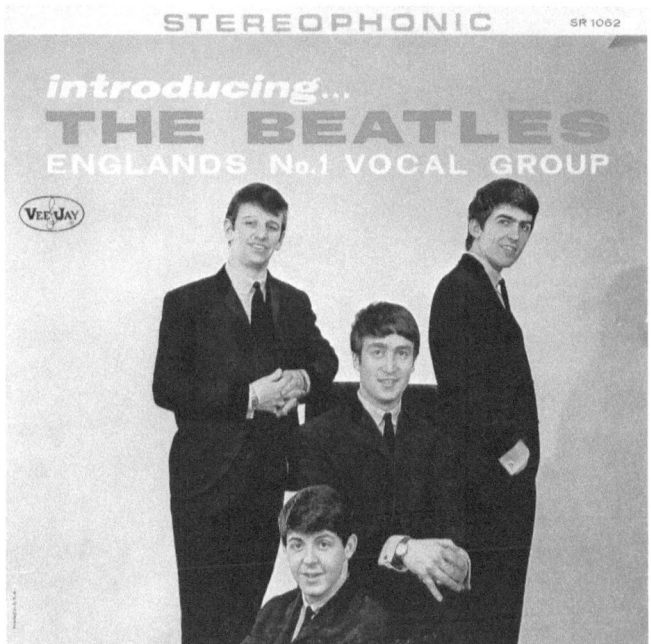

The Beatles, *Introducing The Beatles*: Vee-Jay Records, LP-1062, 1964.

are sold under the "Legacy" label. Argo/Cadet, Riverside, Sue, and Pacific Jazz are labels of the past, but their back catalogues have been purchased by other companies that have made lots of money in the reissue market.

As labels go, Vee-Jay had perhaps the most interesting ending in all of music. The Black-owned, Chicago-based independent label added to its jazz, gospel, and rhythm and blues output by releasing rock 'n' roll records by white bands that included Frankie Valli and the Four Seasons. In 1963, they worked a deal to become the American distributor of a little-known quartet from England; before long, Vee-Jay began selling millions of singles by the quartet, and the group became a phenomenon. After the band began to catch on, Capitol Records fought Vee-Jay for the rights to the group's music. It turns out that the quartet's British record label, Parlophone, was a subsidiary of the large conglomerate EMI, as was Capitol Records in America. The loss of the quartet was one of the factors that led to financial challenges for Vee-Jay. Larger money problems soon ensued, and by 1966, Vee-Jay declared bankruptcy. The name of that quartet from England? The Beatles.

CHAPTER FIVE

The "In" Crowd Goes to the Club

Bars, Taverns, Nightclubs, and the Live Scene

What do the following scenarios have in common: Duke Ellington at the Newport Jazz Festival in 1956; James Brown at the *T.A.M.I. Show* in 1964; Otis Redding at Monterey Pop in 1967; Jimi Hendrix at the same festival in the same year; Michael Jackson at the Motown 25 celebration in 1983; and Janelle Monae's television debut on *The Late Show with David Letterman* in 2010?

They are all examples of live performances by Black musical acts on records, in movies, or in television shows that have become benchmarks for what defines a great live performance.[1] They represent an essential part of the Black performance ethos, known as, according to James Brown, "kill 'em and leave!" Since the earliest days of African American performance, there has been a premium put on the live presentation; so much so that the image of the Apollo Theater crowd either cheering with uncontrolled passion or booing with equally vigorous gusto is etched into the American entertainment psyche. One can hear an example of this on the album *James Brown Live at the Apollo* released in 1963. The crowd's reaction to Brown is as entertaining as Brown's performance, and it is that reaction that is a central key to understanding this live tradition.

Jazz, by its very nature, is music that is best experienced live. Improvisation being at the heart of jazz means that the great players (and even the not-so-great players) will work hard to excel in the live setting, crafting burning solos and ensemble grooves that will inspire and awe listeners. In the jazz world, one of the greatest examples is Duke Ellington's 1956 performance at the Newport Jazz Festival.

Ellington knew that tenor saxophonist Paul Gonsalves, a Bostonian, was practically back home at the performance in nearby Newport, Rhode Island, so he called on him to be one of the featured soloists. Gonsalves, who played with Count Basie and Dizzy Gillespie before joining the Duke in 1950, was inspired on that day in 1956 by friends and family from Boston who came to hear him play. Gonsalves also drew inspiration from a mysterious platinum blonde woman in a black dress who seemed to surrender herself to the music during the band's performance, as well as from his former Basie bandmate Papa Joe Jones. Jones was one of the greatest jazz drummers of all time, but on that July 7 evening, he was not playing with Gonsalves but listening as an audience member. The Newport surroundings, the dancer in the black dress (who inspired others in the crowd to surrender themselves as well), and Papa Joe maniacally beating on the lip of the stage with a rolled-up newspaper sent Gonsalves into a frenzy, and he in turn whipped the crowd into hysterics, soloing over twenty-seven searing choruses of the blues in D-flat.

The tune that Duke Ellington picked as a feature for Gonsalves, "Diminuendo and Crescendo in Blue," had been a regular part of the Ellington band's repertoire since 1938, and the Duke had utilized many different ways to connect what had been two separate tunes ("Diminuendo in Blue" and "Crescendo in Blue"). With Gonsalves's arrival in the band, the Duke used the tenor saxophonist as a soloist to bridge the two tunes. On July 7, with all the inspiration mentioned earlier, Gonsalves and the Ellington rhythm section took off! Columbia Records arranged to have the Ellington Orchestra recorded at Newport for a live performance, so record producer George Avakian was on hand for the performance. Ellington biographer Terry Teachout writes that "Avakian, who was standing in the wings, was floored. 'I'd never heard a rhythm section like that. . . . I'd never heard the Ellington band wailing that way.'"[2] What followed Gonsalves's performances has been described as pandemonium. A reissued recording titled *Ellington at Newport Complete* has a track titled "Riot Prevention," which consists of the Newport crowd sounding very much like they are about to begin tearing the place apart until Duke Ellington steps up to the mic to announce that they will be playing more selections.

The performance, and the resulting album, was a sensation, landing Ellington on the cover of *Time* magazine. A book on the history of Columbia Records notes the importance of the recording: "The album reinvigorated Ellington's career, and several projects with Columbia ensued, including the landmark recording of the soundtrack for Otto Preminger's *Anatomy of a Murder*, one of the first feature films to showcase jazz."[3] On that night, "Diminuendo and Crescendo in Blue," that well-worn selection that Ellington played hundreds of times, had become something that live jazz, on both large and small stages, quite often becomes—a transformative event that lifted everyone who was lucky enough to be there to witness it.

Historically, the way jazz players learned their craft was by witnessing, then apprenticing at live performances. After woodshedding (intense practicing, sometimes in an actual woodshed, sometimes in a basement, wherever one can do so uninterrupted), musicians would emerge ready to go to local jam sessions hoping to get noticed by one of the established bands or by an enterprising musician looking to start a band.[4] Before going to music school and earning a degree in music became an option, most of this apprentice work happened live in front of an audience of paying customers. That was both a curse and a blessing; if you didn't know your stuff, you would find out in real time, really quickly (the stories of Charlie Parker's early failures in Kansas City jam sessions have become legend). But if you could impress a crowd, the success might lead to a spot in a band, a recording contract, fame and fortune, and perhaps a life partner (or a few).

From the earliest days of jazz, players prepared themselves to create tunes and put on a show that would impress the crowd. And in places like Chicago and Harlem, jazz clubs were the places that Black and white folks alike would go to see the finest entertainment. Black Americans migrated to Chicago in large numbers during the first "Great Migration" after WWI, which explains why Chicago became the first city to see significant jazz activity. A biography of Louis Armstrong recounts his move to the city in the early twenties: "[King] Oliver and Jelly Roll Morton had shifted their activity to Chicago, and other musicians were making their way there as well."[5] Chicago jazz tenor sax legend Bud Freeman was one of many young white musicians who would make their way to the Black part of town to hear the great players. "Freeman never forgot the bouncer at the Lincoln Gardens.... The big black doorman weighed about 350 pounds, and every time he saw us he would say, 'I see you boys are here for your music lesson tonight.'"[6]

The live jazz scene in America got some assistance in the thirties from an unexpected place, Prohibition:

> Despite the strong demand for burlesque acts, lavish floor shows set to music now known as jazz dominated a new generation of nightclubs that opened in the wake of Prohibition.... Connie's Inn, which opened in 1923, was one of the first new Harlem jazz clubs with a whites-only policy.... Later the club became a 'black and tan' establishment, letting in light-skinned colored customers after hours. Harlemites were willing to bear such indignities because the entertainment was worth it, especially the club's floor shows.[7]

But the Black population of Harlem had no need for the whites-only clubs or the black and tans; they had their own jazz havens. Harlem also had the most famous Black theater in the world, The Apollo. This venue became the place where jazz musicians could return after long nights on the road doing an endless stream of one-nighters, knowing they had adoring crowds who would welcome them back. The Apollo was also the place that could put a rising star over the top. A book on the history of that great theater notes that "the Apollo was instrumental in nurturing Billie Holiday's career and propelling her to stardom.... Her father, Clarence Holiday, a musician, told her how important an Apollo engagement was."[8] Holiday was known to battle stage fright, and on the night of her Apollo debut in 1935, "she was nervous and unsure of herself.... Once the spotlight hit her, she regained her composure and to his surprise and delight, won the Apollo crowd. They would not let her go without an encore."[9] The desire to gain the approval of the notoriously difficult but engaged crowd is what has made the Apollo Theater the mecca of live Black entertainment.

The Apollo crowd's reaction to Billie Holiday, James Brown, and so many others is an example of the kind of electricity that is central to the live music tradition. In the sixties, that live tradition sustained jazz musicians, and the numerous legendary live albums are the testament to that. Horace Silver's *Doin' the Thing*, Miles Davis's *Four and More*, Jack McDuff's *Brother Jack McDuff Live!*, Wes Montgomery's *Smokin' at the Half Note*, Nancy Wilson's *The Nancy Wilson Show!*, and numerous Cannonball Adderley Quintet albums recorded across America attest to the magic that jazz musicians made in front of audiences, both large (*Four and More* was recorded at New York City's Lincoln Center) and small (John Coltrane's *Live! At the Village Vanguard* was recorded before a full house of 125 people). And even though the Apollo Theater has 1,500 seats, the rapturous crowds make it sound and feel like the most intimate of performance spaces.

The idea of capturing live jazz performances for commercial recordings can be traced back to a series of concerts produced in Los Angeles. Norman Granz learned about putting together concerts while in the Army Air Corp during WWII, and he put that knowledge to use by promoting a series of LA jam sessions. In 1944, Granz was able to assemble a big jazz concert at the Philharmonic Auditorium, the downtown home of the Los Angeles Philharmonic Orchestra. Authors Jim Dawson and Steve Propes note that Granz was able to gain access to the hall by agreeing to donate the profits from ticket sales "to a defense fund to help several Chicanos imprisoned after the infamous 'Zoom Suit' riots in June of the previous year, when a mob of drunken servicemen rampaged through the barrio near downtown, beating up pachucos [the nickname given to the young Chicano men] and tearing off their baggy, draped suits."[10]

For the 1944 Philharmonic concert, Granz's good standing with musicians in LA allowed him access to some of the most popular young musicians in the jazz world including trombonist J. J. Johnson, tenor saxophonist Illinois Jacquet, and a couple of rhythm section players who, at first glance, seem like new players—pianist Slim Nadine and guitarist Paul Leslie. Due to some contractual issues, Nat King Cole had to use the Slim Nadine pseudonym, and army service meant that Les Paul had to become Mr. Leslie. At one point in the concert, saxophonist Jack McVea starts off playing just a standard blues, which would transform into a performance for the ages that was, luckily, being recorded for the Armed Forces Radio Service. Jacquet, who was known as a dynamic performer during his time in Lionel Hampton's band, began to solo after J. J. Johnson. "He began to shriek, squeal. . . . Each new assault on the melody drives the crowd into a frenzy. . . . This was clearly something new."[11] The show was tremendously successful, and that concert led to the series of recordings that became known as *Jazz at the Philharmonic*.

Many changes in the music world are driven by changes in technology, and early recording technology necessitated strict rules of what could be recorded and how it could be recorded.[12] "Because of the still primitive technology, no one had thought to commercially release anything that hadn't been recorded in the controlled environs of a studio."[13] Jazz, however, is a music that has always valued risk-taking. Classical music has always strived for the perfect recording, especially in the earliest days of high fidelity and the emerging home entertainment systems. "But jazz, with its flights of improvisation, was different. Jazz often sounded better live. The JATP concert recordings became the first 'live' album."[14] The success of the JATP concerts also led to Granz's career as the head of numerous record labels, including iconic jazz labels Verve and Pablo.

Due to continuous advances in recording technology, the 1950s brought about a number of great live jazz recordings. One of the first musicians to understand the possibilities of presenting their live performances on records was Dave Brubeck. Brubeck first came to prominence with a series of performances on college campuses, the first being in 1953 at Oberlin College in Ohio. Historians Geoffrey C. Ward and Ken Burns note that "the audience—including conservatory students—responded with ovation after ovation. The concert was recorded, and the album that resulted—*Jazz at Oberlin*—helped build enthusiasm for Brubeck. . . . Black as well as white fans followed the quartet in the 1950s."[15] Other musicians would record highly regarded live albums in the fifties: *Stan Getz at the Shrine*; *Jazz at Massey Hall* (the Quintet, a.k.a. Charlie Parker, Dizzy Gillespie, Bud Powell, Charles Mingus, and Max Roach); *Oscar Peterson at the Concertgebouw*; *A Night at the Village Vanguard* (Sonny Rollins); *'Round About Midnight* (Kenny Dorham); *At the Pershing: But Not for*

Me (Ahmad Jamal). These are just a few of the many live jazz albums from the fifties that have stood the test of time. Two others live recordings by two different gentlemen from Pittsburg, Pennsylvania, deserve special mention.

Erroll Garner came to prominence in the forties playing alongside such musicians as saxophonists Boyd Raeburn, Georgie Auld, and, most notably, Charlie Parker. Garner was a self-taught pianist who never learned to read music, which is interesting considering his elaborately orchestral approach to the instrument. Garner sounded as though he had a grounding in Chopin or Liszt, and he utilized every inch of the piano to draw as many different sounds from the instrument as possible. British jazz historian Stanley Dance noted that "for all the originality of his style, the pianists whom [Garner] referred to as his basic influences were Fats Waller, Art Tatum, and Earl Hines . . . when George Avakian began to work with [Garner] at Columbia, he had decided Garner 'was the greatest thing to come along on the piano since Earl Hines.'"[16] Garner also drew influences from the big bands: "I love the fullness of the piano. I want to make it sound like a big band if I can. . . . I love Duke. I love Jimmy Lunceford, and Count Basie taught me how to keep time."[17]

The characteristic used to describe Erroll Garner most often is "happy." He was called "the happy entertainer" and "the happy pianist." The sense of happiness that he radiated was partly due to his approach to performing. "I always play for my audience. I can't play to empty tables and chairs. . . . You need a public. They are buying your records and putting you where you are."[18] That desire to please his audience was reflected in the repertoire of tunes that made up the bulk of his recorded output. Almost everything that he played came from the Great American Songbook, Broadway shows, movie themes, Tin-Pan-Alley composers, and jazz selections that were known by all. Garner never aimed to set the world on fire—his aim was to please!

That desire to please is what made his 1955 album *Concert by the Sea* a national best-seller. The album, recorded at Carmel-by-the-Sea, California, finds Garner at his peak—he plays stride piano, he plays ballads, he plays mambo and samba style, and he plays the blues. Garner shows off his rhapsodic rubato playing style on song intros, and he shows off a ferocious right-hand chord and octave technique that is a signature stylistic device. But more than anything else, he swings like his life depends on it! You can hear on the recording that the crowd was enthralled. Critic Tom Moon writes, "It's rare to hear applause break out in the middle of a jazz solo, but that's what happens after a particularly spry chorus from Erroll Garner on 'I'll Remember April,' the opening track on this famous live recording from 1955. . . . Though he skips around through several decades, the ride is Cadillac smooth, and extraordinarily assured."[19]

Despite a less-than-perfect sound quality, *Concert by the Sea* clicked with record buyers just as Erroll Garner had with the live audience at the original concert. He was proof that a musician playing at the highest level can easily connect on a grand scale. The great pianist Geri Allen said it best: "Singular yet all-embracing, Garner blurred the line between great and popular art, and he was a staunch journeyman of the blues and his Pittsburgh legacy."[20]

It was another Pittsburgh native who recorded perhaps the greatest live hard bop album. Art Blakey is synonymous with the jazz style called "hard bop," and his bands personified all its stylistic characteristics—playing steeped in the blues that borrowed from Black gospel music, with tunes that had memorable melodies, active background figures behind the solos, and bridge sections that were designed to thrust the tunes into another gear (propelled by Blakey's explosive drum fills and his patented press roll). Throughout the course of the fifties and sixties, Art Blakey and the Jazz Messengers were the keepers of that post-bop groove music that is still being created in the twenty-first century. But in 1954, Blakey was still tinkering with that formula, and at the age of thirty-four, he decided to rely on a crop of young, innovative musicians to help him come up with the musical magic he was seeking.

It is hard for us in the twenty-first century to imagine revered jazz greats as up-and-coming musicians, but that was exactly the situation for pianist Horace Silver, alto saxophonist Lou Donaldson, and trumpeter Clifford Brown. In 1954, they were all in their twenties (Brown was, at twenty-three, the youngest). They were young, but they were the cream of the crop, as stated by Blakey on the stage of the famed nightclub Birdland: "Ladies and gentlemen, I'd like to take the opportunity at this time to mention, with confidence, that I'm working with now, and I hope forever . . . some of the greatest jazz musicians in the country today. . . . Yes sir, Immo stay with the youngsters. When these get too old, Immo get some younger ones; keeps the mind active."[21]

A Night at Birdland, Vols. 1 & 2 was originally released as three separate ten-inch discs, then rereleased as two separate twelve-inch albums in 1956. These records captured the excitement of Blakey and his young cohorts just when they were at their peak (bassist Curley Russell was two years older than Blakey but also an invaluable part of this group). Curiously, the band was not called "The Jazz Messengers"; even though Blakey had used the name "The Jazz Messengers" for his bands as far back as 1947, this band was billed simply as "The Art Blakey Quintet." The "Jazz Messenger" moniker wasn't used again until the release of Horace Silver's 1956 album "Horace Silver and the Jazz Messengers" (on which Art Blakey appears). From that point forward, the name was solely used by groups led by Blakey.

Although they are both wonderful recordings, there are a couple of things that distinguish *A Night at Birdland* from *Concert by the Sea*. The most obvious one on first listen is the sound quality. As described by Tom Moon, "The only downside to *Concert by the Sea* is its sound quality.... The piano sounds as though it's been captured at a distance, muffling Garner's precise attack on the uptempo numbers."[22] By contrast, *A Night at Birdland* was recorded by the legendary recording engineer Rudy Van Gelder, allowing the power and the fire of this ensemble to come through loud and clear. Another difference is in the song selections. As mentioned earlier, *Concert by the Sea* utilized songs that were deeply entrenched in the American music canon, whereas *A Night at Birdland* is almost totally comprised of tunes from the bebop catalogue of Charlie Parker and Dizzy Gillespie as well as the pen of the band's pianist Horace Silver, which began Silver's work of creating a new body of selections that would, themselves, become an invaluable part of the jazz canon. Upon the release of *A Night at Birdland* on twelve-inch albums in 1956, Billboard Magazine noted, "Tremendous modern hard bop session cut at the jazz club during working hours in 1954.... The increased market value of the performers, the superior quality of the solos, and the prevalent excitement throughout should carry sales as far as Blue Note's distribution will allow."[23]

It is assumed that a jazz crowd is a very knowledgeable, very discriminating crowd. Jazz fans know the players' styles, they know the tunes, and there is a standard that is expected when you hear jazz in a live setting. All of those things are true, but there is another side that was apparent that one can hear on the best live recordings that documented the sixties popular jazz scene—the musicians themselves, who make a direct connection with the folks in the audience. You can hear it when Cannonball is announcing the tunes on *Live at "The Club"*; you can hear it in the reaction to the Ramsey Lewis Trio at The Bohemian Caverns in Washington, DC, as they play a new tune that the trio worked up for the first time the day before the recording in 1965. The crowd might have been familiar with the tune, but not as a tune to be played by a jazz trio. Nonetheless, the Ramsey Lewis Trio was a crowd favorite, and when they launched into the new tune, a cover of Dobie Gray's soul music hit "The 'In' Crowd," the recording makes it obvious that they had the audience from the downbeat.

Conventional wisdom within the world of jazz history states that beginning with the bebop era, jazz musicians began to lose their audience. The reasons given run from disdain for the audience on the part of the players to music that became too complicated for people to dance to. The sense that jazz was becoming concert music where audiences sit and watch, much like a classical music performance, is also a common reason given for the demise of jazz.

There is some evidence of the reality of many of those ideas. A great example can be heard on Charles Mingus's 1960 album *Charles Mingus Presents Charles Mingus*, which is an album that recreates, in the recording studio, a Mingus quartet performance at The Showplace in New York. The recreation of the gig on the album includes Mingus's stage banter, which is, to say the least, interesting. Each tune begins with an admonishment to the "audience," including the following that precedes the opening track, "Folk Forms, No. 1"—

> Good evening, ladies and gentlemen, we'd like to remind you that we don't applaud here at The Showplace, or where we're working. So restrain your applause and, if you must applaud, wait till the end of the set—and it won't even matter then. The reason is that we are interrupted by your noise. In fact, don't even take any drinks, or no cash register ringing, etc.[24]

There is a caveat in reading that quote as being representative of every jazz performer's attitude in 1960. Charles Mingus was legendary for being particular about how his music was presented (for more on that, research the 1962 Town Hall performance), and he was legendary, as well, for being a volatile personality. That Mingus would recreate a live album in the studio, complete with calling out the audience, can be considered "pure Mingus." In contrast, however, consider another album also recorded in 1960 but this time in front of an actual audience. *The Cannonball Adderley Quintet Live at the Lighthouse* (in Hermosa Beach, California) is the first of many albums that showcase Adderley's band in a live setting and the first of many that demonstrates Adderley's gift for connecting and engaging with an audience: "I've been trying to figure out a long time what this name means, for this tune that Victor Feldman [pianist on the performance] wrote for us. This one is called 'Azule Serape.' Now he's from England, and I know it's not English, it's somethin' else. 'Azule Serape'—that's what the next tune is!"[25]

On this Lighthouse performance, the audience is clearly enjoying the music, and the album gives one the sense that the sound of the audience, clapping and, from time to time, talking, is an important component of the album. But the real lesson to take away from this is that Cannonball Adderley was, even at a time when there were numerous great live performances captured on albums, an extraordinarily engaging musician in a live setting.

The tale of Julian "Cannonball" Adderley's beginnings in New York has become a part of the "overnight sensation" narratives in the entertainment world. Adderley (1928–1975), who in 1955 was a high school band director in Florida, arrived in New York to attend graduate school at NYU. One night in June, he went to the Café Bohemia to hear a performance by bassist Oscar

Pettiford and his band. Charlie Rouse, the alto saxophonist, asked Adderley if he'd like to sit in, to which he replied yes. Two nights later, Adderley and his cornet-playing brother Nat were in the band, and a week and a half after that, that band was in the recording studio. Comparisons to Charlie Parker could torpedo most alto saxophonists, but Adderley seemed to thrive on the comparison. "Cannon," as he was sometimes known, became the talk of New York. Even Miles Davis was impressed: "After my engagement at the Bohemia, Oscar Pettiford brought a quartet in there that had Julian 'Cannonball' Adderley on alto sax. . . . Everyone knew right away that this big motherf***er was one of the best players around. . . . Man, he was hot that quick."[26]

In no time at all, Adderley assembled the first of many quintets (which always included his brother Nat), and he began recording as a leader, at first for Mercury, followed by a lengthy stay at Riverside Records. But perhaps the most important event in the early part of the Cannonball legacy was his association with Miles Davis. In his almost fifty-year career as an American icon, Miles Davis was known for many things, but his most consistently important role was that of a nurturer of future talent. The list of legendary artists who got their first exposure or first big break with Davis is long: John Coltrane, Sonny Rollins, Herbie Hancock, Tony Williams, Bill Evans (both the pianist and the saxophonist), Chick Corea. In 1957, Davis pulled Adderley into the fold. Davis recounted in his autobiography, "I could almost hear him playing in my band the first time I heard him. You know, he had that blues thing and I love me some blues."[27] If Cannonball Adderley had done nothing but record on Miles Davis's masterpiece *Kind of Blue*, he would still have rated a mention in the history of jazz. On an album that has seven of the greatest jazz musicians to ever play, Adderley manages somehow to stand out. In his book *Kind of Blue: The Making of the Miles Davis Masterpiece*, Ashley Kahn addresses Adderley's solo on "So What": "Cannonball takes a more fluid and melodic approach, injecting an exuberant rhythm in contrast to the subdued mood preceding him. . . . 'The only ones who were really playing on the scales were Bill Evans, Miles, and Coltrane a little bit,' commented Dick Katz, 'but Cannonball was just playing Cannonball.'"[28] Adderley brought a total command of his sound, he adapted and changed to the different styles of each of the tunes that he played on, and he radiated joy in every note.

Adderley's technical brilliance as an alto saxophonist, his jovial disposition, and his skill as a bandleader made him a natural in live performance. But it is his skill as a communicator that made him truly special. Adderley's training as a classroom educator made him not only knowledgeable in the specifics of his art, but it also made him a natural storyteller. Many of the finest music educators know that being an entertainer in front of a class can get you far with the students sitting in front of you. Adderley seemed to relish the role of master of ceremonies/front man/jazz evangelist.[29]

Take, for example, the 1962 album *The Cannonball Adderley Sextet in New York* (on some albums, Adderley added the saxophonist Yusef Lateef to the band, making the quintet into a sextet). The first track on the album is a two-minute Cannonball introduction:

> We've made a lot of records in nightclubs, especially in California . . . we've never made a live album in New York because, for some reason, we have never really felt the kind of thing we wanted to feel from the audience, which has nothing to do with acceptance, applause, or appreciation—it's the atmosphere. You know, you get a lot of people who are supposed to be hip, you know, and they act like they are supposed to be hip, which makes a big difference, you see what I mean. Now we have especially been impressed with the audience here at the matinee performance at the Village Vanguard. We think that this is the kind of audience that is the real jazz audience, and ah, we want to thank you for making it possible, for being so really hip. You know, hipness is not a state of mind, it's a fact of life, you see what I mean. You don't decide you're hip, it just happens that way.[30]

This kind of calm, charming, down-to-earth banter is a hallmark of those Cannonball Adderley Quintet (and Sextet) albums. So engaging are these monologues, they could (and perhaps should) be the subject of their own release minus the musical accompaniment. All of the numerous live releases by this dynamic ensemble feature these Cannon-isms. But perhaps the finest of these Cannonball raps is the intro that accompanies the tune that became the band's biggest hit.

Keyboardist Joe Zawinul joined Cannonball Adderley's band in 1961, and right away, Adderley knew that the man from Vienna, Austria, was not only a gifted pianist but also an imaginative composer. Most of the successive quintet and sextet albums featured at least one Zawinul composition, with many albums featuring multiple Zawinul tunes. In 2003, Capitol Records (Adderley's label home for most of the sixties) released the posthumous compilation titled *Cannonball Plays Zawinul*, and as one would expect, the centerpiece of this album is "Mercy, Mercy, Mercy."

When listening to "Mercy, Mercy, Mercy," the question is this—why does this tune work? What is the reason that the record comes across as the perfect representation of jazz crossed with Black church music and the blues? Is it because this Viennese guy totally appropriated Black culture? Is it the band's interpretation of Zawinul's tune that makes it so incredibly funky? Or is it because Cannonball set the tune up perfectly with his introduction, which allowed the crowd to react as if overcome with the Holy Spirit? The only possible answer seems to be yes to all of those factors!

Adderley starts this tune off with his most memorable introduction—

> You know, sometimes we're not prepared for adversity. When it happens sometimes, we're caught short. We don't know exactly how to handle it [crowd testifies] when it comes up [more crowd testifying]. Sometimes we don't know [long pause] just what to do when adversity takes over [someone in the crowd responds, "Go get on my knees!"]. And uh, I have advice for all of us, and I got it from my piano player, Joe Zawinul, who wrote this tune, and it sounds like what you're supposed to say when you have that kind of problem. It's called Mercy . . . Mercy . . . Mercy!

For the next five minutes, the crowd is all in, hanging on every note and every phrase. What makes it all the more amazing is that the tune itself is very simple—as far as the form goes, it consists of an eight-measure (A) section in the key of B♭, consisting of a four-chord progression played four times, followed by an eight-measure (B) section, consisting of four measures of a build-up over an eighth-note pedal B♭, followed by the entire band playing the climactic figure twice (B♭ B♭ D D E♭ E♭ F—B♭!), followed by section (C), which is just a short, coda-like section that ends on a G minor chord. The simple melody is stated by Zawinul on electric piano and reinforced by the horns, and the only solo, such as it is, is on the electric piano. The fact is that this simple, bluesy song is set up perfectly by Adderley's intro, which gives the audience license to chime in with relaxed, down-home encouragement. The audience then gives the proceedings a looseness akin to an intimate basement performance in front of family and friends. The only way this track could have possibly worked is as a live performance, and it works perfectly.

The album's title is *Mercy, Mercy, Mercy! Live at "The Club,"* and the liner notes are written by E. Rodney Jones, Chicago radio legend, and owner of The Club, which was an 800-seat venue that at one time was known as Club DeLisa. That club, located at 55th and State Street on Chicago's South Side, first opened in 1933, and according to historian/musician Dempsey Travis, "Club DeLisa was the road to glory for many entertainers like Big Joe Williams, who was there when Count Basie discovered him . . . and Billy Eckstine was discovered at the DeLisa in 1939."[31] Club DeLisa became a destination for movie stars who were in the city. Musician Freddie Cole recalled his time at the club: "Lots of times you would hear a police siren blowing full blast, and a motorcade would pull up outside the club with an entourage of movie stars like Bob Hope, Bing Crosby, Gene Autry, George Raft, Mae West, John Carradine, Paul Robeson, Joe Louis,

[and] John Barrymore."[32] In addition to jazz greats like Duke Ellington, Sarah Vaughan, and Earl "Fatha" Hines, the club featured comedians and dancers, and the reference book *The Encyclopedia of Chicago* refers to Club DeLisa as "the largest and most important nightclub in the African American community from the 1930s through the 1950s."[33]

In the mid-sixties, E. Rodney Jones and his fellow deejay Purvis Spann purchased the then-shuttered Club DeLisa and rechristened it "The Club." With 800 seats, The Club was able to draw top-tier, nationally known talent like the Cannonball Adderley Quintet. This new club was, in a way, a lot like the older Club DeLisa; it was a place in the Black community that was a destination—a place to dress up sharp and a place to go to be entertained.

Like many successful deejays in big cities, Jones had access to many of the biggest names in music. In addition to his duties as a deejay, Jones was the music director at WVON, which, in the sixties, was the most popular Black radio station in Chicago. Jones, along with Herb Kent, Purvis Spann, Bill "Butterball" Crane, and Lucky Cordell, made up the "WVON Good Guys," which was the group of WVON deejays who would emcee dances, appear at business openings, introduce acts at places like the Regal Theater, and promote concerts on the side. Jones's smooth, deep-voiced delivery was incredibly distinctive, and at the height of his popularity, Jones and the other "Good Guys" were as popular to Black Chicagoans as were the acts that they promoted and introduced on stage.[34]

Though known for playing blues and R&B, Jones was a former trumpet player who remained a jazz fan. So it was no surprise that one of the first acts to perform in The Club was also one of the best-known jazz bands in America. The fact that the Cannonball Adderley Quintet was known for their live recordings made it obvious that not only should the band play at The Club, but they should also record the performance, to which Capitol Records happily obliged. But there was a problem with the performance as it was recorded on March 18 to 20, 1966. When producer Tom Morgan listened to the tapes, he heard noise on the playback. It was noise being made by the crowd—The Club had some sort of knockers that the audience could use to show approval for what they were hearing, and when Adderley and his band played, the crowd would beat along with the knockers (this seems to be a holdover from the old Club DeLisa). Though the band played as superbly as always, the noise ruined the recordings.

The solution was a rerecording of the same performance, more or less, in October of the same year. The Quintet went into Capitol Studios in Hollywood in front of a live audience (who had access to an open bar) and recorded the performance that became *Mercy, Mercy, Mercy! Live at "The Club."* The album featured liner notes by E. Rodney Jones, and for many years it was assumed that he and Adderley were being less than truthful by promoting the album as being recorded in the Chicago club mainly to help promote Jones's venue. Interestingly, much of the original performances at The Club was released in 2005 on the album titled *Money in the* Pocket, and that performance proves Jones was telling the truth about what happened when he said this in the liner notes to *Mercy, Mercy, Mercy!*—

> Capitol Records came into The Club one night before showtime, strung their equipment all over, and took [the] full evening's performance down on tape. That was one of those great and providential blessings of history. What if there'd been no publisher around to provide a typesetter when Tolstoy wrote *War and Peace*? No Sistine Chapel when Michelangelo got itchy to paint a ceiling? What my friend Cannonball did at The Club is now preserved forever, and it'll be around a long, long time as among the definitive works of a master. I'm proud The Club played a part in it.[35]

The song "Mercy, Mercy, Mercy" was a surprise hit for the band, reaching number eleven on the *Billboard* Hot 100 Chart, and it was awarded the Grammy Award in 1967 for Best Instrumental Jazz Performance—Group, or Soloist with Group. Later in 1967, the tunes was covered by the Buckinghams, a rock band from Chicago, who added lyrics and took the tune even higher up the *Billboard* chart, and the song has been covered by numerous other musicians, including jazz singer Marlena Shaw. "Mercy, Mercy, Mercy," the Cannonball Adderley Quintet song and album, owes much of its success to the sixth member of the band on the recording—the crowd at The Club.

One can get the sense of vibrancy that was created by live jazz played in clubs both large and small in numerous recordings in the sixties. In venues across the country, musicians and record companies were eager to capture the atmosphere of excitement that was experienced on the road. Other Chicago clubs included The Blue Note, The Plugged Nickel, and The Pershing (a particular favorite of the Ahmad Jamal Trio, who recorded two albums there including the 1958 classic *At the Pershing: But Not for Me*, which spent two years on the *Billboard* charts); Detroit had Baker's Keyboard Lounge; New York City was home to numerous venues, from the storied orchestral Carnegie Hall to intimate jazz meccas like Slugs' Saloon and the Village Gate.

Out west, one had quite a few choices—Las Vegas casinos were the site of many significant jazz recordings like *Sinatra at the Sands*, which featured Frank Sinatra with the Count Basie Orchestra; California jazz fans had many choices, from Tsubo in Berkeley and The Blackhawk in San Francisco to The Lighthouse in Hermosa Beach and The Coconut Grove in Los Angeles. Many of these places became a part of jazz lore, with people making pilgrimages to the site where these clubs stood (or still stand, as is the case with the Village Vanguard, Baker's Keyboard Lounge, and others still in operation). But some places operated under the radar of many folks not familiar with the neighborhood in which the clubs existed, like Newark's Front Room (the site of a couple of organ jazz classics—*Brother Jack McDuff Live!* and Shirley Scott's *Queen of the Jazz Organ*), and Bohemian Caverns in Washington, DC.

Bohemian Caverns began its life as a speakeasy called Club Caverns in 1926, so named because the walls were designed to resemble a cave. It was located on U Street. DC historian Paul K. Williams notes that "in the boom days from the 1920s to the 1940s, U Street was the entertainment capital of black Washington and within its corridors were myriad cabarets, jazz spots, supper clubs, dance halls, and cafés featuring the best African American artists of the day."[36] Club Cavern closed in the 1940s but reopened in the fifties as Crystal Caverns, and in the late fifties, it became Bohemian Caverns. Bohemian Caverns hosted top-tier jazz musicians including Duke Ellington, Miles Davis, Bill Evans, and John Coltrane, and Black Washingtonians turned out dressed in their finest to be entertained. The club also featured well-known comedians like Bill Cosby, and according to Williams, "Relatively early in her career, world-renowned performer Aretha Franklin played for several nights at Bohemian Caverns in the fall of 1966. The October 22, 1966, 'After Dark' column [in the *Evening Star* newspaper] wrote, 'No one laughs when Aretha Franklin sits down to play, or for that matter when she stands up to sing. Instead, they yell, stomp their feet, whistle, and generally make a child's final days of school seem like a funeral procession in comparison.'"[37] Another musician who performed at Bohemia Caverns helped to give the club a national presence: Ramsey Lewis.

An internet search of "jazz piano trios" will yield many results, but there are some trios that will always appear—Bill Evans, Oscar Peterson, Ahmad Jamal, Keith Jarrett, Art Tatum, and Bud Powell are sure to be included. There will also be some newer performers like Brad Mehldau, Robert Glasper, and the group The Bad Plus who will usually get a listing on sites that compile "great jazz piano trio albums." And one name that is often left off of those lists is Ramsey Lewis. Lewis's entry in *The New Grove Dictionary of Jazz* is very brief, and it concludes, "His technically competent but repetitive playing has been criticized as being commercially oriented."[38] In his book *Chicago Soul*, Robert Pruter describes Lewis's music as stylish, piano-driven, cocktail-lounge jazz.

Mark Gridley's well-researched textbook *Jazz Styles: History and Analysis* makes this point when noting the connection between jazz and gospel music. "What impact gospel music made on modern jazz was usually felt in the simplest terms. . . . These jazz styles were created by commercially successful players who, although possessing jazz skills, remained on the periphery of jazz developments."[39] Among those groups whom Gridley considered on the periphery were "the piano trios led by Les McCann, Ramsey Lewis, and The Three Sounds."[40] Chapter fifteen of Gridley's book is titled "Bill Evans, Herbie Hancock, Chick Corea, & Keith Jarrett," and the first sentence of that chapter reads, "The most influential jazz pianist to emerge after Bud Powell was Bill Evans. The most widely imitated pianists after Bill Evans were McCoy Tyner, Herbie Hancock, Chick Corea, and Keith Jarrett. All four men combined the influence of Powell and Evans."[41] In reading that chapter, there is no mistaking Gridley's opinion of the importance of Evans, and in particular Evans's classical music background, which can be heard in his jazz playing.

For the record, Ramsey Lewis and Bill Evans began recording jazz trio albums in the same year, 1956. Both pianists were trained at music conservatories, and that training is clear in their earliest recordings. The Lewis Trio's first recording was titled *Ramsey Lewis and His Gentle-men of Swing*, and it leads off with their interpretation of Bizet's "Carmen." This is a reflection of the influence of Lewis's classical studies and his piano professor at Chicago Musical College, a woman named Dorothy Mendelsohn. Lewis speaks fondly of her: "She hammered into me 'you must make the piano sing' and 'listen with your inner ear.'"[42] Lewis's love of classical music as well as his gospel music background did not necessarily make him a natural in regard to jazz playing, and as he began to experiment with playing jazz, his parents were wary. Professor Mendelsohn intervened and reassured his folks: "Can I be honest with you? There's room for one, maybe two, African Americans in classical music, and as good as Ramsey is, he won't be able to make a living. If he has an opportunity to earn some dollars playing jazz, give him a chance and see what he can do."[43]

The classical piano training that seems to give jazz players like Bill Evans and Lennie Tristano an added note of distinction in the eyes of critics and jazz writers seems, in hindsight, to have been denied Lewis when analyzing his output. But his formal music training helped the Ramsey Lewis Trio find an audience right away. Part of that might have to do with the fact that they were in Chicago, which was a place where jazz musicians were not afraid of change. Chicago, in the 1960s, was known for many different types of music. It boasted one of the world's finest symphony orchestras; it was the city where jazz first began to flourish; Chicago-style blues changed the face of rock 'n' roll; and Chicago soul music was beginning to dominate, courtesy of Gene Chandler, The Impressions (and their leader, the great Curtis Mayfield), and the vocal group The Dells. In a book dedicated to jazz fusion in the seventies, Lewis makes note of the fact that Chicago set the tone for that groundbreaking style in the early sixties: "It is obvious that the birthplace of fusion music was in Chicago. It was during the early sixties that musicians such as Eddie Harris, Ahmad Jamal, and a group called the Ramsey Lewis Trio were unknowingly setting the stage for things to come."[44] The word "unknowingly" is crucial; those musicians were not attempting to change the world, they were reflecting the world around them as they saw it and fusing all the music they heard into their art. Noting that jazz gets called different things in different eras, Lewis noted, "Obviously, people living during these particular eras chose to give the music a name which reflected their tastes, and rightfully so. After all, jazz, like other creative art forms, was reflecting culture at the time."[45]

It is also important to note that the Ramsey Lewis Trio developed a style that would work in a couple of the places in Chicago they would often play. The London House and Mr. Kelly's were two nightclubs owned by brothers George and Oscar Marienthal. Unlike Club DeLisa, the Marienthal's clubs were smaller, and they were located in the more upscale Loop (a.k.a. downtown Chicago). The London House began life as a restaurant (ads for the restaurant included the phrase "make a date with a steak tonight") but incorporated jazz in the fifties as a way to stay open later. Sarah Vaughan, Oscar Peterson, and Herbie Hancock were regular performers at that nightclub, with the Oscar Peterson Trio recording four albums at the venue. Herbie Hancock describes the atmosphere this way:

> The London House was an old-school jazz club on North Michigan Avenue, just a few blocks from the Chicago Harbor. It was the kind of place where mostly older, white audiences showed up in suits and dresses to sip martinis and listen to classic jazz. The music was very good, but it wasn't what you'd call avant-garde. George Shearing and Oscar Peterson and Dave Brubeck played there, and the lineup was usually trios or quartets. The jazz there could be described as calmly exciting, not extremely challenging to the ear.[46]

The Ramsey Lewis Trio became the house band, and the London House became well-established as an upscale jazz haven. In the late fifties, the Marienthals opened Mr. Kelly's on Rush Street, the entertainment area just off of Michigan Avenue called "The Magnificent Mile." Both the London House and Mr. Kelly's became known for attracting a mixed-race clientele (a rare thing for the times) that expected great food, great music, and in the case of Mr. Kelly's, cutting-edge comedy. With this clientele in mind, the Ramsey Lewis Trio developed a style built to please people who came out to hear them, which seems to correlate with his basic philosophy: "The average guy, and his wife, they come home from working all day, they don't want to be educated. They want to be entertained."[47]

The Trio's albums were built to appeal to a wide variety of listeners; the selections ran the gamut of classical music, Broadway show tunes, modern blues, jazz interpretations of folk and gospel standards, and Ramsey Lewis originals, and they were able to get a big boost on radio—their manager happened to be one of the most well-known jazz deejays in America, Daddy-O Daylie. The trio also benefited from a contract with Argo Records, which was Chess Record's jazz division. Chess, the legendary Chicago Blues label, had wide distribution across the country, and the Chess Brothers developed a close relationship with Black radio stations in all the major cities. With that as a background and Daddy-O pushing them forward, the Ramsey Lewis Trio became a big draw in clubs across the country like The Bohemian Caverns.

By May 1965, when the Ramsey Lewis Trio was scheduled to record their second live album in the Bohemian Gardens, Lewis, bassist Eldee Young, and drummer Isaac "Red" Holt had been together for ten years. They developed a tight stylistic approach that could be quite varied—anything from classical chamber playing to a soulful, funky bar band sound—and they usually showed their many different sides in all their performances. The allure of popular music also showed itself in the band's repertoire, and soul singer Dobie Gray's hit song "The 'In' Crowd" was suggested by a waitress named Nettie Gray at a restaurant just before the May 1965 gig. Lewis remembers that the trio was trying to come up with a set list. "So Nettie Gray came over to the table to serve us our coffee and [said,] 'What are you guys doing?' So we told her. And she says, 'Well, have you heard this song by Dobie Gray?' Well . . . she went over to the jukebox and played [it]. 'You guys might like this. Listen to this.'"[48]

The trio forgot about the tune until the second night of the three-night gig. As Ramsey Lewis remembered, "When we started playing 'The "In" Crowd,' by the time we got to the middle of the song, everybody—the boppers and our people—everybody was up on their feet. And they were clapping. They were dancing. And we just kind of looked at each other, and we didn't know quite what it meant. It was a big thing."[49] It was a very big thing. Matt Micucci notes, "It sold over a million copies and won a Grammy Award for best small-group instrumental recording of the year. Time Magazine also promptly labeled Lewis 'the hottest jazz artist going.'"[50]

The single went to No. 2 on the *Billboard* R&B chart and No. 5 on the *Billboard* pop chart. The album did even better—it went to No. 2 on the *Billboard* Top 200 chart and No. 1 on the R&B album chart. Despite this (or perhaps because of its chart success), there is rarely any discussion about this monumental jazz success in jazz history, nor is there much discussion regarding Lewis's long and successful career. Popular success is terrain that is unfamiliar and uncomfortable to some of the "keepers" of the jazz tradition. Lewis remembered, "In 1965, we put out a record . . . that clearly drew from the aforementioned styles (black church, rhythm and blues, and jazz). From musicians and critics alike, there were shouts of foul play. At the time they said it was sacrilegious to involve any other kind of music, especially R&B, with jazz."[51]

But Lewis understood something right away that allowed him to capitalize on his success—his audience "got it." "This music was in its early stages, the listener accepted it long before other musicians of that time."[52] And that is obvious in the liner notes to *The "In" Crowd*, written when the album was released (before it would become a phenomenal hit), by jazz radio personality Al Clarke: "The Ramsey Lewis three are among the best-selling jazz artists on record today. A collection of their works shows the many facets of their styles. . . . The scope of jazz today has widened and young men like Ramsey Lewis are improvising, drawing from many sources, blending and putting into jazz something that was not there before, but never losing the source—the blues."[53]

In the years following *The "In" Crowd*, Lewis continued to have success with his crossover approach, recording numerous albums and playing to adoring fans around the world.[54] In 2022, right before his death, eighty-seven-year-old Ramsey Lewis had retired from the road, as well as from making recordings, but to the end of his life still practiced daily and played online concerts on the last Saturday of each month, and he still sounded like the leader of *The "In" Crowd*.

The twenty-first century has seen numerous changes in the world of jazz, but one thing remains clear. The live album continues to be an important document for jazz musicians' creative output. Some of the greatest names in jazz have released live jazz albums since 2000, and the recordings cover the entire spectrum of jazz styles and genres, including big bands like Wynton Marsalis's Lincoln Center Jazz Orchestra and Sherrie Maricle's Diva Jazz Orchestra; jazz singers Gregory Porter and Cécile McLorin Salvant; small group live offerings, like organist Dr. Lonnie Smith's last album *Breathe* as well as nineteen-year-old piano phenom Joey Alexander's *Joey. Monk. Live!* Even the avant-garde continues to be represented in live settings, as evident in a 2020 offering by trumpet player/composer Christian Scott aTunde Adjuah, *Axiom*.

The live jazz experience, and the recordings generated from it continue to be one of the yardsticks by which players measure greatness. That probably has to do, more than anything, with what Cannonball Adderley wanted to "feel from the audience, which has nothing to do with acceptance, applause, or appreciation—it's the atmosphere."[55]

Epilogue

There was one person I thought was crucial in providing a firsthand account of the music scene that I chronicle in this book—Ramsey Lewis. Over the three years that this book was being created, I reached out to Mr. Lewis's management on four occasions. After the first two attempts, his manager emailed me back and said, "Thanks, Michael, let me discuss this with Ramsey and I'll get back to you." I was excited to hear that. Mr. Lewis is a pivotal figure in popular jazz in 1960s Black America, which of course is the subject of the book. I developed a long list of questions to ask him, one of which was "How would you describe the jazz scene in 1960s Black America? As a major participant in it, was it a healthy and dynamic scene? Did it seem vibrant at the time, or did it seem like musicians were always scraping and hustling to survive?" I was really happy that I would get the chance to pick Ramsey Lewis's brain!

Weeks went by, and there was no follow-up from Mr. Lewis's manager. I reached out again, but still no word. Soon a year went by, and I reached out once again, but again no reply. I have performed with musicians who played in his band, so I considered reaching out to one of them to try to act as a go-between. I even considered going to his house because I knew where he lived in Chicago. But I figured that it is best to go through the proper channels—a musician of Ramsey Lewis's stature deserves that respect. However, I had a book to complete, and so I resigned myself to the fact that an interview with Ramsey Lewis would not be part of it.

Today I received a text from my sister: "Ramsey Lewis is gone." One of my thoughts after not receiving a follow-up to the email from his manager was that maybe Mr. Lewis was not in good health. It appears that this hunch was correct. But today's news caused me to reflect on why the interview with Mr. Lewis was so important. More than perhaps any other musician from that era, Ramsey Lewis represented the dichotomy at play when examining the lack of respect afforded popular jazz in the 1960s. Here is a person who represented everything that Black jazz fans loved in the sixties—his music connected with a relentless groove, top-level musicianship, great tunes (both original and covers), class and refinement, plus an abundance of soul! But when reading histories of jazz, Ramsey Lewis is rarely, if ever, included when examining jazz of the sixties. Ramsey Lewis reflected the pride and the aspirations of Black America in the sixties, and he continued to do so through the 2020s. From the first recording in 1956, Mr. Lewis established an elegant piano style and a sense that jazz could connect with a large audience, and those characteristics would serve him well up through his last album, which was scheduled to be released in 2022. The lack of recognition of popular jazz in surveys of jazz in the sixties is a glaring omission, and Ramsey Lewis is the prime example of critical analysis lagging far behind music that best represented what people wanted to hear.

Ironically, it wasn't until I got that text from my sister that I realized that I dedicated many more pages in my book to the music of Ramsey Lewis than I did to any other single musician or group. And it occurred to me that the reason that I wanted to interview him for the book wasn't necessarily for the insights that he would give. Yes, those insights would have been wonderful, but the real reason I wanted to interview him was so that he would know that I wrote a book in which he was a central character. Maybe THE central character. I wanted Ramsey Lewis to know that I wrote a kind of love letter to the music that he, and Eddie Harris, and Herbie Hancock, and Cannonball Adderley, and Nancy Wilson, and Jimmy Smith, and so many others created. I wanted him to know that my dad, who was just a couple of years older than he was, made sure that I knew this music well and that he planted a deep love for this music in me.

I didn't want to interview Ramsey Lewis, I wanted to thank him in person. And I really wanted to present him with this book. But I vow to do the next best thing—I will give a copy of the book (as soon as it is published) to his family. And I will thank them for sharing Ramsey Lewis with the world.

CHAPTER SIX

"When You Go, Let 'Em Know That Daddy-O Told You So"

Black Radio and the DJs that Spread the Sounds

The voice that would introduce the tunes was very relaxed, very mellow, and very hip. "I'm the musical host that loves you the most" or "I'm twice as nice as a mother's advice." When one listened to Daddy-O Daylie on the radio, it was understood that the jazz music on the turntables was only one part of the entertainment. Daddy-O, with his unique rhyming ability, his witty banter with guests, and his calm, cool cadence, was an equal part of the show. At a time when disc jockeys became as well-known as the recording artists listed on the labels (and in some cases, much more well-known), Daddy-O was one of the biggest names of them all.

Chicago's legendary soul music deejay Herb Kent ("the Cool Gent") was a big fan. "Daddy-O was phenomenal. I used to listen to him in high school.... He was so smooth, and he'd play that good jazz in the morning on the way to work, and he'd be rhyming. He was sensational ... the top jazz disc jockey."[1] Daddy-O became a nationally known deejay as well as a civil rights mover and shaker, and upon his death in 2003, there were tributes from around the world. The irony is that none of his successes could have been foreseen in his beginnings as his life emerged from dire circumstances.

Holmes Daylie was born the youngest of thirteen children in Covington, Tennessee, in 1920. His mother died giving birth to him, and at three years old, he was sent to Chicago to live with an older brother. Poverty and a less-than-nurturing home environment left Holmes feeling ashamed and in need of a strategy for keeping schools bullies at bay. Holmes would entertain schoolmates with "jokes I heard on the radio, thinking that if they would laugh with me, they might not laugh at me."[2] Holmes was a talented athlete who played basketball professionally for a while, but eventually he tired of the road and returned to Chicago, where he began working as a bartender. At the bar, Holmes would combine his basketball skills with rhyming as he would flip ice cubes in a glass while reciting a witty line. The owner of the lounge at the DuSable Hotel took notice, and before long, Holmes was bartending at a lounge frequented by some of the most famous Black jazz musicians in America. He remembered that "one morning, Duke Ellington came down to the lounge . . . and Art Tatum came up from the Three Duces downtown and the three of them (including Fats Waller) got into a piano jam session in the lounge that lasted from three a.m. until one-thirty the next afternoon."[3] It was at this time people would come into the bar and say, "Hey, daddy-o, fix me a drink." The nickname stuck, and his given name Holmes was pushed to the sideline—he was now Daddy-O Daylie.

A move in 1944 to a different integrated bar led to a fateful meeting with Dave Garroway, a nationally known white radio deejay who would play jazz records on his show. Garroway was impressed with Daddy-O's rhyming wordplay, and he suggested that Daylie go to school to learn how to become a radio announcer. Daylie followed that suggestion, and the rest is jazz radio history.

Daddy-O was one of many legendary disc jockeys who were crucial in disseminating Black music and Black culture to Black and white Americans via the radio, which was, in the 1960s, the most direct way to get that music and culture. In this contemporary, cyber-connected world of endless unlimited access to media of all kinds at any time anywhere across the globe, it is important to reassess the media landscape of the 1960s. There were no computers or cell phones, and there was no internet or streaming services. Television was dependent on your proximity to transmission antennas and towers; if you lived in or close to big cities, you were likely to get the three major network (NBC, CBS, and ABC) channels' affiliates plus some local station (like WGN, in Chicago). If you lived in small towns, good luck; on a clear day (and especially at night), you might have a chance at good reception to one or two channels.

If you did get good television reception and you were Black, you were not likely to see programming that was aimed at you or your particular cultural needs. In 1965, Bill Cosby made history when he became the first Black man to star in a dramatic television series, *I Spy*, as well as the first Black actor to receive an Emmy Award for dramatic acting. In 1968, Diahann Carroll made history of her own when she starred in *Julia*, the first television series to star a Black woman in a nonstereotypical role. It should be noted that neither Bill Cosby's nor Diahann Carroll's historic casting led to large numbers of television shows starring Black actors in the sixties. Hollywood was, similarly, not a place that one could go to see Black culture. Sidney Poitier's Academy Award win in 1964 for *Lillies of the Field* was only the second time a Black actor won that award (the first being Hattie McDaniel in 1939), and starring roles for Black actors were few and far between (it should also be noted that films about Black life were even rarer; Poitier's role in *Lillies* could have easily been played by a white actor).

Radio, with its potential for long-distance, unrestricted reach, was the only place that Black Americans could regularly turn to for a dose of Black culture. Radio was the lifeline for Black Americans—this was a way to hear the latest songs, hear a sermon from a famous preacher (like C. L. Franklin, Aretha's dad, whose sermons from his Detroit congregation could be heard through the Midwest and the South), get performances from ballrooms or theaters, and get the latest news that pertained to Black life. One of the first people to realize this in the early part of the twentieth century was Jack Cooper, a Black man from Chicago who ran the Washington, DC, office of the *Chicago Defender* (a historic Black newspaper still being published online in 2024). University music professor Aaron Johnson wrote his dissertation on jazz and radio, and in it, he noted that Cooper also had experience with the medium and that "his experience in radio allowed him to recognize an opportunity in Chicago when he returned. In 1929, [Cooper] created the 'All-Negro Hour' on WSBC."[4] Johnson also notes that "Negro-appeal radio, the forerunners of Black-formatted radio stations, first appeared in cities like Memphis, Atlanta, Chicago, and Washington, DC, using this model."[5]

It took the radio networks a while to realize that Black people were an untapped market that had spending power. Oddly enough, a small town in the South was one of the first to capitalize on that market. Noted author and music critic Nelson George reported that "[a] representative example is the *King Biscuit Time* broadcast in the early 1940s from the teeming little metropolis of Helena [Arkansas] . . . At noon, harmonica player Rice Miller (a.k.a. Sonny Boy Williamson II) and guitarist Robert Lockwood Jr. brought listeners fifteen minutes of blues and greetings from the makers of King Biscuit flour."[6] As of 2024, "King Biscuit Time" is still being broadcast!

Soon, the growth of independent record labels that catered to Black musical tastes led to more (and more varied) recording opportunities for Black musicians, which led to more stations that could expand beyond the "Negro Hour" concept, allowing for the emergence of Black radio. These were radio stations owned, for the most part, by white businessmen but staffed by Black announcers, performers, and deejays who understood that there was a segment of the population who wanted to hear music that appealed to them and who would (most importantly of all) spend money on products advertised on the radio stations. There were also Black radio shows that occasionally cropped up on primarily white radio format stations. As a young journalist, celebrated Black novelist Alex Haley (*Roots*, *The Autobiography of Malcolm X*) wrote an article for *Harper's* magazine in the fifties on the impact of Black radio. Nelson George notes that "the future best-selling author made four points: radio helped black as well as white businesses reach potential buyers; helped blacks know where they could shop without fear of harassment; provided prestigious jobs for blacks; and provided outlets for community service announcements by civic and church groups."[7]

An example of one of those black radio stations is WDIA, in Memphis, Tennessee, which calls itself "America's First Black Radio Station." Founded in 1947, WDIA brought in a number of Black on-air personalities to entertain its audience. In 1949, an aspiring young musician named Riley King knocked on the door of the station and asked if he could record a song (in the early days of radio, some stations would double as recording studios). The owner told him that they didn't make records there, but the man looked at Riley and had an idea. He held up a bottle of "Pep-Ti-Kon," a medicinal tonic being sold as a blood builder, from a supplier that bought advertising time at the station. Bert Ferguson, the station owner, asked Riley if he could come up with a jingle to sell the song, to which Riley replied, "Pep-Ti-Kon sure is good, Pep-Ti-Kon sure is good, Pep-Ti-Kon sure is good, you can get it anywhere in your neighborhood!"[8] After conferring with Nat D. Williams, the Black announcer who managed the place, Ferguson gave King a job. According to Christiane Bird's *Da Capo Jazz and Blues Lover's Guide to the U.S.*, "On weekends, [Riley] was required to drive around town and play from the top of a Pepticon truck . . . there was no pay involved in any of this, but Riley was allowed to advertise a gig he then held in West Memphis."[9]

WDIA, which is still on the air, would play an important part in Black radio history even if Riley King had not become B. B. King, because WDIA and other stations proved that Black radio was a viable moneymaker. Black radio was essential because unlike white people, Black America had nowhere else to go for community news and culture. And the music that they used to attract and keep an audience was the music that the Black communities across the country wanted to hear: jazz, gospel, blues, and rhythm and blues. But the most important part of the equation was the radio personalities who, through the magic of radio waves, came into homes and became trusted arbiters of what was hip, in fashion, and good, especially in regard to music.

In the forties and fifties, large national networks had a stronghold on radio, but it soon became clear that local radio stations could create a loyal following by tailoring to the specific needs of the different communities as well as by letting announcers and deejays appear in the community in different capacities. Some of those announcers' names are legendary in the broadcasting world—Jack Cooper, Nat D. Williams, Al Benson, Rufus Thomas (who became an entertainment legend far beyond his radio days), Jocko Henderson, "Jockey" Jack Gibson, Lavada "Dr. Hepcat" Durst, Daddy-O-Daylie, Eddie O'Jay (who became the manager of the legendary soul vocal trio that bears his name), Hal Jackson, Merri Dee, Magnificent Montague, Bob Perkins—not all of them played exclusively jazz, but they were all responsible for creating a demand that sustained jazz, blues, and rhythm and blues musicians.

The Golden Age of Black Radio website has this observation: "Radio in America was never the same after Black deejays came into their own. They introduced the public to a distinct Black style of on-air talk that was a combination of jive, rhythm, and warm affection for the listeners. They became celebrities within their communities, elevated to the role of cultural icons."[10] And for the many white listeners, such as a young Elvis Presley in Memphis, those deejays could be considered cultural ambassadors. Elvis biographer Peter Guralnick writes of the music education Presley was able to receive in the year 1950 in Memphis:

> In fact, if he had never left the apartment, just listening to the radio would have been a big step toward completing his musical education.... Late at night, Elvis could have listened—along with most of the other kids in the Courts and half of Memphis, it seems—to Daddy-O-Dewey, Dewey Phillips, broadcasting from Gayoso on WHBO ... In the morning, there was Bob Neal's wake-up show on WMPS.... If you changed the dial to WDIA, which since its switchover in 1949 to an all-black programming policy had billed itself as 'The Mother Station of the Negroes,' you could hear not only local blues star B. B. King, deejaying and playing his own music live on the air, but also such genuine personalities as Professor Nat D. Williams . . ."[11]

There is no question that Presley frequently had his dial set on WDIA—a few years later, just as he was on his way to becoming the biggest thing in music, Elvis made an appearance at the radio station's annual charity fundraiser. Guralnick recounts an encounter between Presley and B. B. King: "After the show was over, he stood backstage talking quietly and having his picture taken with B. B.... 'To all who are within earshot,' reported the *Tri State Defender* to its black constituency proudly, 'Presley was heard telling King, "Thanks, man, for the early lessons you gave me."'"[12]

Dr. Ted McDaniel, Professor Emeritus of Jazz Studies at The Ohio State University, is a Memphis native who grew up listening to WDIA, and his band director father taught with Nat D. Williams at Booker T. Washington High School. Dr. McDaniel has fond memories of Williams, who was a fellow church congregant as well as a family friend—

> Nat D. Williams was very well-respected for his intellect, there was no b.s. or jive in his delivery, unlike many other radio personalities. Nat was much stronger than that—he was a learned man, a college grad with a commanding voice and a commanding presence. He could take on any subject . . . everybody knew him, he was a major, major radio presence. He might well have been the most notable Black announcer, very civic-minded. Nat was recognized by his peers, and he was a beacon of the community.[13]

McDaniel reiterates a point made earlier—Black announcers and disc jockeys were important people in their communities. "For Black people, the radio announcers and deejays were lifelines for all Black citizens, because even if you couldn't read, you could hear the information that you needed."[14]

Jazz disc jockeys, both Black and white, were an important factor in the demand for jazz records. The recognition that came to jazz players because of the boost deejays gave to their records or live performances could make a huge difference in their careers. Dave Garroway, the white deejay who assisted Daddy-O Daylie and who would go on to become the host of NBC's *Today Show* was an enthusiastic supporter of Sarah Vaughan early in her career. Vaughan biographer Elaine Hayes notes that "Garroway was but one in a quartet of Chicago disc jockeys advocating for Vaughan. Ernie Simon of WJJD, Eddie Hubbard of WIND, and freelancer Linn Burton . . . all used their platforms to voice enthusiasm, praise, and unflinching support for the promising vocalist."[15] These jazz deejays were, in almost all cases, jazz fans who loved listening to the music themselves, which led them to do whatever they could to aid in the careers of the musicians. When remembering her 1960 album *Like In Love*, Nancy Wilson recalled, "Disc jockeys Sid McCoy and Daddy-O Daylie picked up my album and gave it a big play. . . . These two disc jockeys really made it happen for me."[16]

In return for this support, many jazz players wrote tunes dedicated to those loyal deejays. Sid Torin was a very popular jazz deejay in New York City who, despite being white, would talk in Black vernacular while giving a big boost to many young Black jazz players on the radio. Tenor sax player Arnett Cobb was so grateful that he wrote a song titled "Walkin' With Sid." Sax great Lester Young went one better—his tune "Jumpin' with Symphony Sid" became a big hit. Cincinnati deejay legend Oscar Treadwell was also celebrated in song by a couple of saxophonists: Charles Parker's "An Oscar for Treadwell" and Wardell Gray's "Treadin' with Treadwell." Daddy-O Daylie was the inspiration for Nat Adderley's "One for Daddy-O" as well as Oliver Nelson's "Daylie's Double." These tunes and many others illustrate the importance of the airplay and concert promotion provided by the deejays. And because of their association with the greats of jazz, the deejays became big stars themselves; on some occasions, they would appear in concert with the musicians they promoted.

This symbiotic relationship continued in the sixties. Jazz deejays wrote album liner notes, acted as masters of ceremonies for concert appearances, and, in a few cases, hosted television shows where jazz musicians played on-air. Their radio play could make big hits from the songs they featured. An example is the chart success of "Misty" by organist Richard 'Groove' Holmes—notes to the album *Jazz Hits from the Hot 100* recall, "A disciple of Jimmy Smith . . . 'Groove' Holmes enjoyed a sizable pop hit in 1966 with [his] airy take on Erroll Garner's much-covered classic. Short and to the point, Holmes's version was perfect for AM radio and, better still, it swung."[17] This was a relatively common occurrence on sixties radio, and the jazz disc jockeys could regularly influence what their non-jazz counterpart deejays played. Creed Taylor related to Ashley Kahn that "there were certain jazz radio stations that were like bridge stations to the pop world. . . . They had leverage that would get the attention of some of the bigger non-jazz stations. You'd build [a single] at the jazz level and then you'd get it pushed up to the big stations . . . that's the way we worked it."[18] As noted by music journalist Jack Maher in an April 1963 edition of *Billboard*, "Though the number of jazz singles has been at its highest point on the Hot 100 chart, it's not the quantity that's flipping record men, it's the regularity."[19] In his book *A Century of Jazz*, Roy Carr writes about the challenge to jazz posed by music changes in the sixties: "Yet, despite everything else happening around town, straight-ahead modern jazz singles still slipped under the wire to scamper up the charts. Similarly, over on the Hot 100 album listings, jazz sales still flourished no matter which Devil spawn was branded as the latest threat to America's dollar-waving youth."[20]

Radio disc jockeys of all nationalities were superstars in 1950s and sixties America in all styles of music. Alan Freed, Dick Clark, Wolfman Jack, and Dewey Phillips are all names that have come to be well known (the WVON "Good Guys," favorites from the author's childhood, have been chronicled elsewhere in this book). These deejays were the link to a fantastic world that many people could feel as though they were a part of just by turning on the radio, and in those days, stardom afforded the record-spinners a lot of autonomy. The popular jazz DJs were no exception—Aaron Johnson notes, "For the most part, these jazz deejays functioned almost as independent contractors who were free to program their shows as they saw fit, keeping in mind that in this [sixties] era 'personality' deejays enjoyed considerabl[y] more freedom than today.... Jazz record labels knew these jazz deejays and their musical tastes and worked to get their product... aired by these deejays who had an immediate and direct relationship with their listeners."[21] Many of these folks made a handsome living playing the latest jazz for eager audiences who kept these stations alive by spending lots of money, not only on the albums, but also other products that provided big advertising bucks that kept these stations viable well into the late seventies.

During the sixties, jazz radio existed in a number of ways: as a late-night offering on weeknights and on Saturday/Sunday daytime shows on Black commercial radio; on the emerging free-form programming associated with the nascent FM radio band of the late sixties; and most intriguing of all, the "all-jazz" radio format. Beginning in the late fifties, commercial radio began to adopt all-jazz radio in several major markets. These stations could be found across the country: WBEE in Chicago (a particular favorite the author's dad); WLIB in New York; KJAZ in the San Francisco Bay Area; KBCA and KNOB in Southern California; KADI in St. Louis; and stations in Pittsburgh, Kansas City, Cleveland, and Boston, in addition to cities that might not be thought of as Black population hubs, like WJZZ in Bridgeport, Connecticut, and WAYL in Minneapolis–St. Paul. Far from being an old, marginalized style of "cultureless mood music" (as described by Amiri Baraka) that was no longer relevant to civil rights–era Black America, jazz did what jazz has always done. Jazz changed, jazz grew, and jazz adapted to the times, which is reflected in the profitability of these jazz radio stations, jazz labels, and jazz clubs that thrived in the era.

The power and status of Black deejays can be seen in the days surrounding the assassination of Dr. Martin Luther King Jr. All of the major urban areas enlisted the help of Black radio and the star disc jockeys in attempts to quells the anger that erupted when the first reports of Dr. King's death emerged out of Memphis on April 4, 1968. Del Shields, who was a jazz deejay in New York City at the time, shared this memory with writer and critic Nelson George:

> Black radio came of age the night Dr. King was killed. Up until that time, black radio had never been tested nationally. No one ever knew its power. You knew the popularity of black disc jockeys, the power to sell various products. But on the night Dr. King was killed, all across America, every black station was tested and everybody who was on the air at that time, including myself, told people to cool it. We tried to do everything possible to keep the black people from just

exploding even more than they were.... When America looked at black radio in that particular period, it suddenly hit them that this was a potent force.[22]

Those same radio stations played parts of Dr. King's speeches, gave updates on the search for James Earl Ray, his killer (who wasn't caught until June of '68), and played music of all types that helped Black Americans process the loss of the "drum major for peace."

In the 1960s, television newscaster Walter Cronkite was known as "the most trusted man in America." In Black America, that title probably would have gone to a deejay. Probably Daddy-O Daylie.

CHAPTER SEVEN

Pulling out All the Stops

Organ Jazz, the Quintessential Sound of Sixties Jazz

Jazz radio legend Daddy-O Daylie recalled that singer Babs Gonzales was the first person to tip him off. "'Hey, man, there is a cat here in the Apple named Jimmy Smith that is playing more organ than you have ever heard.'... This guy was so fast on the organ that I thought it was a dub. He was just a fantastic musician. I began playing Jimmy Smith LPs on my radio show."[1] What is interesting about this particular anecdote is that it resembles many other people's recollection of the first time they heard Jimmy Smith—his lightning-fast hands seemed to shock and amaze everyone who came out to hear him. And despite the fact that in early 1956 no one could have guessed it, by 1960, the jazz world was signing organists to record contracts as quickly as they could put pen to paper. Jimmy Smith had singlehandedly made jazz organ a phenomenon.

Although it has been used in jazz since the 1930s, the organ, more than any other instrument, signifies popular jazz in the sixties like nothing else. The sound of an organ trio hitting a serious mid-tempo shuffle, a slow, mournful ballad, a well-worn American standard, or perhaps an up-tempo, sweaty blues is the perfect image to evoke all of the splendor of popular jazz in the 1960s. And all the great players gave inspiration to dozens of young musicians who would include the organ in many of the most popular rock, soul, and blues bands of the sixties and seventies.

The electric organ is, in many ways, the perfect instrument for jazz. By pulling out various drawbars (which are the equivalent of the stops on a pipe organ), one can get a myriad of different sounds, and the organ can literally replicate every instrument associated with jazz. In the skilled hands of a great player, the organ can replicate all instruments at the same time and in real time (including drums). But the organ could also be considered the most unlikely instrument to have come to the forefront of jazz in the late fifties mainly because of its close association with skating rinks, television soap operas, and especially its association with church music. Culture critic Mark Anthony Neal notes, "The instrument's use in a jazz context could not have endeared jazz musicians and audiences to the black church, because the organ was in many ways the emblem of gospel music itself."[2] However, the organ did, for many, become the quintessential instrument of sixties jazz. It was an instrument that had a very low profile for most of the fifties, but by the sixties, it was everywhere. And although there are numerous brands and types, the organ that became the gold standard was the Hammond B3—it transformed the jazz landscape, and because of its popularity in jazz, it was able to transform soul and rock music even more than it transformed jazz.

The Hammond organ was built in Chicago by Laurens Hammond, an inventor who had no musical skills whatsoever but who developed patents for various items including 3-D movies and the first electric clock. In need of a new invention after his electric bridge table ("just load in the deck, and the electric bridge table automatically shuffles your cards"[3]) failed to take off during the Depression, Hammond developed the Hammond organ in 1934 by utilizing the same technology that he used to synchronize his electric clocks. In 1935, the Hammond Organ Company began selling the Model A organ to churches as a cheaper and smaller alternative to pipe organs. It wasn't long before jazz musicians began to experiment with the Hammond organ, with Fats Waller being the first, followed closely by Count Basie. But the Hammond organ owes the bulk of its success to two musicians, both of whom shared the surname Smith.

Ethel Smith (1902–1996) was a piano major at Carnegie Tech in her native Pittsburgh. After joining a touring show in the 1930s, she landed in California, where she was offered a job playing organ and accompanying singers at a movie studio. Smith became quite proficient as an organist, and she began playing the instrument on tours with singers and actors, and one of those tours took her to Brazil. It was in Rio that Smith became comfortable playing Latin rhythms, and she also learned the South American standard "Tico-Tico." That song became a showstopper for her, and back in Hollywood, Smith began to be showcased in movies. It is her performance of "Tico-Tico" on the Hammond organ in the 1944 movie *Bathing Beauty* that led to the song becoming a best seller in the States (bebop great Charlie Parker recorded the tune in the early fifties). Despite being largely forgotten today, in the forties and fifties, Ethel Smith was known as the "First Lady of the Hammond organ."

In the forties, the Hammond Organ Company began marketing smaller spinet organs for home usage, which turned out to be very profitable. But it was another invention that would have a huge impact on the world of the organ, and it was an invention that Laurens Hammond fought hard to stifle. The Leslie speaker was invented by Don Leslie in 1940 and, with its patented rotating speaker horns, it transformed the sound of the Hammond organ. Hammond tried in vain to disassociate the organ with the Leslie speaker to no avail, and soon the organ and speaker would become, for many, an inseparable pair. But it wasn't until 1954 that the Hammond organ sound that everyone now knows and loves came into existence with the creation of the Hammond model B3. Soon every Black church that wanted to get the congregation filled with the Holy Spirit purchased the B3, and it became ubiquitous within the sound of Black gospel music. It also drew the attention of a young piano player in Philadelphia.

As mentioned earlier, the organ had a life in jazz before Jimmy Smith discovered it in the fifties. In Leonard Feather's 1957 work called *The Book of Jazz*, he notes that "former jazz pianists who have enjoyed a vogue in the rhythm and blues field through the employment of a hard-driving, voluminous approach to the electric organ include 'Wild Bill' Davis . . . Bill Doggett . . . Jackie Davis, and Milt Buckner."[4] But as Tom Moon notes, it would be Jimmy Smith who would, singlehandedly, become "the man who established the sound and the vocabulary of the Hammond B3 organ in jazz."[5]

Jimmy Smith (1925–2005) seemed to come out of nowhere, fully formed, as the new god of the Hammond B3 in 1956. But in reality, he had been working around Philadelphia for a while, not as an organist at first, but as a pianist—he started out with his father doing a song and dance routine. After military service, Smith began music studies at the university level while also playing piano in Philadelphia and Newark, New Jersey. Playing in jazz and R&B bands brought in money, but he soon became intrigued by the possibilities of the organ, so in 1954, Smith went into the proverbial woodshed (actually, in this case, a warehouse) and didn't emerge for a year until he had the organ perfected. Soon he was the talk of Atlantic City and, not long after, New York City, which is where Blue Note Records' founders Alfred Lion and Francis Wolff caught his act. Wolff remembered it this way: "It was at Smalls in January of 1956. He was a stunning sight. A man in convulsions, face contorted, crouched over in apparent agony, his fingers flying, his foot dancing over the pedals. The air was filled with waves of sound I never heard before . . . Alfred Lion had already made up his mind."[6] Everyone made it out to see what all of the talk was—Richard Havers's book on the history of Blue Note Records notes that "just after Lion signed Jimmy Smith [to a Blue Note Records contract], he went to hear the organist play a club date in Greenwich Village, where he met Miles Davis. The trumpeter told Lion, 'Alfred, he's going to make you a lot of money.'"[7]

Jimmy Smith's story is important to the Blue Note Records legacy, and the numerous books, album compilations, and documentaries about that company never fail to recognize his significance. A two-CD Blue Note compilation from 1997 includes this in the liner notes: "In 1956, Blue Note signed a young Philadelphian named Jimmy Smith who blasted the organ into the modern era with extraordinary technique, a fresh sound, and a strong blues feel. An entire industry built around soul-jazz organ groups sprang up around this innovator."[8] But that was not a newfound reverence by the label in the nineties; Smith's original Blue Note albums also lauded his style in the album notes. *Home Cookin'*, Smith's 1961 Blue Note classic, has this Ira Gitler statement: "Jimmy has explored the myriad combinations possible on the Hammond more than any other jazz organist today. He is able to express many moods through tasteful employment of his instrument's broad tonal palette. His footwork is extraordinary, too."[9] And there was good reason for Blue Note and Verve, Smith's other long-term record label, to sing his praises. He didn't sound like an organist—he sounded like Charlie Parker, a fact that was noted by the organist himself, when he said, "I'm not a keyboard player—I'm a horn player, I'm a voice."[10] Smith had blinding hand speed combined with an endless amount of imagination that he'd use to play chorus after chorus of the blues, but he never played the same idea twice and never failed to keep listeners, both live and on records, enthralled.

Jimmy Smith was a jazz superstar in the sixties, and he sold a lot of records. Notes jazz producer/writer Bob Porter, "His recordings . . . were enormously successful. He was the best selling of all jazz artists in the 1960s. No fewer than ten of his albums reached the Top Forty pop charts!"[11] (Blue Note Records released fifteen albums by Jimmy Smith between 1956 and 1959.) And it seems that was Smith's plan from the beginning—he wanted to have a lot of people listening to his music. As noted in a Verve compilation of Smith's hits, "He can play bebop and ballads with the best of them, but he's not afraid of the familiar, even the seemingly overfamiliar . . . at times his repertoire seems positively retro. . . . He knows exactly what he is doing. Defying musical snobbery, he said in a famous *DownBeat* interview, 'I bow to the masses.'"[12] And he understood quite well that he was the originator of a new revolution in jazz. Referring to the numerous jazz organist who began to record after his success, Smith said, "I like all my pupils—Don Patterson, Jack McDuff, Groove Holmes, Shirley Scott, Larry Young, George Fame . . . Freddie Roach is a Jimmy Smith copy . . . John Patton, he's a fair organ player. . . . They're my understudies."[13] And that was no mere hyperbole; Jimmy Smith reinvented what the jazz organ could do and defined what all subsequent organists must do.

Many of the organists cited above have, like Jimmy Smith, become legends. Of this group, the person who came the closest to being considered Smith's peer was Jack McDuff. McDuff (1926–2001), who hailed from Champaign, Illinois, started his professional musical life as a bassist in Chicago in the 1950s, playing in bands led by pianist Denny Zeitlin and saxophonist Joe Farrell. McDuff switched to piano, and after hearing the possibilities brought to the fore by Jimmy Smith, switched once again, this time to the organ. McDuff was prolific—he recorded twenty-four albums for Prestige Records between 1960 and 1966, then continued his voluminous sixties output with Atlantic, Cadet, and Blue Note Records.

McDuff was no mere Jimmy Smith clone. His bass-playing experience made him equal to Smith in regard to the organ's bass pedals (which allow organists to play bass lines on records and in live settings without bass players), and McDuff also had very quick bebop-like lines as a soloist. But one of the major differences between the two is that Smith tended to feature himself in a trio setting with a guitarist and a drummer. McDuff's preferred ensemble was a quartet with a saxophonist sharing the melodic duties. His work as a sideman with tenor saxophonists Joe Farrell and Willis Jackson provided the blueprint for success for McDuff's ensembles. His groups featured saxophonists Red Holloway, Harold Vick, Ben Branch, and others, and he frequently collaborated with sax greats Sonny Stitt and Gene Ammons. McDuff also featured some fine guitarists; both Kenny Burrell and Grant Green were featured on recordings with McDuff (they both played with Jimmy Smith as well), and McDuff took a chance on a young guitarist from Pittsburgh named George Benson, who, in a 1967 *DownBeat* interview remembered it this way: "I never thought I'd leave Pittsburgh . . . I was eighteen when Jack McDuff came through and hired me. . . . The McDuff group gave me a different conception, but I think the greatest thing was that it gave me the chance to hear what everyone else was doing from coast to coast."[14]

McDuff's bands were revered for their live recordings, which provided a perfect representation of what the band could do in a club. They were well known for being able to bring down the house with their no-frills approach to jazz. In his book on hard bop, author David Rosenthal described the popularity of the organ groups in Black clubs in the sixties: "Among them were Shirley Scott . . . and Richard 'Groove' Holmes. . . . Still another was Jack McDuff, who in the sixties led a quartet with tenor saxophonist Red Holloway, guitarist George Benson, and drummer Joe Dukes that could get into one of the meanest, most absorbing grooves ever heard or—alternately—generate enough heat to lift the roof off any club or dance hall. . . . As McDuff put it: 'We play that good-time thing. We play the way we feel . . . it's always been a happy thing; play and swing and have a good time. No formula.'"[15]

Because of the popularity of organ jazz in those communities in the sixties, the Black population centers in all the major cities had numerous taverns that kept a Hammond B3 organ in house. Part of this had to do with economics; historian Roy Carr notes that post-World War II, "Suddenly organ, guitar and drums, and more frequently, sax, became the ideal club combo, capable of kicking up as much dust as a big band and at a fraction of the cost."[16] Legendary Philadelphia DJ Bob Perkins remembered it this way: "Let me add a bow to [Philadelphia's] small bars that once featured jazz, the ones along old Columbia Avenue, Ridge Avenue, and in other neighborhoods during the jazz organ heyday. Bar owners looking for more bang for their buck always included the hiring of an organist, saxophonist, and drummer in their budget, knowing that they could make a small room rock and bring in the patrons."[17] On a segment of NPR's *Jazz Night in America* dedicated to the jazz organ tradition in Philadelphia that aired in 2018, Philly resident Thelma Anderson reminisced that back in the day "you had places all over Philadelphia that you could go and be comfortable in and listen to the music.... It's like going to church ... I can see the places that we've gone."[18] Ms. Anderson, who, based on info provided in the NPR segment, was in her late eighties at the time of the broadcast, goes on to mention numerous venues, large and small, where Philadelphia jazz organists could show their stuff to enthusiastic audiences.

As has been noted, Jimmy Smith made lots of money for Blue Note Records in the late fifties and early sixties, and his star power drew the attention of Verve Records, which at the time had more financial resources than Blue Note that allowed them to lure him away. Richard Havers's book on the history of Blue Note Records notes that "Jimmy Smith signed to Verve on a long-term contract in February 1963, at which point he was, somewhat ironically, back on the *Billboard* chart with another Blue Note album, the fabulous *Back at the Chicken Shack*."[19] Smith would continue to have great success during his time at Verve, but now he was frequently recording in large ensemble configurations with arrangements by Lalo Schifrin and Oliver Nelson. Of special interest is Smith's Verve album *Peter and the Wolf*, a jazz interpretation of Russian composer Sergei Prokofiev's symphonic fairy tale. Smith's musical interests ran the gamut of classical, soul, jazz, and blues music, and Verve allowed him to chase his muse wherever it led him.

Jimmy Smith's parting left a void at Blue Note, which they would soon fill with numerous other organists. Havers notes that "Blue Note would sign a number of others over the next decade. "Baby Face" Willette recorded his debut, *Face to Face*, in 1961; the following year, Freddie Roach cut *Down to Earth*; in 1963, Big John Patton issued his debut as a leader, *Along Came John*, and a year after that, Larry Young recorded *Into Somethin'*, which was his first as a leader for

Blue Note."[20] A bit later in the sixties, Blue Note found considerable success with Reuben Wilson and Lonnie Smith, an organist from Lackawanna, New York, who benefited from the presence of trumpet great Lee Morgan on his first couple of albums. Dr. Lonnie Smith, as he became known, was active until his death in September 2021.

Of this large group of Blue Note organists that followed Jimmy Smith, Big John Patton and Larry Young had the most impact. Patton (1935–2002), who started out playing piano with R&B star Lloyd Price, switched to the organ in the early sixties. After recording on Blue Note with saxophonist Lou Donaldson, the label gave Patton a shot as a leader with the album *Along Came John* in 1963. Patton formed a close working relationship with guitarist Grant Green and drummer Ben Dixon, and their tight rapport made for some very fine albums with grooves that would play an important role in the Acid Jazz club scene in 1980s London. Larry Young (1940–1978), who, musically speaking, tended more to the experimental side, would get credit, along with drummer Tony Williams and guitarist John McLaughlin, for initiating the fusion movement with their 1969 album *Emergency!* To many ears, Young is the least "organ-like" of the great sixties organists. Tom Moon observes that on his 1965 album *Unity*, "Young becomes the first wizard of the Hammond B3 to step out of the barn-burning game to explore more freely.... An alert accompanist, Young peppers the soloists with zinging chord clusters that push things forward."[21]

Prestige Records would, in many ways, top Blue Note in regard to organ jazz releases in the sixties. In addition to Jack McDuff, their organ roster included Don Patterson, Sonny Phillips, Johnny "Hammond" Smith, and Charles Earland, as well as two others who would have quite an impact on the charts, Shirley Scott and Richard "Groove" Holmes.

Scott (1934–2002), one of the numerous Philadelphia organ jazz greats (along with Jimmy Smith, Charles Earland, and Jimmy McGriff; Groove Holmes was from nearby Camden, New Jersey), was as prolific in her early sixties output as Jack McDuff. In addition to her numerous solo recordings, she would also play on her husband's (tenor saxophonist Stanley Turrentine) recordings, leading Ira Gitler to make this observation regarding their musical coupling: "Shirley gained recognition in a combo with tenor man Eddie 'Lockjaw' Davis. In the sixties, they [Turrentine and Scott] joined musically and followed by becoming man and wife.... Both Stanley and Shirley have a great deal of warmth in their playing and they complement each other well."[22] Scott's style was unique—despite being tutored on the instrument by Jimmy Smith, she often approached the organ more like a pianist with bop-like solo lines and a melodic touch, and her trio consisted of bass and drums (which was unlike many organists who played in a trio setting with guitar and drums), covering the basslines themselves with their left hand and the pedals. For a time in the sixties, Scott released albums on Impulse Records simultaneously with her recordings on Prestige. Of note are a few large ensemble albums that she recorded with arrangements by Oliver Nelson, including one in 1964 titled *Great Scott!!*

Richard "Groove" Holmes (1931–1991) began his solo career in 1961 on Pacific Jazz Records; in 1965, he switched to Prestige Records and immediately had a massive radio and jukebox hit with his interpretation of Erroll Garner's *Misty*. Holmes played in traditional trio settings with guitar and drums, but he would, like Jimmy Smith and Shirley Scott, also play in a large ensemble setting. On those recordings, he forged a close working relationship with the legendary arranger Gerald Wilson, who spoke highly of his collaborations with Holmes: "Well, just being able to work with Groove was really a great thrill in my career, I'll tell you that. . . . We kinda kept in touch all the time when he would come to town. We were very good friends, and it's one association that I really enjoyed every moment of."[23] Holmes, like Jack McDuff, started out as a bass player (Jimmy Smith, who originated on piano, was known to be a fine bass player), and he taught himself to play the organ after hearing Smith. Holmes collaborated with a number of great tenor saxophonists including Ben Webster, Gene Ammons, Houston Person, and Grover Washington Jr., and he was a very popular live entertainer as well as a beloved collaborator all the way up to the time of his death in 1991.

One of the more interesting things to note about all this organ activity is the number of crossover collaborations of the musicians playing on those records. Grant Green and Kenny Burrell played guitar on numerous organ albums; Harold Vick played tenor with Jack McDuff, John Patton, Shirley Scott, Jimmy McGriff, and Groove Holmes; trumpeters Lee Morgan and Blue Mitchell were guests on many of these albums as well. And these organ players were guests on solo albums by numerous horn players. This gives one the sense of the vitality of the organ in popular jazz in the sixties.

So popular was the organ in Black communities in the sixties that many of these players had tunes that would show up on the *Billboard* charts, get lots of radio play, and become jukebox hits. Jimmy McGriff (1936–2008), another of the great Philadelphia organists, had a hit with a cover of Ray Charles's "I've Got a Woman" on the small, independent Sue Records in 1962. McGriff was a policeman in the fifties who played bass in his spare time. Says British music journalist Rob Finnis, "McGriff was inspired to take up the organ after hearing Richard 'Groove' Holmes's entertaining guests at [McGriff's] sister's wedding in 1957. . . . McGriff enrolled in the Juilliard School of Music and received further tuition from Milt Buckner . . . Jimmy Smith and 'Groove' Holmes himself."[24] In the seventies, Holmes and McGriff recorded a couple of albums together, billing themselves as the "Giants of the Organ!"

Hank Marr (1927–2004), who stayed close to his home base of Columbus, Ohio, developed close relationships with some of the local legends, many of whom became nationally known, like saxophonists Rahsaan Roland Kirk and Rusty Bryant, and the great song stylist Nancy Wilson. In 1964, Marr recorded a single for King Records titled "The Greasy Spoon." Rob Finnis notes that "'The Greasy Spoon' became something of a minor classic, notching up steady sales in the R&B market over the next few years."[25] Because of Marr's success as well as the success of one of his protégés, Don Patterson, Columbus has become a haven for jazz organists. One of those Columbus players is Bobby Floyd, who has played with Ray Charles, the Count Basie Orchestra, and Dr. John, among many others. Floyd is one of the finest organists in the world today, and he still calls Columbus home. Twenty years after his death in 2004, Hank Marr is still a highly revered Ohio jazz legend.[26]

Smith, Scott, McGriff, Earland, Bill Doggett (whose organ playing predates Smith), and Holmes, all Philadelphia natives (or in the case of Holmes, right next door in Camden, New Jersey) contributed to the city's reputation as the Organ Jazz Capital of the World. But there were players all across the country who found success on the organ—the aforementioned Marr and Patterson in Columbus and McDuff in Chicago; Johnny "Hammond" Smith from Louisville, Kentucky; Melvin Rhyne from Indianapolis, Indiana; Sonny Phillips from Mobile, Alabama; Freddie Roach from the Bronx, New York; Charles Kynard from Kansas City, Missouri; Sam Lazar from St. Louis, Missouri; Reuben Wilson from Mounds, Oklahoma; Larry Young from Newark, New Jersey; Dr. Lonnie Smith from Lackawanna, New York (not to be confused with Lonnie Liston Smith, a very fine organist in his own right, who would make a name for himself starting in the seventies); Billy Larkin from way out west in Portland, Oregon; and Rhoda Scott form Paris, France via New Jersey! There are numerous other organists who made a name for themselves in the sixties in cities like Cleveland, Houston, Los Angeles, and especially Baltimore.

One byproduct of all of this jazz organ activity was the arrival of numerous guitar greats who were members of these organ trios and quartets. Jimmy Smith set the tone for the trio configuration of guitar, drums, and of course organ. This, along with the meteoric rise of Wes Montgomery (who led a trio that included organist Mel Rhyne in addition to Montgomery's later recording duet albums with Smith) led to a bumper crop of jazz guitarists who would use their positions in these organ trios to make their mark. Some, like Kenny Burrell, Grant Green, George Benson, and Pat Martino, became legends in their own right. Many of the others flew a bit more under the radar, but they made great recordings and became heroes to numerous jazz guitarists who came after them. Ivan "Boogaloo Joe" Jones, Melvin Sparks, Jimmy Ponder,

Gene Edwards, Floyd Smith, and others created a comping (accompanying) style in these organ trios and quartets, a very specialized way of playing that has become a part of guitar pedagogy. In order to consider oneself well versed in jazz guitar, aspiring players must listen to and learn the grooves these great players laid down.

The importance of the jazz organ in popular music in the sixties cannot be overestimated. The stylistic revolution set off by Jimmy Smith had far-reaching reverberations that were felt beyond the world of jazz. Soul and rock 'n' roll musicians adapted the instrument after witnessing the results of organ jazz's popularity. Powered by a jazz-influenced organ blues riff, "Green Onions" by Booker T. & the M.G.'s was a Top Ten *Billboard* hit in 1962. Soon, the sound of the Hammond organ was everywhere on the pop charts—The Young Rascals' "Good Lovin,'" the Spencer Davis Group's "Gimme Some Lovin,'" Sly and the Family Stone's "Dance to the Music," and Deep Purple's "Hush" are just a few of the many popular songs in the sixties that utilized the distinctive Hammond B3 sound. Soon, other organs, such as the Wurlitzer and the Farfisa, began to be utilized on numerous popular music recordings as well.

Those sixties' organ jazz stars would also have a huge influence on rock music in the seventies. The list of American and British rock keyboardists who derived inspiration from this music is long. Keith Emerson of Emerson, Lake & Palmer was one of the most prominent. In an appreciation piece written upon the organist's death in 2016, music journalist Jim Allen wrote, "Jazz was a huge part of Emerson's musical education too, and Dave Brubeck, Jimmy Smith, and Jack McDuff loomed large on his list of heroes. He would come to call 'Rock Candy,' the opening track of 1963's *Brother Jack McDuff Live!*, the one that started it all for him. (He'd eventually cover that one too.)"[27] Jon Lord of Deep Purple was another; when asked whom his biggest influences were, Lord commented, "Jimmy Smith was like a god to me."[28] One would be forgiven for mistaking "Lazy" from Deep Purple's 1972 album *Machine Head* for a Jimmy Smith original. Yes, Genesis, Traffic, and many other seventies rock bands featured a Hammond B3 organ at the center of their sound.

Other British keyboardists beyond the world of rock felt the call of the organ. For example, Brian Auger is one of the early players to fuse jazz and rock together. Reminiscing about an early jazz trio that he played in with guitarist John McLaughlin, Auger notes that "the band folded, and toward the end of 1964, I was really beginning to listen to Jimmy Smith; also heard Jimmy McGriff, Jack McDuff, and people like that. And so the organ became one of those things that I wanted to experiment with."[29]

The influence of organ jazz is ubiquitous on today's classic rock radio. Billy Preston was prominently featured on rock classics by many musicians and bands, among them the Beatles and the Rolling Stones, and he was inspired by both jazz and the church. Preston, considered by many to be the "Fifth Beatle," learned to play the organ in Black churches in his native Texas and Los Angeles, and he went on to become an organ legend, playing the Hammond B3 on recordings by Sam Cooke, Little Richard, Ike and Tina Turner, and so many others, as well as his own very popular recordings in the sixties and seventies.

It should be also noted that Ray Charles and James Brown, the two most important musicians in regard to rhythm and blues and soul music of the fifties and sixties, were both inspired by the organ jazz explosion. Charles, well known as one of the finest R&B and jazz pianists, had a huge hit in 1961 with *Genius + Soul = Jazz*, his first album for ABC/Impulse Records. On that album, Charles is backed up by a big band and featured exclusively on the Hammond organ while providing vocals for only two selections. "One Mint Julep," the instrumental hit single from the album, landed the organ front and center on the very top of the *Billboard* R&B chart while reaching number eight on the pop chart. James Brown recorded a number of singles and a couple of albums featuring himself playing the Hammond organ. While no one would consider him in the same league as Smith, McDuff, or Ray Charles, Brown was a more than adequate player and occasionally landed some of his instrumental tunes on the R&B charts in the early sixties.

There have been times where jazz organ activity has slowed a bit. An article on miscellaneous instruments in jazz in *The Oxford Companion to Jazz* notes that "with the growing popularity of electric pianos and synthesizers, the 1970s saw a decline in younger players using the B3. However, in the 1990s, several players—including Dan Wall, Larry Goldings, John Medeski, Joey DeFrancesco, and Barbara Dennerline—have renewed its presence and sought innovative uses for the B3 in modern jazz settings."[30] Despite some ebbs and flows, without fail, jazz organ always seems to come roaring back. Almost all of the great players mentioned above continued to have great impact beyond the sixties.[31]

Upon his death in 2005, Jimmy Smith was celebrated around the world. At the time of his passing, Smith had just completed a recording with DeFrancesco and was scheduled to go on tour. NBC news had this remembrance: "The world has lost one of its greatest musical innovators . . . [Smith's] virtuosity over the instrument combined with his brilliant infusion of gospel, blues, and R&B riffs and melodies into bebop-inspired improvisations place him alongside other jazz pioneers such as Charlie Parker, Art Tatum, and John Coltrane—artists who revolutionized the way their respective instruments were played and who are continuing to have a profound influence of other instrumentalists."[32] The Acid Jazz and Northern Soul music scenes that began in 1980s London have made people like Big John Patton and Reuben Wilson heroes to a younger generation of music fans. And upon his untimely death in 2022, Joey DeFrancesco was, like his mentor Jimmy Smith, celebrated worldwide. His *New York Times* obituary had the headline "Joey DeFrancesco, Reigning King of the Jazz Organ, Dies at 51."[33]

The vibrancy and vitality of organ jazz and its importance to Black jazz listeners of the sixties seem to have escaped many of the historians and critics. Historian Mark Gridley does note organ jazz's popularity but seems to negate its relevance: "But the highest record sales went to the organ-guitar-drums and piano-bass-drums groups of Jimmy Smith and Ramsey Lewis, respectively. These are players who musicians and critics do not ordinarily consider to be within the mainstream of jazz developments."[34] This statement is at the heart of the challenge when contemplating popular jazz in the sixties, especially as practiced by the great organ jazz players. There seems to be a consensus among many in the world of jazz history and jazz criticism that the music made by these musicians wasn't pushing jazz forward, and to those critics and historians, the proof that organ jazz wasn't important is that it was so popular (as mentioned, popularity and big record sales have become anathema to jazz critics as well as some jazz musicians and fans). David Rosenthal notes that "in interviews and liner notes, soul-jazz artists often sounded defensive about the fact that they were not pushing back the boundaries of Afro-American music."[35] The truth is that those organists were the mainstream of jazz in Black communities in the sixties, and to that community, this was the best of what jazz had to offer.

Mark Anthony Neal, who is a professor at Duke University, has written much about the importance of music as a Black cultural marker. In terms of jazz, he has noted that "hard bop's popularity was largely based on its ability to remain malleable to the full range of musical influences and tastes contained within a still largely segregated black public.... Throughout the sixties, many black jazz musicians, under the banner of hard bop and later, soul jazz, recorded music that was extremely popular to a larger black mainstream audience."[36] This truth is reflected in the incredible number of records sold by Jimmy Smith, Jack McDuff, Shirley Scott, and all the others. Perhaps it has been forgotten. Nevertheless, the organ, backed up by a full-bodied, bluesy tenor sax player or just guitar and drums, was everywhere in the musical world of Black America in the 1960s.

Organ jazz, as a subgenre, is still quite alive and well in 2024, with a diverse group of players such as Lonnie Liston Smith, Rhoda Scott, Reuben Wilson, Pat Bianchi, Larry Goldings, Chris Foreman, Cory Henry, Tony Monaco, Carla Bley, Sam Yahel, Atsuko Hashimoto, Brian Auger, Bobby Floyd, John Medeski, and Barbara Dennerlein continuing to draw large crowds at clubs, theaters, and festivals around the world. The world that Jimmy Smith created still lives!

CHAPTER EIGHT

Mean Greens, Fried Neckbones, and Home Cookin' at the Greasy Spoon

Black Cultural Identity and Popular Jazz

The photo on the cover of Jimmy Smith's 1961 album *Home Cookin*[1] shows the organist standing in front of a luncheonette advertising four different flavors of Italian icicles (green, orange, red, and lime), two different "Drink Coca Cola" signs, and a smaller 7 Up sign as well. The official name of the restaurant, which was located in Harlem, was Kate's Home Cooking, and the window made it clea—"Food Served at All Times." According to the liner notes by Ira Gitler, "Performers such as Ruth Brown, Cozy Cole, Count Basie, Fats Domino, James Moody, Art Blakey, and Horace Silver make it their prandial headquarters during the course of a week when they are playing the big A [the Apollo Theater]."[2] Gitler goes on to say that Jimmy Smith is also a fan of the eatery and that the album is dedicated to Kate O. Bishop, the restaurant's owner: "The distance from grits and gravy to swing, sounds, and soul is a short one for Jimmy Smith."[3] The photo was taken in Harlem, but you could find a home cookin' restaurant exactly like that one on Madison Street on the West Side of Chicago, on Central Avenue in Los Angeles, on Mt. Vernon Street in Columbus, Ohio, and just about any major business district in Black America.

The cover of *Home Cookin'* was a perfect signifier of a specific trend that started in the fifties, which, by 1961, was becoming much more common—the outward presentation of Black cultural identity. Author Mark Kurlansky, writing about "the Black Arts Movement," notes that "their art would express a black

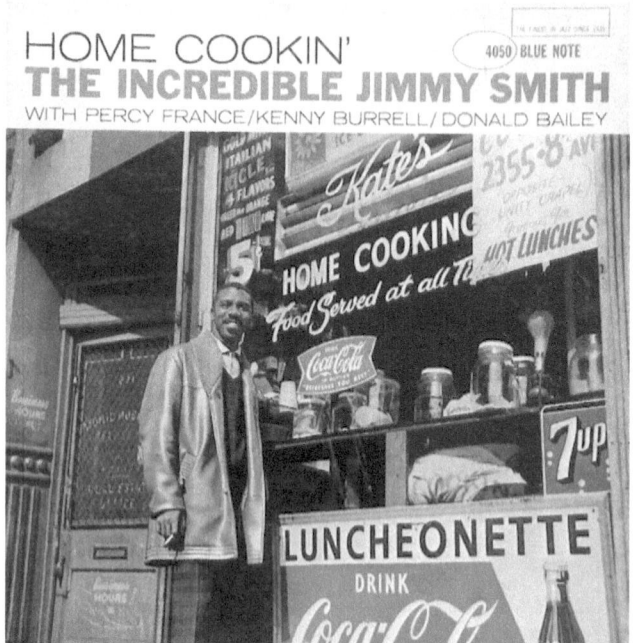

Jimmy Smith, *Home Cookin'*: Blue Note Records, BLP 4050, 1961.

perspective, something totally distinct and apart from white art. The movement went beyond art to the fashion of wearing African-style clothes and the emergence of 'soul' food restaurants."[4]

It should be noted that in 1961, such outward shows of Black American culture were risky in regard to album covers. Motown Records was just beginning to make its mark in the early sixties, and the company was very careful not to show their artists on record jackets so as to not curtail potential sales in white communities. Albums by Mary Wells, the Marvelettes, and Martha and the Vandellas were released with illustrations or inanimate objects on the cover. But the jazz world would embrace these signifiers of emerging Black pride. Abbey Lincoln's 1961 album *Straight Ahead* not only included a song titled "African Lady" (accompanied by African-styled hand percussion and a 12/8 Afro groove), it also featured Lincoln on the cover with a "natural" hairdo. This embrace of Blackness took many forms on jazz albums in the sixties: the look of the graphic arts, the titles of the albums as well as the tunes included on them, the sound of the records, even the way the musicians dressed—and the jazz world would lead the rest of Black America's soulful makeover.

There is something about jazz that is very personal to Black people, even to those Black people who don't regularly listen to it. Part of this has to do with how jazz helps define America for Black Americans. The imminent scholar,

Mary Wells, *Bye Bye Baby, I Don't Want to Take A Chance*: Motown Records, M-LP 600, 1961.

Abbey Lincoln, *Straight Ahead*: Candid Records, CJM 8015, 1961.

writer, and blues philosopher Albert Murray explains it this way: "Jazz is an Afro-American form. Everybody identifies with it because it is an adequate metaphor for the truth of the American experience.... That's why everybody feels 'that's ours.' And they identify with it because they're telling the story about America, the basic story of all Americans: you've got to be resilient."[5] Part of it may be that it is the only African American form of expression that is revered worldwide, and it may also be that, stylistically, it just feels right to Black folks.

But there may be another, more obvious reason for Black pride in jazz. From the very earliest days, jazz has been a style of music within which the practitioners have felt very comfortable sharing the vernacular and the everyday trappings of Blackness. One of the most consistent views of the Black world was through songs about food, soul food, to be specific. Jelly Roll Morton wrote and recorded a stride/blues solo piano piece about the joys of "Fat Meat and Greens" in 1926; in 1927, Louis Armstrong seemed to be happy to be "Struttin' with Some Barbecue"; in 1933, Bessie Smith famously sang, "Gimme a Pigfoot and a Bottle of Beer"; in 1945, the only way to make Nat King Cole happy was to give him "The Frim Fram Sauce" (with a side of "chafafa"); 1949 saw Louis Jordan intervening in a fight between "Beans and Cornbread" (Jordan, himself, needed some intervention that same year when he went to the "Saturday Night Fish Fry"!).

In the fifties and sixties, the culinary signifier was everywhere within the titles of the tunes and albums in the jazz world. We can imagine that Horace Silver was, like Jimmy Smith, at Kate's luncheonette, looking for some "Home Cookin'," (Smith himself ended up *Back at the Chicken Shack*). Organist Freddie Green was begging for *Mo' Greens, Please* (he was there at the recommendation of Eddie Harris, who told Green that the place had some *Mean Greens*), and it's possible that he met up with Lee Morgan at "Kate's Home Cooking" partaking of *Cornbread*. At that same joint, Kenny Burrell's favorite must have been "Chitlins Con Carne" (seems like an awful lot of meat, but oh well), while Brother Jack McDuff preferred *Hot Barbecue*. Tenor saxophonist Willis Jackson asked for "Cool Grits," but there was a mix-up in his order; when organist Johnny "Hammond" Smith joined him at the table, they ordered "Neck Bones." What they got instead was "Fried Neckbones and Some Home Fries"—that order should have gone to percussionist Willie Bobo! And George Benson wasn't picky about his order, just as long as it was smothered in *Giblet Gravy* (fellow guitarist Burrell told Benson that he should try the "Wavy Gravy"—he said it went well with "Chitlins Con Carne").[6]

The culinary signifier was but one of many Black cultural tropes that could be found in sixties jazz. The jazz world would lead the way for the decade-long celebration of Black pride, and much of it keyed in on the concept of soul.

Although soul as a concept has come to denote Black popular music of the 1960s (best exemplified by the Motown sound, James Brown, Aretha Franklin, etc.) and the Black cultural esthetic that was an outgrowth of the civil rights era and the Black Power movement, soul as a connection to a Black mode of expression comes primarily from jazz. In the book *The Meaning of Soul*, Emily J. Lordi notes that "before it came to note a musical genre or to encompass a cultural logic, soul was most often used to describe a quality of jazz performance.... The 'soul' of 'soul jazz' described the music's soulful feeling."[7] In fact, the word "soul" began to show up regularly in jazz in the fifties—Horace Silver wrote a funky AABA blues titled "Soulville" in 1957 followed closely by Mal Waldron's "Soul Eyes," which was covered soon after by John Coltrane. Around that same time, Coltrane had a tune written for him by Tadd Dameron titled "Soultrane" (Coltrane released an album with that same title but it did not include the song "Soultrane").

In the sixties, soul became the inspiration for many compositions and album titles. There was *Soul Station* and "Hank's Other Soul" by tenor saxophonist Hank Mobley; *Silk and Soul* and "Soulful Drums" by Jack McDuff, who also played on *Soul Summit* by saxophonists Gene Ammons and Sonny Stitt; and *Soul Finger* by Art Blakey and the Jazz Messengers, which predated by two years the well-known instrumental soul song of the same name by the Bar-Kays. The concept of soul turned up often on records by organist Johnny "Hammond" Smith—three of his albums utilize "soul"—*All Soul, Soul Flowers*, and *Soul Talk*. Kenny Burrell had a "Soul Lament," and even Duke Ellington felt the need to make a *Soul Call*. The Red Garland Trio met up at *Soul Junction*, and organist Charles Kynard became a member of *The Soul Brotherhood*. Tenor sax great Houston Person found some *Underground Soul!* and found a place to do a *Soul Dance*, while Willis Jackson celebrated *Soul Night Live*, where he could become a *Soul Grabber*. And three tenor sax greats, Oliver Nelson, King Curtis, and Jimmy Forrest met on "Soul Street" where they engaged in a *Soul Battle* (spoiler alert: they all won!).

The truth is that there were hundreds of jazz albums that utilized "soul" in the title and hundreds more that had at least one song title that held the word "soul." One could compile all of the mentions of "soul" in sixties jazz into a book, and it would be quite long!

Everywhere you looked, there were symbols of Blackness in ways that were not seen in earlier decades. Throughout his career, Oliver Nelson was at the forefront of celebrations of Black pride. His 1961 album *Afro/American Sketches* is a concept album whose tracks include "Jungleaire," "Emancipation Blues," "Going Up North," and "Freedom Dance." Nelson also recorded a tribute album to Dr. Martin Luther King Jr. titled *Black, Brown and Beautiful*, which is detailed

Nina Simone, *Silk and Soul*: RCA Victor Records, LSP-3837, 1967.

Art Blakey and the Jazz Messengers, *Soul Finger*: Limelight Records, LM 82018, 1965.

Houston Person, *Underground Soul!*: Prestige Records, PR 7491, 1966.

Duke Ellington, *Soul Call*: Verve Records, V-8701, 1967.

in the chapter devoted to jazz and civil rights. Duke Ellington, whose extended work *Black, Brown and Beige* from 1943 inspired Nelson's *Black, Brown and Beautiful*, wrote a stage play and recorded the album *My People* in 1963. Of particular note is the composition "King Fit the Battle of Alabam," an uncharacteristically direct and confrontational (for Ellington) piece of music based somewhat loosely on the spiritual "Joshua Fit The Battle of Jericho." Ellington (along with Billy Strayhorn) was very clear in his indictment of southern racism as well as his show of Black pride. The song includes this lyric—

> Now when the dog saw the baby wasn't afraid, he pulled his uncle Bull's [Connor] coat and said, "that baby looks like he don't give a damn, are you sure we're still in Alabam?"[8]

Black vernacular and slang became prominent in jazz, and you began to see the influence of the Black Power movement on display in album titles such as Max Roach's *Speak, Brother, Speak*, guitarist Ivan "Boogaloo Joe" Jones's *Right On Brother*, Brother Jack McDuff's *The Natural Thing* and *Down Home Style*, and Charles Earland's *Black Talk!*, which has become an enduring album from the era because of the hit song "More Today than Yesterday." To a certain degree, pianist Bobby Timmons was at the forefront of the inclusion of Black vernacular in song titles; his twin tunes "This Here" and "Dat Dere" became instant classics recorded by many, including Art Blakey and The Jazz Messengers, Oscar Brown Jr. (who write lyrics to Dat Dere), and Cannonball Adderley, who took "This Here," and for reasons of soul and description, we have corrupted it to become "Dis Here."[9] On Timmons's 1960 album *Soul Time*, he titled the last selection "One Moe."

Pride in African heritage also became clearly represented in 1960s Black jazz. There is "Afro Blue," composed by Mongo Santamaria but popularized by John Coltrane (as well as the version with lyrics written by Oscar Brown Jr. and recorded by Abbey Lincoln in 1961), "Africaine," composed by Wayne Shorter for the Jazz Messengers, and "Man from South Africa" on Max Roach's album *Percussion Bitter Suite*, which is an album filled with African-inspired percussion and grooves. Lee Morgan composed numerous tunes with African themes including "Zambia," "Mr. Kenyatta" (a tune dedicated to Jomo Kenyatta, the first prime minister of Kenya), and "Afrique" for the Jazz Messengers. Art Blakey and his Jazz Messengers recorded numerous tunes that exhibited African stylistic grooves, melodies, and harmonies, and Blakey recorded a one-off album with a group called the Afro-Drum Ensemble titled *The African Beat*. John Coltrane's first album for Impulse Records was *Africa/Brass*, Ellington recorded the album *Afro Bossa* for Reprise Records in 1963, and Cannonball Adderley recorded two

Black Cultural Identity and Popular Jazz

Miles Davis, *Miles Ahead* (sailboat cover): Columbia Records, CL 1041, 1957.

Miles Davis, *Miles Ahead*: Columbia Records, CL 1041, 1957.

Africa-inspired albums: *African Waltz* in 1961 (the title tune was composed by Canadian composer Galt McDermot, who fell in love with the music of Black South Africans while studying at Cape Town University; Adderley's recording won McDermot a Grammy Award), and *Accent on Africa* in 1968.

There are certain concepts that were radical in their day but, with the passage of time, now seem quaint. In regard to jazz and Black culture, one of those quaint concepts concerns models on album covers. There was a time when record companies routinely used beautiful models to sell albums. This was done to sell jazz albums, pop music albums, and occasionally classical music albums. Interestingly, through the fifties and into the sixties, the models were always white women (one of the most famous, or perhaps infamous, was *Whipped Cream and Other Delights*, by Herb Alpert and the Tijuana Brass in 1965). This explains why the original album art for Miles Davis's 1957 masterpiece *Miles Ahead* features a white woman on a sailboat. According to George Avakian, the album's producer, after the album was released, Davis said to him, "'Why'd you put that white bitch on there' . . . his next sentence, delivered with a chuckle, was merely a quiet, 'You should have used a black girl.'"[10] Columbia replaced the model on *Miles Ahead* with a photo of the trumpet star himself, but from that point onward, Davis would make sure that Black women were depicted on his album covers. Being Miles Davis, he need look no further than the beautiful women who happened to be in his life. This included his wife Frances Davis, who appeared on two of his albums, *Someday My Prince Will Come* in 1961 and *ESP* in 1965; Cicely Tyson (Davis's future wife) on *Sorcerer* in 1967; and Betty Mabry (soon to be Betty Davis) on *Filles de Kilimanjaro* in 1968.

In the sixties, numerous album covers were used as platforms to show Black feminine beauty. There was Willis Jackson's *The Good Life* in 1963, the 3 Sound's *Out of This World* in 1965, Stanley Turrentine's *Easy Walker* in 1966, Donald Byrd's *Slow Drag* in 1967, Horace Silver's *Serenade to a Soul Sister*, and Lou Donaldson's *Midnight Creeper* in 1968, and of course the numerous albums where women were the featured artist. *Uncompromising Expression*, the expansive retrospective book that celebrates Blue Note Records, makes note of this important cultural change: "Some covers also featured a striking image of a black woman—a real step forward for the record industry. Freddie Roach's *Brown Sugar*, Big John Patton's *Oh Baby!*, or Grant Green's *I Want To Hold Your Hand* may look safe and not particularly Miles-esque, but all these albums were cutting edge."[11] Miles-esque, in this case, is a reference to Reid Miles, the award-winning head of graphic design at Blue Note Records in the sixties.

Curiously, some record labels continued the practice of using white models to sell albums by Black jazz musicians. Verve Records placed white models on albums by Wes Montgomery (*California Dreaming*, 1965) and Jimmy Smith (*Who's Afraid of Virginia Woolf?* 1964), and even Blue Note wasn't immune to

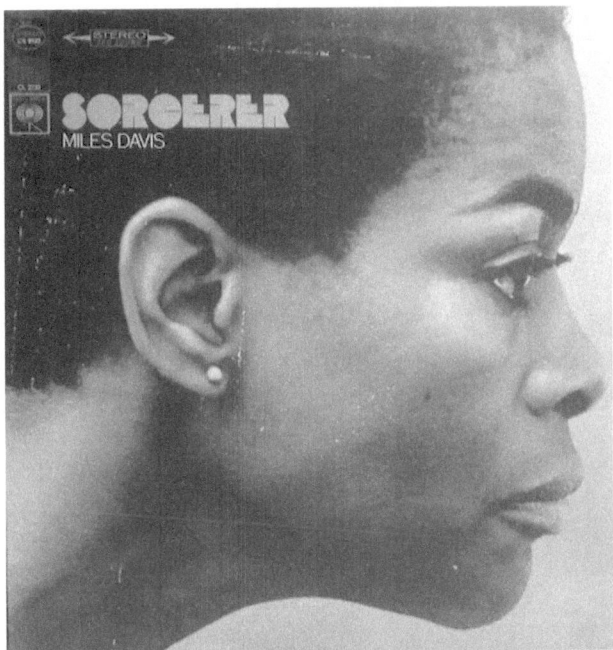

Miles Davis, *Sorcerer*: Columbia Records, CS 9532, 1967.

The Horace Silver Quintet, *Serenade to a Soul Sister*: Blue Note Records, BLP 4277, 1968.

Lou Donaldson, *The Natural Soul*: Blue Note Records, BLP 4108, 1963.

Freddie Roach, *Brown Sugar*: Blue Note Records, BLP 4168, 1964.

the practice, placing the same white model on Lou Donaldson's *Alligator Boogaloo* in 1967 and *Mr. Shing-A-Ling* in 1968. One can assume that it might have been an effective way to get those albums to appeal to white audiences, but at a time of so much Black pride on parade, those efforts seem somewhat regressive at best, especially considering the Black model with the short, natural hairdo who had already appeared on the cover of Donaldson's 1963 album *The Natural Soul*. Gene Ammons, like Donaldson, was a leader in using Black vernacular and imagery in his music, but the cover art for the album *The Soulful Moods of Gene Ammons*, released in 1963, consists almost totally of a white woman's face (an unknowing record buyer would be excused for thinking that, based on the album cover, Gene Ammons was a white woman!). These decisions were made by the graphic art departments of the different record companies. Most jazz musicians didn't have the clout that Miles Davis had to get a photo removed but perhaps Ammons did because he would rectify the situation with three stunning displays of Black feminine beauty—*Boss Soul!* in 1963, *Velvet Soul* in 1964, and *Angel Eyes* in 1965.

This groundswell of authentic Black jazz expression seemed to come from a real desire to show a true view of the life that the artists lived. This desire inspired one of the seminal recordings of the era, Herbie Hancock's *Watermelon Man*. Hancock reflected back on his past: "I wanted to write something that was authentically from the African American experience . . . so I though, *Okay, why not try to write something that speaks to my own experience as a black person from Chicago?* And that's when the figure of the watermelon man, the most ethnic character from my childhood, popped into my head."[12] As provocative as this might seem in the twenty-first century, the watermelon man (or the fruit man or the vegetable man) was constant in Black neighborhoods. The sound of the shouts of these vendors as they made their presence known still echoes in the memory of those who heard it.

Unfortunately, there has been scant coverage of this very important display of Black pride in sixties jazz. The book *Jazz: A History of America's Music* (which in many ways is a wonderful source of jazz history) seems to minimize this jazz era: "Even the titles of the tunes Jimmy Smith and his cohorts recorded celebrated the African American world from which they came—'Home Cookin',' 'The Sermon,' 'The Preacher,' 'Cornbread,' 'Grits [and] Gravy,' 'Back at the Chicken Shack.' It was all good-time music, and it worked for a time."[13] What is missed in this somewhat shallow view is how the jazz world was in the lead in this cultural and racial pride movement. At a time when soul musicians were glamming it up with gowns and tuxedoes (á la the Temptations and the Supremes), the jazz world was dressing in hip dashikis; when "processed" hair (hair that was permed and straightened) was in vogue with soul musicians, jazz musicians would wear afros; when soul musicians were (successfully) reaching out to the white market, the jazz world promoted what was happening in the neighborhood. It would take the rest of the Black music world a few years to catch up to the progressive lead in the jazz world.

In regard to the theme explored earlier of the culinary tropes in jazz, consider this true anecdote. Pianist Les McCann was an early booster of organ great Richard "Groove" Holmes. Holmes, who recorded the albums *A Bowl of Soul*, *Soul Message*, *Living Soul*, *Soul Mist!*, *Super Soul*, and *Soul Power*, was a large man and, according to McCann, he loved to eat. A website dedicated to Holmes shares the story: "Les played a key role in Groove's career when in 1960 he met up with him in a Pittsburgh, Pennsylvania, restaurant. 'I remember going to look for him, and I was told to look in this little restaurant—and it's one of the soul kinda places with greens and beans—and I walked in and I saw this huge person sitting at the table and the whole table was covered. I thought l could eat! But when I saw this! And then the capper was that he asked for a Diet Coke. I started laughing, and we hit it off right away somehow.'"[14]

CHAPTER NINE

"Why Am I Treated So Bad?"... "Compared to What?"

Popular Jazz and Civil Rights

From almost the very earliest days of recording technology, Black musicians have used their musical platforms to address discrimination, inequity, injustice, and civil rights. Bert Williams was considered by many to be the finest performer to come out of minstrelsy and vaudeville, and his admirers included comic legend W. C. Fields, who called Williams "the funniest man I ever saw, and the saddest."[1] In 1906, Williams wrote, performed, and recorded a song titled "Nobody," in which he sings

> When winter comes with snow and sleet,
> and me with hunger and cold feet,
> who says "here's twenty-five cent, go get something to eat"?—Nobody.

The notes to the CD compilation *Really The Blues? A Blues History 1893–1959* make this observation: "'Nobody' is (or may be) Williams's not-so-subtle way of depicting himself, and everyone else of color, as ultimate outsiders in a land of dominant white images, even as those images, under the growing hegemony of African American culture, were changing radically."[2]

It makes sense that Bert Williams would use the only means available to him to address the harsh inequities in twentieth-century America. Music has always been a balm for Black Americans in work songs, field hollers, spirituals (or, as W. E. B. Du Bois calls them, the "Sorrow Songs"), and even minstrel songs that were composed by Black performers. The blues was an especially effective mode of soothing the continual wounds that were suffered. Peter Muir notes that this was obvious in the earliest days of blues music-making: "A truth widely acknowledged, if little discussed, is that the basic purpose of blues is to cure its performers, and by extension its audience, of the condition of the blues. As Paul Oliver, doyen of blues histories, puts it: "It is generally understood that a blues performer sings or plays to rid himself of the blues."[3] W. C. Handy was more succinct: "Blues music was created to chase away gloom."[4]

Black protest lyrics on records and/or in performance was not looked upon favorably, so quite often it was censored. The instances that we find before the 1960s are that much more fascinating, in part, because the musicians were banned from performing them, but also because some of the most popular Black entertainers of the times got away with it. Lead Belly wrote his discrimination anthem "The Bourgeois Blues" in 1937, but despite his popularity, the song was not widely adapted until the folk boom that would come about a decade later. Fats Waller, on the other hand, was at his creative and popular peak in 1927 when he and Andy Razlaf composed "Black and Blue." The lyrics are searing, especially for the 1920s:

> How will it end? Ain't got a friend
> My only sin is in my skin
> What did I do to be so black and blue?

The song would be performed by Waller, Ethel Waters, and Louis Armstrong, three of the most famous Black jazz musicians of the twenties and thirties.

Throughout his fifty-year career as a composer and bandleader, Duke Ellington was always interested in finding ways of portraying the African American experience through music. He composed numerous suites, portraits, tone poems, and even an opera that he hoped would become the equivalent of the European masters' musical depiction of their homelands. To that end, Ellington wrote the extended work *Black, Brown and Beige* for his 1943 debut performance in Carnegie Hall. The most well-known piece to come from the three-movement suite was "Come Sunday," which was a part of the *Black* movement. This beautifully somber plea to God has been recorded and performed hundreds of times, most notably in a 1958 Ellington recording featuring Mahalia Jackson. It is sometimes interpreted as an instrumental, but in its original form, the lyrics convey a message that works as both a religious and a secular call for mercy—

> Lord dear Lord above, God almighty, God of love
> Please look down and see my people through

Ellington biographer Terry Teachout wrote, "Duke Ellington was never ostentatious about his religious observances . . . but he was deadly serious about them. . . . 'Come Sunday,' the best-known section of *Black, Brown and Beige*, is a 'tone parallel' of a church service, and when Mahalia Jackson sang it on record in 1958, even the most skeptical of listeners could not doubt its composer's faith"[5]

But the early jazz protest anthem that continues to inspire, amaze, and, sadly, seems relevant in 2024 is "Strange Fruit," the anti-lynching polemic composed by Abel Meeropol but brought to life, against all odds, by Billie Holiday. The imminent blues scholar Albert Murray calls "Strange Fruit" "a political torch song, a lament about unrequited patriotic love. We have loved and fought and died for this country for all these many years, the song asserts, because it has been our official homeland for this many generations, and now just look at what some of these other folks think they have a right to do to somebody because they want to think that they are better than them."[6] The story of Holiday recording the song against the wishes of Columbia Records (she recorded it for Commodore Records instead) and her performance at Café Society in 1939, as well as the consequences of those actions, has become an American legend and the subject of a 2021 feature film titled *The United States vs. Billie Holiday*.

The end of the Depression and WWII brought new focus to the issues of race and discrimination, particularly in the Jim Crow South. Two incidents, both in 1955, brought sharp focus to the struggles of Black Americans—the murder of fourteen-year-old Emmett Till in Money, Mississippi, and Rosa Parks's defiant action that began the Montgomery Bus Boycott in Alabama. After those early civil rights beginnings, it became increasingly difficult for famous African American entertainers and athletes to remain silent in the face of the atrocities faced by Black folks, particularly, but not exclusively, in the South.

One of the more interesting stories of jazz and civil rights involves Louis Armstrong. Armstrong, who was, by the 1950s, a major recording and movie star, was criticized within the Black community partly for his affable, avuncular presence and partly because many Black Americans felt that he didn't lend his voice to civil rights causes loudly enough. Armstrong was very well known throughout America and the rest of the world, so much so that in 1957, he was chosen by President Eisenhower to lead a delegation of musicians on a goodwill tour of the Soviet Union. Around the same time, Orval Faubus, the governor of Arkansas, used federal troops to prevent nine Black students from entering Little Rock Central High School, an action that went in opposition to the *Brown v. Board of Education* ruling that banned school discrimination. Faubus's action, as well as the US government's inaction to stop him, angered Armstrong so much that he decided against embarking on the Soviet Union goodwill tour. Armstrong, who was derisively referred to by some Black folks as an Uncle Tom, told a reporter that "Ike (Eisenhower) and the government can go to hell," going on to call Governor Faubus a "no good motherf***er."[7]

Interestingly, it was the same Little Rock Nine event that inspired Charles Mingus (1922–1979) to compose one of the most majestic jazz protest songs, "Fables of Faubus." There was, however, one problem—Mingus was recording for Columbia Records, the very same major label that denied Billie Holiday's "Strange Fruit" twenty years earlier. Twenty years was not enough time for Columbia to change, because Mingus, too, was denied his incendiary lyrics. Mingus, like Holiday before him, had a plan B—he recorded "Fables of Faubus" as an instrumental on the 1959 Columbia album *Mingus Ah Um*, and a year later, recorded the original version with lyrics on the independent Candid record label. Now titled "Original Faubus Fables," Mingus, singing and chanting along with his drummer Danny Richmond, did not hold back:

> Name me a handful that's ridiculous, Dannie Richmond.
> Faubus, Rockefeller, Eisenhower.
> Why are they so sick and ridiculous?
> Two, four, six, eight, they brainwash and teach you hate!

"Fables of Faubus" and "Original Faubus Fables" are beloved parts of the Mingus canon, and Mingus, in his lifetime, recorded the songs numerous times.

Charles Mingus is sometimes known as "the Angry Man of Jazz," but most of his ire was targeted on racial injustice. A recurring theme in his music is freedom, both literally and figuratively. Jazz musicians are particularly interested in freedom because it is easy to make the step from freedom to live as an equal in America with freedom to compose and play what and how one wants to play. Freedom, as a noun and as a signifying goal, began to appear in jazz in the fifties most notably on Sonny Rollins's groundbreaking album and composition *Freedom Suite*. Rollins laid the foundation, both musically and thematically, for freedom explorations that would become commonplace in the sixties. Max Roach was the drummer on that album, and perhaps it was the inspiration from those sessions that spurred the creation in 1960 of *We Insist! Freedom Now Suite*. Created in the wake of the Greensboro, North Carolina, lunch counter sit-ins (with an album cover evoking the event), *We Insist!* is a tour-de-force ensemble piece. Abbie Lincoln is particularly effective in her delivery of the lyrics written by Oscar Brown Jr., which not only allows her to sing, but she also, in the words of Tom Moon, "moves through a series of wordless moans, eddying cries, and shrieks that is unlike anything else in music."[8] This towering achievement set the tone for unblinking, unvarnished expressions of musical indignation, and although Roach was signed to Mercury, which at that time was a major label, *We Insist!* was released on the Candid record label just as Charles Mingus's "Original Faubus Fables" had been, for essentially the same reasons.

The Black college student sit-ins of 1960 and the worsening treatment of Black Americans throughout the South began to inspire more musical activity. The composer and big band leader Oliver Nelson created an entire album motivated by the causes being brought to the forefront titled *Afro American Sketches*. The album included such tunes as "Message," "Emancipation Blues," "Disillusioned," and "Freedom Dance." In Texas, a group of young musicians put together a band styled somewhat after Art Blakey and the Jazz Messengers, so it seemed that the name Jazz Crusaders would be an appropriate way to give people the sense of what they were all about. Their 1961 debut album was titled *Freedom Sounds*, and the title track, composed by the pianist Joe Sample, sets up a martial groove akin to the sound of freedom marchers. *Freedom Sounds* began a long list of very popular albums by that band in the sixties, which ironically has been overshadowed by their successes in the next decade. In 1969, the Jazz Crusaders dropped the "Jazz" part of their name, becoming "The Crusaders," and by the end of the seventies, "Crusaders." The Crusaders were one of the best-selling jazz-fusion bands of the seventies and eighties, and their crossover appeal packed people in concert halls around the world.

As mentioned earlier, singer/songwriter Oscar Brown Jr. (1926–2005) provided the lyrical content to Max Roach's music on *We Insist!* That same year, Brown would record his debut album titled *Sin and Soul*. Despite this being his first recording, Brown displays a musical and lyrical maturity seldom matched by artists with decades of recorded works. He managed to do something quite extraordinary—he gave a twelve-song glimpse into the world of Black America in 1960 that ran the gamut—songs about love, songs steeped in folklore, songs about the blues, songs displaying humor, and songs displaying pathos. Brown added lyrics to three tunes (Nat Adderley's *Work Song*, Bobby Timmons's *Dat Were*, and John Coltrane's *Afro Blue*), and in the process, made them instant additions to the Great American Songbook. But it is his original composition "Bid 'Em In" that is simply astonishing—in one minute and thirty-eight seconds, Brown's portrayal of a slave auctioneer gives the sense of the heartlessness and brutality of the process:

> Don't mind those tears, that's part of her tricks
> Five fifty's the bid who'll say six,
> She's healthy and strong and well-equipped,
> Make a fine lady's maid when she's properly whipped!

This album is a masterpiece of Afrocentrism; from beginning to end, Brown gives the listener a sense of the depth and breadth of life in Black America: the joy of childhood, the pain of discrimination, the monotony of the "Humdrum Blues," where one gets frustrated by "fighting the future and mad at the past." *Sin and Soul* heralded a new and important voice in the music world. It's worth noting that Oscar Brown Jr. was signed to Columbia Records two years before Bob Dylan. Considering Brown's brilliance as a singer-songwriter, his lovely singing voice, and his good looks and charisma, one can only guess what might have happened if he had gotten the same kind of promotion as Dylan. In a perfect world, Brown Jr. would be celebrated at least as much as Dylan, who has become an unquestioned American music icon.

Years later, Brown remembered those days of jazz and protest this way: "Everybody was up in arms at the time! The character of the work that we did went off into a more nationalistic or militant tone . . . it's not like we had a formal organization. There was no one person who was the leader—we were kindred spirits and we would run into each other during that period."[9] As the civil rights protests and marches throughout the South gained momentum, so did the backlash against them, and that backlash became much more violent and deadly. Perhaps no backlash was sadder and more tragic than the 16th Street Baptist Church Bombing on September 15, 1963, in Birmingham, Alabama. The bombing, carried out by local Ku Klux Klan members (who weren't brought to justice for decades), killed four girls—Addie Mae Collins, Denise McNair, Carole Robertson, and Cynthia Wesley, all between eleven and fourteen—and injured twenty-two others. Over the years, there have been numerous tributes to and commemorations of this act of hate and oppression, and among the first was by John Coltrane. Three months after the murder of the four girls, Coltrane and his quartet went in the studio and recorded "Alabama," a beautifully mournful meditation that would set the template for the "Psalm" movement of his masterwork *A Love Supreme*. Coltrane biographer J. C. Thomas called *Alabama* a "eulogy, a lament, and an elegy . . . more than any other Coltrane composition during that period, it expressed the deep, profound melancholy that was revealing itself more and more frequently."[10]

Jazz musicians became very comfortable lending their name, their time, and their talent to the cause of civil rights. The brazen nature of the attacks on civil rights workers was becoming difficult to stand by and ignore, and jazz musicians were some of the most high-profile Black people in America. As jazz scholar Ashawnta Jackson notes, "This might have been why a political agnostic like Monk performed at a 1963 civil rights benefit for the Student Nonviolent Coordinating Committee.... This was a move that fit well into the long history of jazz musicians performing for explicitly activist causes. In the past, musicians had performed at benefits for the Scottsboro Boys, the Freedom Riders, the NAACP, and, later, the lunch counter sit-ins. Monk would be part of a tradition that included musicians like Duke Ellington, Abbey Lincoln, and Clark Terry, musicians who were contributing their talents to the fight."[11]

Musical protest in the jazz world utilized many different approaches, some subtle, some powerful and direct. One of the most fiery retorts starts off, "The name of this song is Mississippi Goddam! And I mean every word of it."[12] And with that intro, Nina Simone (1933–2003) tears into the song "Mississippi Goddam," which she describes as "a show tune, but the show hasn't been written for it yet."[13] The song is remarkable in the sense that it really does sound like a 1960s Broadway-style show tune, complete with rapid two-beat rhythm and major key tonic-dominant harmony, but the lyrics tell a different story:

> Alabama's got me so upset,
> Tennessee made me lose my rest
> And everybody knows about Mississippi, goddamn

Another striking thing about this recorded performance is that it took place in 1964, in Carnegie Hall! The April 9, 1964, edition of *Jet Magazine* made note of the concert: "Nina Simone, who gave a concert at Carnegie Hall, left them with a lot to smoke in their pipes. A song on the segregation mess which she penned herself, *Mississippi [Goddam]*, was one of the high points of the concert."[14] In the tune, Simone unleashes a torrent of fury: "Don't tell me, I'll tell you, me and my people are just about due.... This whole country is full of lies, You all gonna die, and die like flies."

Mississippi Goddam, I Wish I Knew How It Would Feel to Be Free, and *Young, Gifted, and Black* are just a few songs written or recorded by Nina Simone that have become civil rights anthems written between the time of the 1961 Freedom Riders and "Freedom Summer," the activities in the year 1964 that would result in passage of the Civil Rights Act, which banned segregation and employment discrimination. Freedom Summer was brutal, and the number of kidnappings, lynchings, bombings, torture, and murders made it difficult for musicians of all styles and genres to look away. Art Blakey's response was a seven-and-a-half minute solo drum suite titled "The Freedom Rider," which would also become the name of his 1964 album with the Jazz Messengers; guitarist Grant Green, who in 1961 wrote and recorded "Freedom March," returned to that theme once again in 1965 with "The Selma March"; Charles Mingus, ever the provocateur, recorded the song "Freedom" in 1965, which lamented "freedom for your brothers and sisters, but no freedom for me"; Eddie Harris's "Freedom Jazz Dance" became an anthem after its inclusion on Miles Davis's *Miles Smiles* album in 1965—it seemed that the demand for freedom was everywhere in the jazz world.

But it wasn't just the jazz world; soul, pop, and folk musicians began to openly express concern and disgust at the treatment of Black Americans in the Jim Crow South as well as everywhere else in the US. It became impossible to ignore, in large part due to television. The network news shows began broadcasting directly from the protest lines, the confrontations, and the over-the-top police reactions, bringing the reality into everyone's household regardless of locale. The Little Rock Nine incident inspired Pops Staples, legendary guitarist, songwriter, and leader of the Staple Singers. Mavis Staples, a legend in her own right, recalled the story to journalist and radio show host Greg Kot: "Pops was sitting in his recliner watching the news on TV, and as those kids walked up to enter the schools, a [National Guardsman] told them to turn around. And Pops says, 'Why would he do this? Why are they treated so bad?' And he wrote that song that night."[15]

That song would become one of the many Staple Singers' songs that propelled them to the forefront of groups that used their talent and creativity to help to do what musicians can do better than most other artists in aiding the cause of freedom around the world. Because they started out singing a mixture of gospel and folk songs, the Staple Singers gained credibility in areas where other popular acts had problems connecting—they became trusted messengers. The Staple Singers "combined spirituality with social significance in an important genre known as the 'message song.'"[16] "Why Am I Treated So Bad?" became a landmark "message song" inspiring musicians and nonmusicians alike. Greg Kot states further that "Martin Luther King was enthralled by 'Why? (Am I Treated So Bad).' 'Stape,' King would say nearly every time he saw Pops, 'You gonna play my song tonight?'"[17] Among the musicians who got the "message" were Cannonball Adderley and Duke Ellington, who met the Staple Singers at a performance in 1961. "It was a very small audience . . . but Cannonball Adderley told [gospel critic Anthony Heilbert] he was a big fan of the Staple Singers, because they reminded him of down-home singing. . . . Ellington told Pops he loved what the group was doing; it's where he saw the family play 'gospel in a blues key' for the first time."[18]

Adderley was inspired enough to record his own version of "Why Am I Treated So Bad!" in 1967 for the album of the same name. Adderley, over a relatively short twenty years (he died in 1975 at the age of forty-six), was an amazingly prolific recording artist both as a sideman and as a leader of his own bands. As stated in the chapter on live music, one of the traits that made Cannonball Adderley special was his ability to connect with audiences. His background as a band director in his native Florida became useful on the bandstand; Cannonball was part music educator, part historian, and part motivational speaker because he used every opportunity available to inspire the audience, especially in regard to Black pride. A classic example of this is his spoken intro to "Walk Tall," a tune released as a single from another 1967 album *74 Miles Away*: "Like I said before, there are times when . . . there are times when things don't lay the way they're supposed to lay. But regardless, you're supposed to hold your head up high and walk tall . . . WALK TALL!"[19]

That sense of Black pride and celebration of Black culture began to appear in many areas of the African American community in the sixties, and jazz is no exception. As in "Walk Tall," messages of inspiration and togetherness, as well as connectedness to the larger diaspora, became common. Duke Ellington composed an entire stage show around the concept of commemorating the Emancipation Proclamation titled *My People*; Jomo Kenyatta's election as Kenya's first indigenous prime minister and president in 1964 inspired Lee Morgan to compose and record the tribute "Mr. Kenyatta" on his album *Search for the New Land*; Ramsey Lewis would have a hit with the title song from his 1966 album *Wade in the Water*, a jazz take on the traditional spiritual; Brother Jack McDuff recorded Sam Cooke's somber but hopeful plea for equality, *A Change Is Gonna Come*, the title track on a 1966 album; Art Blakey and the Jazz Messengers got in the spirit with the 1965 tune "Freedom Monday"—along with some of the great soul songs, like the Impressions' *Keep on Pushing*, Cooke's aforementioned *A Change Is Gonna Come*, and Sam and Dave's classic *Soul Man*, which, in 1967, extolled the virtues of coming through the Black struggle:

> Got what I got, the hard way,
> and I'll make it better each and every day.
> So honey, don't forget,
> That you ain't seen nothing yet![20]

Isaac Hayes was inspired to write *Soul Man* while watching news coverage of the riots in Detroit. As he described it, "I saw the news flash where they were burning [the neighborhoods]. Where the buildings weren't burnt, people would write 'soul' on the buildings. . . . So I said, 'Why not do something called 'Soul Man' and kind of tell a story about one's struggle to rise above his present conditions . . . . 'Soul Man' came out of that whole black identification."[21] For a brief window of time, one could detect some hopeful signs of progress, at least in Black artistic expression. That window closed shut on April 4, 1968, when an assassin's rifle cut down Black America's drum major for peace, Martin Luther King Jr., in Memphis, Tennessee. All hope seemed lost—pride turned to sadness and anger, hope to hopelessness.

For many in the jazz community, Dr. King was a hero, or at the very least, greatly admired. Alice Coltrane, speaking about her husband's admiration for Malcolm X and Martin Luther King, recalled "John was very interested in the civil rights movement; he appreciated both men from their different perspectives.... He knew that Dr. Martin Luther King was an intelligent man and as a preacher could reach the heart of the people."[22] In the sixties, religion played a big role in John Coltrane's life and music. Author and musician Charley Gerard notes that "the composition 'Reverend King' was composed as a demonstration of how these various religious strains could be combined."[23] Miles Davis also spoke of his admiration of Dr. King, calling him "a great leader and a beautiful guy."[24] Carmen McRae, speaking of civil rights, notes, "The one who really made it prominent was our Martin Luther King. He changed the whole economic structure of Alabama. That was the beginning, and it all stemmed from that."[25]

Dr. King understood well the power of music. He knew that W. E. B. Du Bois loved the "Sorrow Songs," and both his mother and his wife were superb musicians (Coretta Scott King was on a scholarship, studying at the New England Conservatory of Music, when she first met her husband, who was also studying in Boston). Throughout his work across the country, he met and developed friendships and kinships with musicians in all styles and genres. And the civil rights movement was awash in music: Greg Kot's book on Mavis Staples tells of a *Newsweek* article written during the civil rights era: "'History has never known a protest movement so rich in song as the civil rights movement,' *Newsweek* declared in 1964. 'Nor a movement in which songs are as important. Martin Luther King called them 'vital.' ... At nightly get-out-the-vote meetings, singing always came first, the singers gilded with sweat starting off with 'We've been 'buked and we've been scorned ... but we'll never turn back.'"[26]

The year 1964 was a consequential one for Dr. King. He would be a key component in the passage of the Civil Rights Act, and he would win the Nobel Peace Prize. But one of his lesser-known writings came from that year as well—a beautiful tribute to jazz. The organizers of the inaugural Berlin Jazz Festival invited him to write a foreword to the festival program. King was known to have much love and respect for jazz, so for the festival program, King wrote the following:

> God has wrought many things out of oppression. He has endowed his creatures with the capacity to create—and from this capacity has flowed the sweet songs of sorrow and joy that have allowed man to cope with his environment and many different situations.

Jazz speaks for life. The Blues tell the story of life's difficulties, and if you think for a moment, you will realize that they take the hardest realities of life and put them into music, only to come out with some new hope or sense of triumph.

This is triumphant music.

Modern jazz has continued in this tradition, singing the songs of a more complicated urban existence. When life itself offers no order and meaning, the musician creates an order and meaning from the sounds of the earth which flow through his instrument.

It is no wonder that so much of the search for identity among American Negroes was championed by Jazz musicians. Long before the modern essayists and scholars wrote of racial identity as a problem for a multiracial world, musicians were returning to their roots to affirm that which was stirring within their souls.

Despite the constant public threats, the stabbing and bombings, the dogs and water cannons, and the rock, bottles, and intimidation that were captured and shown by the press that followed him everywhere he went, Dr. King's death stunned America and the rest of the world. Black America saw King's fight as their fight. He was the visual manifestation that was needed: brilliant, articulate, steadfast, and unafraid despite the very real danger that was ever-present. When he was gunned down on the Memphis hotel balcony, Black America's dreams of freedom and equality seemed to be gunned down as well. *Keep On Pushing*—why? *A Change is Gonna Come*—you really think so? *Walk Tall*—why, so we can be easier targets?? As reported by Walter Cronkite, known as the most trusted man in news in 1968, "There was shock in Harlem tonight when word of Dr. King's murder reached the nation's largest Negro community. Men, women, and children poured into the streets, they appeared dazed, and many were crying."[27]

Across the spectrum, rage, anger, and sadness gripped Black America. Miles Davis recalled, "I just never could go for his non-violent, turn-the-other-cheek philosophy. Still, for him to get killed like that, so violently—just like Gandhi—was a goddamn shame. He was like America's saint."[28] Motown Records founder Berry Gordy was known for being very conscious of the company's image—he was careful to project a non-threatening, positive, and polished image of Black life to America. But author Mark Kurlansky's book centered around Motown in the sixties notes that Dr. King's death rattled Gordy as well. "'I couldn't contain my anger,' [he said].... He agreed to hold a Motown benefit concert to raise money for the Poor People's Campaign that King had planned. Gordy even marched side by side with Sidney Poitier, Mary Wilson, and Sammy Davis Jr."[29]

Memphis was the home of Stax Records, one of the most successful soul music record labels, and the studio was relatively close to the Lorraine Hotel, the site of Dr. King's murder. Although almost all the hit records produced there were by Black singers and groups, Stax was well-known for being one of two southern studios that utilized white and Black musicians working together (the other being Fame Studio in Muscle Shoals, Alabama). One of the most popular groups at Stax was Booker T. & the M.G.'s, who struck it big in the early sixties with the hit record "Green Onions," and the evenly integrated quartet provided the background for most of the sessions that emerged from the studio, including one on April 4, 1968. Music journalist Peter Guralnick writes that "William Bell recalls being in the studio the day of Martin Luther King's death and finding out about the assassination only after the session was over. He and the other black musicians had to walk Steve Cropper and Duck Dunn [the M.G.s' white guitarist and bassist] to their car through an ugly mob that had formed outside."[30] Isaac Hayes and Booker T. Jones were also at the session that night. "'I went blank,' said Hayes, 'I couldn't write for almost a year—I was filled with so much bitterness and anguish, till I couldn't deal with it.' 'That was the turning point,' echoed Booker T., 'the turning point for relations between races in the South. And it happened in Memphis.'"[31]

Eileen Southern, the dean of African American musicology, wrote of the importance of freedom songs to the civil rights movement in general and to Dr. King in particular, and she had this poignant observation of that terrible time in Memphis:

> As the black masses began to realize that nonviolence was powerless against the entrenched racism in the United States, the singing stopped. Instead, there were angry slogans and riots. Only for one day was there singing—on April 9, 1968, the day of the funeral of the martyred Martin Luther King.... Many songs were heard during the open-air service held after the funeral procession on the grounds of Morehouse College, but the most moving of them was Mahalia Jackson's singing of King's favorite, the gospel song *Precious Lord, Take My Hand*.[32]

Southern goes on to note that "King's death left black Americans numb. The different segments of the black population gave vent to their feelings of desolation in varied ways."[33]

The jazz community was a part of the Black population that needed to vent their desolation and devastation. Herbie Hancock, who, in 1968, was juggling his time between membership in Miles Davis's celebrated sixties quintet, a very active life as a session musician, and his own very hot solo career, was compelled to expresses himself on his final Blue Note album *The Prisoner*: "It was a concept album focused on the struggle for civil rights. Like most black Americans, I was shattered by the assassination of Martin Luther King Jr. in

April of 1968 and Bobby Kennedy two months later.... Most of the songs on *The Prisoner* were about Martin Luther King Jr.... *The Prisoner* didn't sell very well, but it's a record that's close to my heart."[34]

Oliver Nelson, who, in 1967, wrote and recorded an album commemorating an earlier assassination titled *The Kennedy Dream*, once again used his pen to express his pain and sorrow, this time on the album recorded in 1969 titled *Black, Brown and Beautiful*. But where that earlier album could be viewed as poignant and mournful, *Black, Brown and Beautiful* has a different feel altogether, which is made obvious on the first track, "Aftermath": the first sounds are that of police sirens, machine guns, breaking glass, and footsteps engaged in a quick-step march. The cacophony becomes more unsettling as it's joined by a very dissonant orchestral tone cluster with different rhythmic motifs played between the piano and the lower string section. Soon, a tenor sax begins to play a melody that is a bluesy, plaintive moan accompanied by sliding diminished chords in the strings; eventually, the strings mirror that plaintive saxophone melody only to have the band join in with a free and open musical expression of disharmony and discord, both literal and figurative. "Aftermath" ends with the same dissonant orchestral tone cluster heard earlier.

This album is one of the finest representations of tone painting, which is the concept of using tones, timbre, notes, scales, and phrases to give a symbolic representation of a person, event, time period, etc. And what Nelson does so effectively is to convey multiple facets of what Black Americans (and many non-Black Americans) were feeling at the time. If "Aftermath" is a pure expression of anger and rage, "I Hope in Time a Change Will Come" represents hope despite the evidence to the contrary. "Martin Was a Man, a Real Man" is a "final salute to a Great Man, a Great American."[35] Oliver Nelson wrote an extensive essay as album notes that accompany the record. And he does not hold back his disgust one bit:

> Writing the liner notes seems to be more difficult than having composed the music for this album. Mainly because I'm confused about the meaning of words. For instance, the words riot, revolt, dissent, civil disturbance, civil disobedience, violence.
>
> Our country was born from violence, riot, revolt, dissent, civil disobedience, but we record these historical events as the War of Independence, the Boston Tea Party, the Civil War, Conquest of the West, etc. However, when American people of African descent are involved in efforts to achieve Freedom, Justice, the Right to Work, to Educate Their Children, etc., the words Treason and Communism are included with the words Riot, Revolt, Dissent, and Civil Disobedience.

> The concept that this country is moving toward two separate societies is true. Our country is Racist, the Churches have failed completely, Uncle Tom is gone forever and the Black, Brown, and White Militants are here to stay.[36]

Of interest to readers in 2024 is Nelson's own description of his idea for the song "Self Help Is Needed" where he writes, "I have always felt that the Federal Government wasn't going to do a damn thing and American Blacks were going to have to do it for themselves. However, you can't have a foot on your neck making it impossible to help yourself. That seems logical—doesn't it?"[37]

Another jazz tribute to Martin Luther King is made more poignant because it is an album recorded by the person whom Dr. King was talking to at the moment he was killed. Ben Branch was a Memphis-born tenor saxophonist who came up through the ranks by playing with the greats of that city. Branch worked with B. B. King, Phineas Newborn, Hank Crawford, and many others before making his way up to Chicago, where he was, among many other activities at the time, the music director for Jesse Jackson's "Operation Breadbasket" broadcasts (Cannonball Adderley references "Brother" Ben Branch on the intro to "Country Preacher") as well as a well-known and highly regarded musician for various civil rights causes. The National Civil Right Museum website has a section on Ben Branch that reads:

> Branch recollected his last conversation with the reverend. King had asked Branch to play "Precious Lord, Take My Hand" at a rally later that day, as Branch's instrumental rendition of this gospel song was one of MLK's favorites. "Play that song tonight—I want you to play it like you've never played it before in your life," Branch remembered the civil rights leader saying. Just minutes after this conversation, an assassin's bullet would take Dr. King's life on the balcony of the Lorraine Motel.[38]

That last conversation was the inspiration for the album *The Last Request*, which Ben Branch recorded with the Operation Breadbasket Orchestra and Choir. This musical tribute is of a very different nature than Oliver Nelson's *Black, Brown and Beautiful*. Stylistically, the music on this album draws heavily on gospel sounds, with the piano and organ played in a style that says "Sunday Morning." Vocal soloists and the choir contribute to that church service feel, but Branch's tenor sax playing presents his jazz bona fides quite well, and the band accompanying him is playing a mixture of soul music and jazz that was very representative of the time. Included in the list of songs is "Precious Lord, Take My Hand," which truly was Dr. King's last request. (Branch would go on to become the director of Cultural Development for the City of Chicago, where the author of this book worked for him during the summer of 1977.)

Nina Simone had a take-no-prisoners approach to her message when civil rights was at issue. But Dr. King's death seemed to break her spirit, at least temporarily. Just days after the assassination, Simone and her band played a concert in Long Island, New York, and on the intro to the song "Why? (The King of Love is Dead)," she sounded as if she'd lost the will to fight that was so present on *Mississippi Goddam*. In a very hushed tone, almost a whisper that is simultaneously intimate, reverential, and sad, Simone speaks:

> We want to do a tune written for today, for this hour, for Dr. Martin Luther King. We stated before that this whole program was dedicated to his memory, but this tune was written about him, and for him, and so we had yesterday to learn it and so we'll see.[39]

"Why? (The King of Love is Dead)" was written by Gene Taylor, the bassist in Simone's band, on the day that they performed and recorded it, April 7, just three days after Dr. King's assassination. In a remembrance forty years after the concert, Sam Waymon, Simone's brother and the band's organist, said, "We didn't have a chance to really, like, have two or three days of rehearsal, but when you're feeling compassion and outrage, and wanting to express what you know the world is feeling, we did it because that's what we felt."[40] The concert was released in 1968 on the album *'Nuff Said*. The album is typical of Simone's output—some pop tunes, some jazz, a blues, and a show tune, this time by the Gershwins. But also among the tunes she performed that evening is her version of the gospel standard "Precious Lord, Take My Hand," a song now forever tied to history as the last song on the mind of Dr. King.

After the death of Dr. King and the riots that followed, as well as the death in June 1968 of Senator Robert F. Kennedy (who was well on his way to securing the Democratic nomination for president), the message songs became more strident and more direct. And they began to come from surprising places. Motown's Berry Gordy was well aware that much of his success was due to the crossover nature of his music. To make the albums marketable in the South, Motown would purposely not put photos of some of the groups on the covers in the early sixties. But even at Motown, there was a change in the air: The Temptations, perhaps the biggest sellers for the company in the sixties, began to deal with issues facing the inner cities with songs such as "Cloud Nine," "Runaway Child," and "Message From a Black Man"; The Supremes, known to all at the company as the group that Gordy groomed for mainstream success, tackled unwed motherhood and poverty with "Love Child" and "I'm Living in Shame."

Elsewhere in the world of soul in 1969, Donny Hathaway kept it basic, singing a wordless, bluesy, church-like moan and setting a funky groove with a band that included Afro-Latin percussion for a trip to "The Ghetto"; James Brown had a big hit with "Say It Loud, I'm Black and I'm Proud," but his attempt at a call for Black pride was not received well by all, getting him banned from some radio stations while losing some of the white fans that he picked up over the years. Sly and the Family Stone's 1969 album *Stand* is a prime example of the post-King music world; there is the social uplift of the title track as well as on the songs "Everyday People" and "You Can Make If You Try"; there is the direct racial confrontation of "Don't Call Me Nigger, Whitey"; there is the soulful psychedelic funk of "I Want to Take You Higher"; and there is the LSD-inspired, drugged-out extended jam of "Sex Machine." Sly and the Family Stone was representative of the rock psychedelia that was beginning to become a part of Black music as well, and Sly himself was beginning to have a big influence on the jazz world via one of his most famous fans.

Miles Davis, the man who was in constant motion in regard to his music, his stage presence, and just about everything else in his life, was once again about to change his persona and in the process, change the jazz world. Davis always had his ears open for new sounds, and those sounds always made their way into his recordings. He counted on the younger musicians in his band as well as the younger musicians on the radio to point the way to the new directions that he should take. Guitarist Carlos Santana became a trusted friend to Davis in the late sixties, and he remembers it this way: "Around that time, Miles always seemed to be in the company of a group of women.... They changed the way he dressed, the places he went, and the music he listened to. Largely because of their influence, Miles really began to check out James Brown and Sly Stone, and he started hanging out with Jimi."[41] Davis himself said, "The music I was really listening to in 1968 was James Brown, the great guitar player Jimi Hendrix, and a new group who had just come out with the hit record 'Dance to the Music,' Sly and the Family Stone."[42] Davis developed a relationship with Hendrix, and the two jammed together quite a lot. "He influence me and I influenced him, and that's the way great music is always played.... He was a great blues guitarist. Both him and Sly were great natural musicians; they played what they heard."[43]

Not only was Davis influenced by the music on the streets, he also began to pick up on the fashion and the art. "Everybody was into blackness, you know, the black consciousness movement, and so a lot of African and Indian fabrics were being worn. I started wearing African dashikis and robes and looser clothes ... I had moved away from the cool Brooks Brothers look and into this other thing, which for me, was more what was happening with the times."[44] This new acknowledgement of Black consciousness by Miles Davis would result in his most radical shift yet, the album *Bitches Brew*. In the notes to the box set of

The Complete Bitches Brew Sessions, Quincy Troupe (who co-authored *Miles: The Autobiography*) notes that despite the critics' negative reactions to his new direction, Davis always led by incorporating everything that was happening at the time of his different recordings. "Looked at in this light, *Bitches Brew* was pointing our ears in the direction musical production was about to go, even if many didn't like or understand it.... And in many ways, *Bitches Brew* was a summing up of the musical, political, and cultural changes that the era of the 1960s had just ushered us through."[45]

With *Bitches Brew*, Miles Davis was able to accomplish something unique; he recorded an avant-garde album that connected with the masses despite confusion by the critics. The music on *Bitches Brew* is, at times, dissonant, loud, atonal, brooding, and confrontational. It is also, many times, danceable, melodic, mellow, funky, and on "Sanctuary," it even manages to be tender. Most of the tracks are incredibly long, but they never seem to meander—part of this is due to the incredible musicians playing on the album, and part of it is in the editing that Davis and his producer, Teo Macero, performed on the tracks, something Davis had never done before. Despite all of the uniqueness put forth on this double album, it became Davis's biggest seller (until being surpassed in later years by his 1959 classic *Kind of Blue*). Writer, professor, and historian Gerald Early writes in the notes to a CD compilation of Black Power music: "Miles Davis tried to adopt aspects of the music of Sly Stone, James Brown, and Jimi Hendrix with indifferent critical success, but considerable popular appeal in some quarters, especially with his 1969 album *Bitches Brew*."[46] *Bitches Brew* is the big bang that would create the world of jazz-rock fusion in the seventies, and in the introduction to her book on fusion, Julie Coryell noted Davis's importance: "Though some of jazz's more traditional critics viewed the emergence of this 'new music' with disdain, its box-office appeal was clearly evident. Davis was able to sell out rock halls such as the now-defunct Fillmores—a sure sign of popular status—while his record sales soared."[47]

The reason that *Bitches Brew* connected is because it sounded like 1969. It sounded like an album that reflected the loss of the most important civic leaders to the people who depended on those leaders for hope. It sounded like revolution in the streets, waged against racism, against poverty, against a war that no one understood. *Bitches Brew* sounded like a battle between generations, waged between those who hated the idea of drugs and those who wanted the freedom to experiment. *Bitches Brew* sounded like Shirley Chisholm and her battles in the U.S. Congress that began in 1969; it sounded like battle for women's rights; it sounded like the riot at the Stonewall Inn in 1969 for LGBTQ rights. Miles Davis created a post-King jazz masterpiece that spoke to the times without uttering a word. As Troupe notes, "it shouldn't be lost on the listener that Miles

Davis recorded *Bitches Brew* in 1969, the year of that chaotic, tumultuous era of change in America—and in the world—with the album being released in 1970, the first year of the next decade.[48]

There was another huge selling jazz album that was recorded in 1969, but this album was powered by perhaps the most direct jazz protest song, one with an unusual backstory but one that also had quite a big impact. "Compared To What" was the eight-minute-and-eighteen-second opening track from the album *Swiss Movement* by Les McCann and Eddie Harris, and the story of the song's success is as unlikely as it is fascinating.

Gene McDaniels was a singer who had a top ten hit in 1961 with the song "A Hundred Pounds of Clay," and he followed that up with a few others. McDaniels's innocuous style on those early sixties hits is very much in the mode of white pop singers, which was somewhat unique considering that McDaniels was Black. Though his records did appear on the R&B charts, his singing, as well as the production, was not what would have been considered soulful—many of the songwriters who supplied McDaniels with tunes also had success in the sixties and seventies with Elvis Presley. After his initial success performing, McDaniels took some time away. In his own words: "I dived out of the nightclubs because of the smoke, the loud talking, the booze, the irreverence to the music, I mean it drove me nuts. So I have been out of the nightclub scene since about . . . more like 1968 as a general overall picture."[49]

What Gene McDaniels did next is what makes the story somewhat unusual—he reverted back to his birth name, Eugene, and he became a songwriter. Considering that his first big hit as a singer was a pop song about God taking *A Hundred Pounds of Clay* and forming man, the fact that his first success as a songwriter would become a countercultural milestone was either a stroke of luck, a stroke of genius, or a bit of both. According to McDaniels, "Compared to What" was inspired by "the right-wing push toward globalization and privatization, etc. etc. kinda acing out the normal people in the world like myself . . . so I started writing about it."[50] In the song, McDaniel rattles off a list of challenges and concerns: "Slaughterhouses killin' hogs, twisted children killin' frogs, poor dumb rednecks rollin' logs, tired old ladies kissin' dogs."

He goes on to talk about the Vietnam War, preachers in churches "filling us with fright," and in the final verse he seems, like most Black Americans, left with more questions and no answers:

> Where's that bee and where's that honey,
> Where's my God and where's my money
> Unreal value's a crass distortion,
> Unwed mothers need abortion

Eugene McDaniels seemed like a totally different performer than Gene McDaniels, and "Compared to What" was the beginning of a transformation that would blossom into a magnificent but totally underrecognized career as a recording artist in the seventies—his 1971 album *Headless Heroes of the Apocalypse* is a relatively little-known masterpiece—but he had significantly more success as a songwriter. When he composed "Compared to What" in 1966, the first person he thought of was Les McCann, the pianist/bandleader from Kentucky, with whom McDaniels performed in the early sixties. McCann recorded "Compared to What" on his 1966 album, *Les McCann Plays the Hits*. Three years later, "Compared to What" resurfaced twice. The first time was as the lead track on *First Take*, the debut album of singer/pianist Roberta Flack. This version features a funky groove that is equal parts soul and jazz. The tempo is laid back, allowing Flack to sing with a calm and cool delivery. *First Take* became a best-seller, mainly on the success of the single "The First Time Ever I Saw Your Face," and it is considered a classic album, with a fiftieth anniversary reissue in 2019.

But "Compared to What" took off as the lead single from another 1969 album derived from an impromptu performance. Eddie Harris and Les McCann were both featured performers at the 1969 Montreux Jazz Festival in Switzerland. McCann heard Harris play earlier in the festival and invited him to play on McCann's performance on the final day. According to the liner notes:

> This album was recorded at the Montreux Jazz Festival in Montreux, Switzerland, in June 1969. Both the Eddie Harris Quartet and the Les McCann Trio performed with great success at the Festival. Later in the week, Eddie and Les felt like playing together. The great American trumpet player, Benny Bailey, who has been living in Europe for several years, was also at Montreux, and he was asked by Eddie and Les to join them in the impromptu jazz concert which can be heard on this album.[51]

Tom Moon, in his book *1,000 Recordings to Hear Before You Die*, makes the observation that "the tone is set from the first notes of the opening track, 'Compared to What,' which became the unlikeliest of hits. A showcase for McCann's gruff vocals, it's a litany of complaints about decaying American society and the Vietnam War."[52] Among the things that make this version an unlikely hit is its 8:18 length (chopped down for radio airplay) as well as the use of the words "goddamn" and "God damn it." Curse words were very unusual on any recordings in the sixties, let alone recording prepared for airplay. But "Compared to What" was very prominent on Black radio stations, usually, but not always, with the expletive "bleeped" out. The groove laid down by the band was infectious and the solos were burnin' hot (of particular note is trumpeter Benny Bailey, who was blowing fire!), but it is the righteous indignation in Les McCann's vocal delivery that really struck a chord with listeners. From the first word, McCann seemed to seethe, and from there, he continued to ramp up the outrage on each successive verse. In a very long career that includes albums recorded in the twenty-first century, this performance in Switzerland is a peak for McCann.

Another thing that makes this album's success unlikely is that, as an unplanned performance, the idea of recording it for an album was not at the top of anyone's mind. There was no rehearsal, and chord changes were, at times, shouted out across the stage. But it works because Harris, McCann, and the rest of the musicians were all great players at the top of their game, with the commitment to making great music while keeping their egos in check. Moon calls *Swiss Movement* "the essence of jazz, the notion that thrilling for-the-ages music can be created by near-strangers, on the fly, with very little advance preparation."[53]

At some point after the release of *Swiss Movement*, Eugene McDaniels received a call at his home. "A guy says to me, 'congratulations . . . you've got the number one jazz tune in the world!' . . . I said, 'What's the title?' He said, 'Compared to What,' and I said, 'THAT'S MINE! YES!!!'"[54] "Compared to What" sold more than one million copies, and the *Swiss Movement* album did in fact top the jazz album charts as well as made it to number twenty-nine on the *Billboard* chart of all albums. "Compared to What" would also become the lead track on the album *Breathless*, the 2015 Blue Note release by trumpet player and Academy Award–nominated composer Terence Blanchard. This new version is as timely, relevant, and fiery now as it was in 1969.

"Compared to What" and the album *Bitches Brew* seemed, in retrospect, to perfectly represent the end of the decade of the sixties in jazz in particular, as well as the post-King music world in general. The sound of these two records, the lyrical sentiment in "Compared to What," the artistic layout of the album jacket for *Bitches Brew*, and even the name *Bitches Brew* and the use of the word "goddamn" could not have been anticipated in 1960, where there was nothing at that time that looked or sounded anything like those two seminal works. *Bitches Brew* and "Compared to What" represent the common thread that weaves throughout the entirety of Black music history; the understanding that music can change hearts, soothe wounds, and demand change in ways that might not be heeded otherwise.

And even though the look, the sound, or the lyrical sentiment of *Bitches Brew* and *Swiss Movement* could not have been anticipated in 1960, there is something that could have been anticipated—the brisk record sales. It is very important to remember one other point as it pertains to "Compared to What"— it is an illustration of the main premise of this book, which is that jazz was a consistent seller in the music world of 1960s Black America. That was proven to be true in 1961 on the Eddie Harris album *Exodus to Jazz*, and as pointed out here, it was proven to be true once again on the 1969 album *Swiss Movement* by Les McCann and Eddie Harris. And the question that was asked in that earlier chapter is worth revisiting. With all those records being sold as well as all of the folks going out to hear live jazz, one has to ask, why does the jazz world refuse to acknowledge all of this success? Who's afraid of Eddie Harris?

CHAPTER TEN

How Did We Forget, Why Did We Forget?

The Revising of the Sixties Jazz Narrative

For every Lee Morgan and Ramsey Lewis and Jimmy Smith and Nancy Wilson and Stan Getz and Eddie Harris who released an album that made a splash on the national charts and garnered airplay on radio across America, there were numerous musicians playing behind them, making those albums burn.

There were the drummers: Billy Higgins, Mickey Roker, Grady Tate, Joe Chambers, Otis "Candy" Finch, Bernard "Pretty" Purdie, Leo Morris/Idris Muhammad, Ben Dixon, Donald Bailey, Redd Holt, Lex Humphries, Freddie Waites, Albert "Tootie" Heath, Roy Brooks, Joe Dukes, Bill English, Ed Shaughnessy, Osie Johnson, Billy Hart, Louis Hayes, and so many others....

Then, of course, we should talk about the bass players: Bob Cranshaw, Sam Jones, Gene Taylor, Larry Ridley, Milt Hinton, George Duvivier, Richard Davis, Leroy Vinnegar, Eldee Young, Bill Lee, almost too many to name....

We can't forget about the pianists: Barry Harris, Cedar Walton, Harold Mabern, Bobby Timmons, Patti Brown, Roger Kellaway, Hank Jones, Willie Pickens, Herbie Lewis, so many fine ones....

And how about the guitarists: Phil Upchurch, Melvin Sparks, Mel Rhyne, Jimmy Ponder, Ivan "Boogaloo Joe" Jones, Gene Edwards, Floyd Smith, and one could list many more....

These are some of the rhythm section players who powered the popular 1960s jazz and laid down grooves so relentless as to make even the most mundane melody sound like greatest thing you ever heard, and in the process, create singles or albums you just had to own. These are the players who stoked the engines that made jazz in the sixties burn. These great players were men and women of their time—they took inspiration form everything that was happening in the music world as well as inspiration from the world around them outside of music.

It's easy to forget that working musicians in every era of jazz had to incorporate changes in their world into their mode of expression. If there is any doubt about that fact, all one has to do is listen to the track "Blue Pepper (Far East of the Blues)" on Duke Ellington's 1967 album *Duke Ellington's Far East Suite*. This track makes it obvious that the Duke, who started out as a bandleader in 1923, was well aware of James Brown's dominance in Black popular music in '67. Another music giant who understood that change in music is inevitable was Miles Davis. One of the reasons that Davis is, arguably, the most important single musician in post-bebop jazz is he lived by that change concept throughout his almost fifty years in music. When speaking of the moment in the late sixties that he began to add electric instrument to his band, Davis said this: "Musicians have to play the instruments that best reflect the times we're in, play the technology that will give you what you want to hear."[1] The marketplace makes that a reality—you have to give the people what they want right along with the personal things that you need to say. Here too, Miles proved that he had his finger on the pulse of the music world of the late sixties: "Nineteen sixty-nine was the year rock and funk were selling like hotcakes.... I had seen the way to the future with my music, and I was going for it like I had always done."[2] The last album that Davis completed before his death in 1991 was the album *Doo Bop*, which featured Miles performing with hip-hop musicians.

The numerous rhythm section musicians listed above (as well as so many others) worked very steadily in the sixties because they understood they had to adapt their art. Some of them became well known in their own right; many of them even led their own bands and recorded their own albums. Some never led their own bands, and some were forgotten. As of the year 2024, most have passed away, but a few of them are still here, and some are still making music! All of them, however, made important, lasting artistic contributions to the music culture outlined in this book.

One might notice some names that are not listed above—the names of those that became godlike on their respective instruments: drummers Tony Williams, Elvin Jones, and Billy Cobham; bassists Ron Carter, Ray Brown, and Dave Holland; guitarists George Benson, Grant Green, and Jim Hall; and pianists/keyboardists Herbie Hancock, Joe Zawinul, Bill Evans, Keith Jarrett, and Chick Corea. Many of those musicians are included elsewhere in this book, and the ones who aren't are so well known and revered as to not needing to be named in the list of those who may have been forgotten. But make no mistake; Benson, Green, Hancock, Corea (who passed away during the writing of this book), and the rest worked just as hard at making jazz in the sixties into a unique and important leap forward for a style that has always been dependent on forward motion.

A theme that runs throughout this book is that much of the music outlined within has, seemingly, been erased from the historical record. This emphasis on historiography has to do with the fact that many people who didn't get to experience this music firsthand will assume, if they read much of the history of jazz as presently written, that nothing of consequence happened in the jazz world of the sixties except for the avant-garde. That statement is not meant to be hyperbole—that is the real, true impression that is given in so many books on jazz. That is the way the story has come to be told. And sadly, because of that, many of the musicians above as well as many of the musicians already chronicled in this book have never been given their due. Their music, in its time, was the heart and soul of jazz for a large segment of America, specifically Black America in the sixties. And it must be stated that this music culture outlined in these pages was much more a part of Black America in the sixties than the music that is etched deeply in the historical record—the music of the avant-garde Black jazz world of the sixties.

It is here that clarity is needed; that avant-garde Black jazz world, the "New Thing," as it came to be known, was a vibrant and beautiful world. There were many wonderful musicians in that world who left some incredible artistic documentation, and they pushed the music forward in ways that were necessary. Their contributions matter, and it goes without saying that the names Ornette Coleman, John Coltrane, Cecil Taylor, Albert Ayler, Sun Ra, and Fred Anderson are important parts of the story of jazz in the sixties as well as the story of Black America in the sixties.

In that regard, it is important to note that one of the founders of one of the most important musical organizations to come out of the avant-garde jazz scene is partially responsible for this book. The Association for the Advancement of Creative Musicians, or AACM, was founded in Chicago in 1965 by Muhal Richard Abrams and Kelan Phil Cohran, and that organization is still going strong today. Some of the most groundbreaking musicians that the world has ever known have been a part of the collective: Pulitzer Prize–winning composer/musician Henry Threadgill, the members of the Art Ensemble of Chicago, Maurice White and Fred White of Earth, Wind & Fire, and so many more. In 1982, Kelan Phil Cohran employed a drummer in his band, the Circle of Sound, who would play with him for two years, and all the while the young drummer was getting his musical soul rewired in the process. That drummer is the author of this book, and so much of what he holds to be important in the world of jazz (and the general world of music) was set in motion by his two years under Maestro Cohran.

But that world is only a part of the story, and the part of the story that is outlined in this book is an even more significant part of the story, not because it is better or worse, but because it is truer of the total experience of Black Americans in the sixties. This music reflects the way that Black folks lived, the way that Black folks thrived; the values in this music are the values held dear to the people who consumed this music. Black people are more than their struggles—that was true in the sixties, and it continues to be true in 2024. That truth is not stated nearly as much as it should be stated.

The question becomes how did we forget? Why did we forget?

One significant factor in this misrepresentation of sixties jazz is who tells the story. And to that end, one of the issues is that some of the folks who write about music in all genres are either not musicians or they are not musicians with experience in the style they write about. Many well-known media critics and many arts columnists come by their jobs because they were given an assignment by a newspaper, television or radio station, website, etc. and were told that they are going to write about "the arts" or going to cover music or "popular culture." Nothing wrong with that per se, but the challenge comes when looking beyond the incorrect narratives that are written that become accepted as truth. Stories get told and retold until they become part of the record, even if they are incorrect. Writings about music of all styles and genres suffer from stories that were told incorrectly early on but continued to be rehashed. With jazz, there has always been so much to know and so much more to hear, and that makes it an impossible style to cover unless you immerse yourself deeply into the subject matter. There have been so many changes in jazz, often in such a short amount of time, and sometimes stories get created to explain the changes in order to fill a void of information, which then become part of the "official" historical record.

There are numerous examples, but one that comes to mind as among the more egregious and incorrectly told stories in jazz is about bebop. Numerous books tell the story that bebop never caught on with the public because the musicians' strike and recording ban of 1942 (described in detail in chapter two) prevented bebop from being recorded early on, and the public didn't get a chance to hear it and form an appreciation of it. Scott Yanow's book *Bebop*, which is, in most ways, an excellent resource, has a section on "Why Bebop Did Not Become Popular." In it, he writes, "Due to the first Musicians Union Strike and World War II, the general population never had an opportunity to be introduced gradually to Bebop. It just seemed to spring out of nowhere.... When Bebop was first heard in 1945, some listeners questioned not only whether it was good or whether it was considered jazz but whether it was music at all!"[3]

The reality is just the opposite; because the recording ban was focused mostly on the major labels (Columbia, Decca, and RCA), independent labels, like Savoy Records in Newark, New Jersey, were established to fill in the gap, and the smaller labels focused on music that the major labels looked past. Musicologist Scott DeVeaux notes, "Bob Theile, who had begun a modest program of recording on the Signature jazz label in 1940, kept the label active during the ban by reissuing old recordings and had resumed recording new small combos by the end of 1943."[4] DeVeaux goes on to say that "Commodore, Blue Note, and Signature were soon joined by others who realized that 'hot Jazz' was an attractive specialization.... Jazz proved to be particularly lucrative for Savoy, and during 1944, the company moved aggressively to establish a presence in the market."[5] Bebop, which actually began being recorded before the 1942 recording ban (Thelonious Monk's "Epistrophy" was first recorded in 1942), actually benefited from the establishment of independent labels during the recording ban. And bebop did, by and large, catch on with many segments of the public. The reason the bebop era didn't last very long mainly had to do with the fragmentation of the recording industry in the wake of the recording ban, which led to the rise of other styles. White pop singers, who, because of American Federation of Musicians' classifications, could continue to record during the ban since singers weren't considered "musicians," became popular with white listeners, and Black audiences saw the rise of bebop as well as rhythm and blues, which was played by former big band musicians like Louis Jordan, who figured out how to make the swinging Kansas City–styled, riff-based big band approach work with a small group. It is also true that all the bebop innovators and originators branched out into many other ways of playing while also continuing to play bebop. All the bebop innovators knew they needed to play many styles to survive (Dizzy Gillespie and his Latin jazz creations and Charlie Parker's pop music explorations with strings are examples of this). Hard bop in the fifties is just an extension and variation of bebop. And if you don't think that the Cannonball Adderley Quintet was playing bebop in the sixties, you should listen again. Jazz has a history with lots of twists and turns, and they mirror the world in which the great players lived.

Returning to the story of jazz in the sixties, another issue, as it pertains to Black America, is that a number of the contemporary historians who have written this history are not African Americans who experienced the sixties personally. But here again, clarity is important—based on the histories that they have written, those historians do, indeed, love jazz, and they don't seem to have a personal agenda that fuels their writing outside of wanting to align the story of jazz in the sixties with the greater narrative of that decade. In particular, the narrative that says the sixties was a time of revolt and seismic social shifts seems to drive most of the stories told in all the histories that revolve around jazz during that time. As has been pointed out many times in this book, there were, indeed, many changes in the sixties, and many of them had monumental effects not only in the Black communities, but in communities and cultures of all kinds. But that isn't the entire story. And those who lived it will tell you that most of the time, Black Americans were living, as Sly and the Family Stone said, like "Everyday People." In his book *What the Music Said*, Africana Studies professor Mark Anthony Neal makes an astute observation: "Without formal articulations of a black mainstream perspective, many of the counternarratives of black public life emerge as primary conduits of black expression."[6] And because of that, many of those counternarratives missed the diversity and vitality of 1960s Black America.

There are times, it seems, when history seems to forget that Black people are more than just their struggles. It is easy to frame the African American community by the challenges faced by the folks living in places deemed "crime-ridden," "poverty-stricken," or "at risk." But in the sixties, just as it is now, Black America was a dynamic place. There were rural Black communities as well as urban; there were Black folks in small communities and in big cities; Black people lived in tenement buildings, brownstone apartments, and single-family homes. And in all these places, Black Americans found comfort in community. All those places deemed "crime-ridden," "poverty-stricken," and "at risk" were places where people built communities around social organizations, church congregations, school districts, political precincts, park district sports leagues, movie houses, bars, restaurants, and places of entertainment. When all that is seen is crime, the impulse by many well-intentioned civic leaders is to remove people from what is perceived as a bad situation, or, worse yet, to not even see the people who are there. And that is what allows people to forget that there is a vital history and community in those places.

An example of this can be seen in the protests that followed the plan to demolish the Robert Taylor Homes in Chicago. The housing community, completed in 1962, was one of the most visible examples of the challenges of what came to be known as "the Projects," the low-income, high-rise structures that could be found on the south and west sides of the city. Regarding visibility, the Robert Taylor Homes were impossible to miss—they ran along the east side of the Dan Ryan Expressway (the major artery into downtown Chicago from the south), from 39th Street to 55th Street. The "homes" looked like both a perfect example of Chicago's skyscraper architectural style, and, at the same time, like models for the prison-industrial complex that would ensnare so many Black men. As the decades progressed, the concept of piling people atop one another in apartment units that were small, ill-maintained, and difficult to properly police because of the way that they were enclosed proved to be a bad plan. In the nineties, the city devised a plan to demolish the Robert Taylor Homes as well as other high-rise projects throughout Chicago. The plan also included building low-rise housing units across the South Side of the city that were more like townhouses than the skyscraper projects, and to disperse the residents of the Robert Taylor Homes to the low-rise units in new neighborhoods throughout the city.

What should have been obvious to the folks at the Chicago Housing Authority (but sadly wasn't) was that the Robert Taylor Homes was just that—home to the people who lived there, and the residents didn't want to leave. In 2007, NPR reporter Cheryl Corley filed a report about critics of the Chicago Housing Authority plan—

> Beauty Turner, an activist and journalist with the magazine *Residence Journal*, stands at the head of a yellow school bus today, leading academics, journalists, and the simply curious to neighborhoods where public housing used to be prolific. Turner says people need to be aware of what's happening, to know that public housing was not always about gangs and drugs and shootings, but also about a sense of community and good stories often ignored. First stop on the tour: 53rd and State. Turner used to live in the public housing developments that were here. Now her voice floats over an empty field.[7]

The story of the Robert Taylor Homes is an illustration of what happens when struggles and trauma are all that is seen in a community. But Beauty Turner, the late activist and journalist, understood that there was beauty in her community, which is why she led the "Ghetto Bus Tour," with "Ghetto" standing for Greatest History Ever Told To Our people. Ms. Turner won numerous awards for her efforts at bringing dignity to the story of people who live in housing projects in Chicago as well as throughout America.

What Turner and the other residents knew was that the overwhelming majority of people who live in projects and other "at-risk" communities are people who want the same thing that people across the urban landscape want: safety, dignity, and the ability to grow and prosper, for themselves and for their neighbors. And she knew that the projects produced many people who would go on to find fame and fortune, like athletes Maurice Cheeks and Kirby Puckett, actor Mr. T, and legendary soul musicians Jerry Butler and Curtis Mayfield.

The story of the Robert Taylor Homes and the late Beauty Turner is also analogous to the conventional story of jazz in the sixties as it has been told. Where historians remember the strife and struggles, the people who were there during those times remember that as well, but more than that, they remember how they overcame the strife and struggles. And they remember that most of the time they weren't focused on their struggles and strife—quite often, they were too busy enjoying life to notice or worry about the struggles. Specific to the story of the Robert Taylor Homes and the beauty to be found there is this—Club DeLisa, which was chronicled in chapter five as it changed and reverted to "The Club," was in the same neighborhood as the Robert Taylor Homes. Record Row, the three-block independent record label district on Cottage Grove Avenue that was headquarters to, among others, Chess and Vee-Jay Records (both of which are chronicled in a few places in this book), was also located in the same neighborhood as the Robert Taylor Homes.

The neighborhood was also home to the Regal Theater, one of the jewels in the crown of African American entertainment palaces in the twentieth century. The Regal was the destination in many Black musicians' wildest dreams of success, and it was the place that many everyday people went to celebrate and enjoy their favorite acts. In his book on *The Chitlin' Circuit*, author Preston Lauterbach writes of promoter Ben Bart's efforts on behalf of 1940s R&B singer Roy Brown: "Bart sold blocks of Brown dates to the chitlin' circuit's most powerful promoters . . . and booked Roy 'Around the World,' as the upper-echelon northern black theaters, Harlem's Apollo, Baltimore's Royal, Washington's Howard, the Paradise in Detroit, and the Regal in Chicago, were collectively known."[8] Timuel Black, the great Chicago historian who chronicled the world that he witnessed in his 102 years, wrote about the Regal Theater and the surrounding neighborhood:

> And I saw Ella Fitzgerald up on Forty-Seventh Street coming out of the Regal. She had just become famous with "A-Tisket, A-Tasket," and I saw Billie Holiday—because I got to know them both as people that I really knew. But they were right here. They were in the neighborhood. . . . So in some places at least, some of that old flavor has been retained, and I don't care who lives where—we *all* used to have those cultural centers. Literary, musical, athletic. You know, if a guy wanted to learn how to be a boxer, there were lots of clubs where he could learn how to

be a boxer. If he wanted to learn how to play tennis, there was a place out there on Fifty-Seventh Street, and there used to be a little place down on Thirty-Fifth Street where women had a tennis club. So you had all that around to draw from.[9]

The vibrant neighborhood that Timuel Black described, which was also the neighborhood where Louis Armstrong, Nat King Cole, and so many other jazz legends lived and which would later be labeled as crime-ridden and not worthy of saving, was quite literally central to many of the stories chronicled in this book as well as much of the music outlined here. When the stories are forgotten, when the people are not seen, their history gets left out of the of the narrative. And as stated in the introduction, when the need or desire to create a narrative that fits within a general social history eliminates an entire era of music from the historical record, it also eliminates the culture and the people who created and lived that culture.

A large part of what is being discussed in this chapter deals with musicology, which is the study of music from multiple viewpoints; from a historical standpoint, from the standpoint of certain periods or eras, as a part of society, as it is practiced in different regions, and as it is performed by specific people, as well as purely aesthetic considerations (is it good, is it beautiful, is it artistic, is it tasteful). In regard to musicology, the historical view is important but only a part of the equation, especially as we look back at an era gone by. Much of the established writing on jazz in the sixties is very selective in regard to who is included and who is left out. In a doctoral studies class that was taken years ago, the author of this book made an observation that he wrote in the margins in the fourth chapter of Alastair Williams's book *Constructing Musicology*: "There is indeed an established rock musicology being practiced, and it is built around the enshrined legends of the Boomer generation (Beatles, Dylan, Springsteen, etc.). Just like traditional musicology, it is defined as much by what it leaves out as it is by what it includes."[10] That statement is as true for jazz musicology as it is for the topic of rock 'n' roll (which was the subject of "Identities," the fourth chapter of *Constructing Musicology*). Even though writers on jazz span many generations, the established jazz musicology is defined as much by who and what is left out as it is by who and what is included. To illustrate this point, consider saxophonists. As mentioned above, the saxophonists that are usually covered when telling the story of sixties jazz are John Coltrane, Ornette Coleman, and Albert Ayler, plus Archie Shepp and Pharoah Sanders (both Sonny Rollins and Wayne Shorter were very active in the sixties, but discussions regarding Rollins are usually reserved for the fifties, whereas Shorter is usually discussed in the seventies).

Consider some of the saxophonists left out of traditional historical discussions of the sixties jazz scene—Eddie Harris, Hank Mobley, Cannonball Adderley,

Stanley Turrentine, Dexter Gordon, Eddie "Lockjaw" Davis, and Johnny Griffin. Why are many of the most popular and listened-to saxophonists left out of the history? Why are the musicians who were on the radio and in the clubs, like Harris, Adderley, and Turrentine, not considered worth covering? And who decided that they were not worth covering? We often talk about John Coltrane as a saxophone influence and rightfully so. Coltrane looms large in regard to the post-1960s jazz scene and saxophone playing that followed in his wake. Numerous jazz saxophonists of the past and present are identified as having been influenced by John Coltrane. But why do we rarely, if ever, read or hear discussions about a Stanley Turrentine school of saxophonists (which would include, among others, Grover Washington Jr.)? What about a Hank Mobley school?

We are beginning to witness contemporary music studies that emanate from the cultures and the people who created it. There is now an attempt to chronicle the history of specific musical styles and eras through a thorough examination of the true lives lived by the people of that era. Work is being done to analyze and chronicle hip-hop and focus beyond the East Coast versus. West Coast trope to now include the numerous different communities that have created it, like the Houston scene, Chicago House music scene, southern rap and hip-hop, and hip-hop in various Latino communities. A new spate of books and documentaries have been released examining the singer-songwriter movement of the late sixties and early seventies, and much of the scholarship surrounding that time is now focused on Laurel Canyon, the community outside Los Angeles where much of that music was made. The stories are being told by the musicians who were there. Another example is punk. Great care has been made to examine the different scenes that were involved during that music's heyday, including NYC, Detroit, LA, Washington, DC, and London. Part of the changes that we are seeing in these histories is that the storytellers lived in the cultures that nurtured these styles. The stories are coming from within. The hope is that this book is just the beginning of a whole new narrative regarding jazz in the sixties.

As stated in the introduction, jazz is an important component in Black cultural identity. Part of that is pride in the visibility that jazz brought to the contributions of Black people to American culture. All the white teenage musicians from Chicago who lined up outside Lincoln Gardens on Chicago's South Side in the twenties that led to the Black bouncer acknowledgement "I see you boys are here for your music lesson tonight"[11] is an example of that. Charley Gerard, in his groundbreaking (and somewhat controversial) book *Jazz In Black and White*, also notes that jazz has been looked upon in the Black community as an opportunity for advancement—noting the difference between jazz and "race records" (blues and other popular types of Black musical expressions in the twenties), Gerard writes, "While race music held blacks to their roots like an ethnic glue, jazz released them into a world of opportunity in which talented, savvy musicians with the right connections could compete with whites."[12] Gerard also makes observations regarding African Americans as an ethnic group. "From the black music perspective, black music is the ethnic expression of the African American people. Adherents to the black perspective dispute the view that jazz, blues, gospel, rap, and other idols are disparate entities. Instead, they see all the music created by African Americans as one unified idiom rather than as a composite of different styles."[13]

Yet another factor is explained by Samuel Floyd Jr. in his seminal work *The Power of Black Music*. Floyd adds the components of signifying (a form of narrative expression critically important to African and African American culture) and cultural memory to the mix:

> In spite of what we might know and understand about the mechanics of improvisation in black music, its full nature is elusive, for its essential musical facilitators are based in cultural memory, where the intuitive resources and instinctive assets of Call [and] Response reside.... The technique, the knowledge of structure and theory, and the external ideas that facilitate and support improvisation, then, must be called on to convey, in coherent and effective presentations, what emerges from cultural memory. It is this dialogical effectiveness that jazz musicians strive for as they create and recreate, state and revise, in the spontaneous manner known as improvisation; it is this signifyin(g) revision that is at the heart of the jazz player's art.[14]

Floyd's larger point, connecting jazz to African-based forms of communication that are essential in understanding Black musical expression, helps to bolster the larger theme of this book. These histories and the stories that are being told are a part of the larger culture, and by centering it on the people who lived in the culture that nurtured these musical styles, there is a more complete understanding.

The hope is that this is just the beginning of a whole new narrative regarding jazz in the sixties that comes from people who lived in the community that supported new and popular forms. It is important to reiterate that the style being labeled "popular jazz" here was not, in its time, some hybrid fusion-type form that differentiated from the mainstream of jazz in the sixties. This WAS the mainstream of jazz in the sixties. Put another way, this was the natural progression of jazz in the 1960s—the natural place where it morphed from what is had been in the previous decades. It was a form of jazz that was a vibrant, living music that reflected the totality of what was happening. This is a chronicle of a community that was not struggling; this is a look at a community that was surviving, striving, and thriving. This was a community that discovered pride in who they were at a time when they needed to see that pride in themselves.

You could see that pride displayed proudly on the faces of the beautiful women on the covers of Freddie Roach's 1965 album *Brown Sugar*, on Miles Davis's 1967 album *Sorcerer* (the woman on this album was celebrated actress Cicely Tyson, who would marry Davis two decades later), and Horace Silver's 1968 album *Serenade to a Soul Sister*. You can hear that pride on display as Cannonball Adderley urged the audience on the live album that he recorded in 1967 to *Walk Tall*, and you hear it in the voice of Eddie Jefferson, as he sings, in 1968—

> I'm so glad I'm up off my knees now,
> and I'm so glad I've made up my mind, I've got to be free.
> Talkin' 'bout no more taking second best, I'm in pursuit of happiness,
> and I just can't settle for nothing less, now see if you can get to that![15]

You could see that pride on the face of Oscar Brown Jr. as he introduces Nancy Wilson on his 1962 television show *Jazz Scene USA*. And you could see that pride in Wilson herself, as well as her fans, when she became the first Black woman to host her own television show, which won an Emmy in 1968. Despite the ongoing struggles, the pride was able to shine through.

The larger point here is this: jazz is and always has been an important mode of Black musical expression, because in jazz you can get recognition of pain and struggles and you also get affirmations of triumph and joy. In an interview with Wynton Marsalis, the great jazz scholar Albert Murray noted that "the spirit of jazz, the spirit of the blues and jazz, is always to counterstate adversity and negative feelings about the outcome of things. . . . To me, jazz is a form [that] includes all of that: it's tragedy, comedy, melodrama, and farce. . . . You have to have a slapstick behavior for slapdash situations, which means: you are ever trying to maintain that dynamic equilibrium. That's the *fate of man*. Jazz is the music that does this."[16]

If nothing else is accomplished by this chronicle of popular jazz in the 1960s, a spotlight has been shined on some truly wonderful music as well as some fantastic artists who, in their time, connected with a large group of people. Some of those people have been widely celebrated, and some have been forgotten. Some, like Herbie Hancock, have benefited from a long career in the spotlight, and some, like trumpeter Booker Little and alto sax star Eric Dolphy, had a very brief time in the spotlight. But all of them helped to define a place and a time; all of them added to the dynamic view of Black life in all its hopes and joys, pains and sorrows, tragedies, and ultimately, triumphs.

What a hip time it was!

APPENDIX A

1960s Popular Jazz Listening Guide

POPULAR JAZZ SONGS OUTLINED IN *IN WITH THE IN CROWD* ... THAT APPEARED ON THE *BILLBOARD* HOT 100 CHARTS			
Artist	"Song"	*Album*	Label/Year
Eddie Harris	"Exodus"	*Exodus to Jazz*	Vee-Jay / 1961
Etta Jones	"Don't Go to Strangers"	*Don't Go to Strangersw*	Prestige / 1960
Ray Charles	"One Mint Julep"	*Genius + Soul = Jazz*	Impulse / 1961
Nancy Wilson	"Saving My Love for You"; "A Sleeping Bee"	*Nancy Wilson/ Cannonball Adderley*	Capitol / 1962
Herbie Hancock	"Watermelon Man"	*Takin' Off*	Blue Note / 1962
Jimmy Smith	"Walk on the Wild Side"	*Bashin': The Unpredictable Jimmy Smith*	Verve / 1962
Mongo Santamaria	"Watermelon Man"	*Watermelon Man!*	Battle / 1963
Lee Morgan	"The Sidewinder"	*The Sidewinder*	Blue Note / 1964
Stan Getz	"The Girl from Ipanema"	*Getz/Gilberto*	Verve / 1964
The Ramsey Lewis Trio	"The 'In' Crowd"	*The "In" Crowd*	Argo / 1965
The Cannonball Adderley Quintet	"Mercy, Mercy, Mercy"	*Mercy, Mercy, Mercy! Live at "The Club"*	Capitol / 1966
Richard "Groove" Holmes	"Misty"	*Misty*	Prestige / 1966
OTHER EXAMPLES OF POPULAR JAZZ IN 1960S BLACK AMERICA			
Artist	*Album* (hit song, if applicable)	Label/Year	
Ahmad Jamal	*At the Pershing: But Not for Me* ("Poinciana")	Argo / 1958 (Listed here because it remained on the *Billboard* chart into 1960)	
Jimmy Smith	*The Sermon!*	Blue Note / 1959	

Appendix A

Artist	Album (hit song, if applicable)	Label/Year
Ray Bryant Combo	*Madison Time* ("The Madison Time")	Columbia / 1960
Cannonball Adderley Quintet	*At the Lighthouse* ("Sack O' Woe")	Riverside / 1960
The Jazztet	*Meet The Jazztet* ("Killer Joe")	Argo / 1960
Oscar Brown Jr.	*Sin & Soul* ("Dat Dere")	Columbia / 1960
Art Blakey and the Jazz Messengers	*The Big Beat* ("Dat Dere")	Blue Note / 1960
Hank Mobley	*Soul Station*	Blue Note / 1960
Bobby Timmons	*This Here Is Bobby Timmons* ("This Here/Dat Dere")	Riverside / 1960
The Jazz Crusaders	*Freedom Sound*	Pacific Jazz / 1961
Dinah Washington	*Unforgettable* ("This Bitter Earth")	Mercury / 1961
Herbie Mann	*At the Village Gate* ("Comin' Home, Baby")	Atlantic / 1961
Oliver Nelson	*The Blues and the Abstract Truth* ("Stolen Moments")	Impulse / 1961
Jimmy Smith	*Home Cookin'*	Blue Note / 1961
Grant Green	*Solid*	Blue Note / 1962
Lorez Alexandria	*Deep Roots*	Argo / 1962
Vince Guaraldi Trio	*Jazz Impressions of Black Orpheus* ("Cast Your Fate to the Wind")	Fantasy / 1962
Lou Rawls	*Stormy Monday*	Capitol / 1962
Stan Getz and Charlie Byrd	*Jazz Samba* ("Desafinado")	Verve / 1962
Gloria Lynne	*At the Las Vegas Thunderbird*	Everest / 1963
Kenny Burrell	*Midnight Blue*	Blue Note / 1963
Brother Jack McDuff	*Live!* ("Rock Candy")	Prestige / 1963
Duke Ellington	*Money Jungle*	United Artists / 1963
Ella Fitzgerald and Count Basie	*Ella & Basie!*	Verve / 1963
Willis Jackson	*The Good Life*	Prestige / 1963
John Coltrane and Johnny Hartman	*John Coltrane and Johnny Hartman*	Impulse / 1993

Artist	Album (hit song, if applicable)	Label/Year
Oscar Peterson Trio w/Clark Terry	Oscar Peterson Trio + One ("Mumbles")	Mercury / 1964
Horace Silver	Song for My Father ("Song for My Father")	Blue Note / 1964
Herbie Hancock	Empyrean Isles ("Cantaloupe Island")	Blue Note / 1964
Stanley Turrentine		Hustlin' Blue Note / 1965
Grant Green	His Majesty King Funk	Verve / 1965
Donald Byrd	Up with Donald Byrd	Verve / 1965
Aretha Franklin	Yeah!!! ("Muddy Water")	Columbia / 1965
John Patton	Oh Baby!	Blue Note / 1965
Wes Montgomery	Tequila ("Bumpin' on Sunset")	Verve / 1966
Chico Hamilton	The Dealer ("For Mods Only")	Impulse / 1966
Eddie Harris	Mean Greens ("Listen Here")	Atlantic / 1966
Frank Sinatra & Count Basie	Sinatra at the Sands	Reprise / 1966
Wayne Shorter	Adam's Apple ("Footprints")	Blue Note / 1966
Dizzy Gillespie	Swing Low, Sweet Cadillac	Impulse / 1967
Miles Davis	Miles Smiles ("Freedom Jazz Dance")	Columbia / 1967
Hugh Masekela	The Promise of a Future ("Grazin' in the Grass")	Uni / 1968
Ramsey Lewis	Maiden Voyage	Cadet / 1968
Roy Ayers	Stoned Soul Picnic	Atlantic / 1968
Les McCann & Eddie Harris	Swiss Movement ("Compared to What")	Atlantic / 1969
Charles Earland	Black Talk! ("More Today Than Yesterday")	Prestige / 1969
Herbie Mann	Memphis Underground ("Memphis Underground")	Atlantic / 1969
Harold Mabern	Rakin' and Scrapin' ("Rakin' and Scrapin'")	Prestige / 1969
Quincy Jones	Walking in Space ("Killer Joe")	A&M / 1969
Freddie Hubbard	Red Clay ("Red Clay")	CTI / 1970
Miles Davis	Bitches Brew	Columbia / 1970

NOTES

INTRODUCTION—WHERE'S NANCY?

1. Dr. Martin Luther King Jr., *The Other America*; speech at Stanford University, April 16, 1967.
2. King, *The Other America*.
3. King, *The Other America*.
4. Charley Gerard, *Jazz in Black and White: Race, Culture, and Identity in the Jazz Community* (Westport, Connecticut: Praeger Publishers, 2001), xiii.
5. Albert Murray et al., *Murray Talks Music* (Minneapolis: University of Minnesota Press, 2016), 235.
6. United States Congressional Act, H.Con.Res.57, (100th), Jazz Preservation Act of 1987. Rep. John Conyers Jr. [D-MI-1], sponsor.
7. Jonathan Gill, *Harlem* (New York: Grove Press, 2011), 211.
8. Gill, *Harlem*, 221.
9. Bruce Crowther and Mike Pinfold, *Singing Jazz: The Singers and Their Styles* (San Francisco: Miller Freeman Books, 1997), 23.
10. Crowther and Pinfold, *Singing Jazz*, 245.
11. Todd Gitlin, *The Sixties: Years of Hope, Days of Rage* (New York: Bantam Books, 1987), xiii.
12. Howard Mandel, *Future Jazz* (New York: Oxford University Press, 1999), 24.
13. Mandel, *Future Jazz*, 24.
14. Frank Tirro, *Jazz: A History* (New York: W. W. Norton & Company, 1993), 371.
15. Ashley Kahn, CD booklet to *Four Women: The Nina Simone Philips Recording* (2003), CD, Verve Records 440 065 021-2.
16. Barbara Gardner, "Nancy Wilson: The Baby Grows Up" *DownBeat*, November 19, 1964 (accessed online http://downbeat.com/archives/detail/the-baby-grows-up).
17. Tim Owens, "Remembering Nancy Wilson: The Best of Jazz Profiles." https://www.npr.org/2018/12/15/676919863/remembering-nancy-wilson-the-best-of-jazz-profiles.
18. "Radio-TV" *Jet Magazine*, July 11, 1963, p.66 (accessed online https://books.google.com/books?id=GMEDAAAAMBAJ&printsec=frontcover&dq=Nancy+Wilson&hl=en&sa=X&ved=2ahUKEwiojPfq_IrwAhVbbcoKHVbPC2w4ChDoATACegQIAxAC#v=onepage&q=Nancy%20Wilson&f=false.

19. Clarence Waldren, "Nancy Wilson Celebrates 50th Year in Music with New CD R.S.V.P.," *Jet*, October 4, 2004, 60.

20. Will Friedwald, *A Biographical Guide to the Great Jazz and Pop Singers* (New York: Pantheon Books, 2010), 539.

21. Ted Fox, *Showtime at the Apollo* (New York: Holt, Rinehart and Winston, 1983), 292.

22. Geoffrey C. Ward and Ken Burns, *Jazz: A History of America's Music* (New York: Alfred A. Knopf, 2000), 456.

23. John Fordham, *Jazz* (New York: Barnes and Noble Books, 1999), 44.

24. Roy Carr, *A Century of Jazz* (London: Hamlin, 2005), 150.

25. Tom Moon, *1,000 Recordings to Hear Before You Die* (New York: Workman Publishing Co., 2008), 30.

26. Alastair Williams, *Constructing Musicology* (Hampshire and Burlington: Ashgate Publishing, 2001), 18.

27. Williams, *Constructing Musicology*, 19.

28. Rob Finnis, notes to *The Jazz Hits from the Hot 100 1958–1966* (2008), CD Ace Records, CDCHC 1188.

29. Sean Wilentz, *360 Sound: The Columbia Records Story* (San Francisco: Chronicle Books, 2012), 193.

30. Cornel West, *Prophetic Reflections* (Monroe [Maine]: Common Courage Press, 1993), 16.

31. Henry Louis Gates Jr., *The Black Church* (New York: Penguin Press, 2021), 8.

32. Gates, *The Black Church*, 71.

33. Samuel A. Floyd Jr., *The Power of Black Music*, (New York and Oxford: Oxford University Press, 1995), 185.

34. Richard M. Sudhalter, "Hot Music in the 1920s: The 'Jazz Age,' Appearances and Realities," in *The Oxford Companion to Jazz*, edited by Bill Kirchner (Oxford and New York: Oxford University Press, 2000), 149.

35. Mark Anthony Neal, *What the Music Said: Black Popular Music and Black Popular Culture* (New York: Routledge, 1999), 31.

36. Scott Deveaux and Gary Giddings, *Jazz (2nd Edition)* (New York: W. W. Norton and Co., 2015), 373.

37. The 1959 Project. https://the1959project.com/about, accessed June 12, 2021.

38. The 1959 Project. https://the1959project.com/about, accessed June 12, 2021.

39. Rachel Martin and Vince Pearson, "More Than 'Kind Of Blue': In 1959, a Few Albums Changed Jazz Forever." https://www.npr.org/2019/04/29/717579612/more-than-kind-of-blue-in-1959-a-few-albums-changed-jazz-forever.

CHAPTER ONE: WHO'S AFRAID OF EDDIE HARRIS?

1. Eddie Harris. https://www.eddieharris.com/biography.

2. Vee-Jay is written both with a hyphen and without. Since Concord Records, the label in charge of reissues, refers to the label as Vee-Jay, it is written with a hyphen throughout this book.

3. Robert Pruter, *Chicago Soul* (Urbana and Chicago: University of Illinois Press, 1992), 26.

4. Nelson George, *The Death of Rhythm and Blues* (New York: Plume, 1988), 84.

5. Pruter, *Chicago Soul*, 26.

6. Michelle Mercer, *Footprints: The Life and Work of Wayne Shorter* (New York: Tarcher/Penguin, 2004), 72.

7. Julie Coryell and Laura Friedman, *Jazz-Rock Fusion* (New York: Dell Publishing Co., 1978), ix.

8. Association for the Advancement of Creative Musicians. https://www.aacmchicago.org/about.

9. Frank Tirro, *Jazz: A History* (2nd edition), (New York: W. W. Norton & Co., 1993), 399.

10. Geoffrey C. Ward and Ken Burns, *Jazz: A History of America's Music* (New York: Alfred A. Knopf, 2000), 436.

11. Stanley Crouch, "On the Corner: The Sellout of Miles Davis," in *Reading Jazz*, ed. Robert Gottlieb (New York: Vintage Books, 1996), 898.

12. Gene Seymour, "Hard Bop," in *The Oxford Companion to Jazz*, ed. Bill Kirchner (Oxford and New York: Oxford University Press, 2000), 384.

13. Richard B. Woodward, "Kind of Blue: Jazz Competes with Its Past, Settles for the Hard Sell," in *Rhythm and Business: The Political Economy of Black Music*, ed. Norman Kelley (New York: Akashic Books, 2005), 165

14. Grover Sales, *Jazz: America's Classical Music* (New York: Da Capo Press, 1992), 5.

15. Richard Crawford, *America's Musical Life: A History* (New York and London: W. W. Norton and Company, 2001), 383.

16. Terry Waldo, *This Is Ragtime* (New York: Da Capo Press, 1976), 19, 20.

17. *Igor Stravinsky: An Autobiography* (New York: W. W. Norton and Company, 1962), 77, 78.

18. Crawford, *America's Musical Life*, 567.

19. *Etude Magazine, The Jazz Problem*, August 1924: accessed online https://www.amherst.edu/media/view/107149/original/Etude%2B-%2BThe%2BJazz%2BProblem.pdf.

20. *Etude Magazine, The Jazz Problem*, August 1924: accessed online https://www.amherst.edu/media/view/107149/original/Etude%2B-%2BThe%2BJazz%2BProblem.pdf.

21. *Etude Magazine, The Jazz Problem*, August 1924: accessed online https://www.amherst.edu/media/view/107149/original/Etude%2B-%2BThe%2BJazz%2BProblem.pdf.

22. *Etude Magazine, The Jazz Problem*, August 1924: accessed online https://www.amherst.edu/media/view/107149/original/Etude%2B-%2BThe%2BJazz%2BProblem.pdf.

23. Crawford, *America's Musical Life*, 460.

24. Edward Jablonski, *Gershwin* (London: Simon and Schuster, 1988), 62.

25. Jablonski, *Gershwin*, 62.

26. Jablonski, *Gershwin*, 62.

27. Crawford, *America's Musical Life*, 574.

28. Mark C. Gridley, *Jazz Styles: History and Analysis* (Englewood Cliffs: Prentice Hall, 1994), 214.

29. John Fordham, *Jazz* (New York: Barnes and Noble Books, 1999), 39.

30. Tom Moon, *1,000 Recordings to Hear Before You Die* (New York: Workman Publishing Company, 2008), 181.

31. Geoffrey C. Ward, notes to *Ken Burns Jazz* (2000), CD box set, Columbia Records, 61432.

32. Ashley Kahn, *A Love Supreme: The Story of John Coltrane's Signature Album* (New York: Viking, 2002), xv.

33. Kahn, *A Love Supreme*, 68.

34. Throughout this book, Amiri Baraka (1934–2014) will be referred to as Jones/Baraka. There is no disrespect meant; this is to reflect that many of his writings are ascribed to

LeRoi Jones, his birth name, and many to Amiri Baraka, his adopted Muslim name. This acknowledges that Jones/Baraka are one and the same.

35. LeRoi Jones (Amiri Baraka), *Black Music* (New York: Akashic Books, 2010), 13.

36. Kwami Coleman, "*Free Jazz* and the "New Thing": Aesthetics, Identity, and Texture, 1960–1966," *The Journal of Musicology*, Vol. 38, Issue 3 (Summer 2021), 269.

37. Ashley Kahn, *The House that Train Built: The Story of Impulse Records* (New York and London: W. W. Norton & Company, 2006), 140.

38. Annunzio Mantovani, an Italian-born British composer and orchestra leader who specialized in light classical/pop music whose albums were best-sellers in the fifties and sixties.

39. LeRoi Jones, *Blues People* (New York, William Morrow & Co., 1963), 235.

CHAPTER 2: SERENADE TO A SOUL SISTER

1. Arthur Taylor, *Notes and Tones: Musician-to-Musician Interviews* (New York: Perigee Books, 1982), 156.

2. Leonard Feather, *The Book of Jazz: From Then till Now* (New York: Horizon Press, 1965), 158–59.

3. Ted Fox, *Showtime at the Apollo*, (New York: Holt. Rinehart and Winston, 1983), 269.

4. Elaine M. Hayes, *Queen of Bebop: The Musical Lives of Sarah Vaughan*, (New York: Ecco, 2017), 42, 43.

5. Hayes, *Queen of Bebop*, 49.

6. Sean Wilentz, *360 Sound: The Columbia Records Story*, (San Francisco: Chronicle Books, 2012), 107, 109.

7. Hayes, *Queen of Bebop*, 86.

8. Charlotte Greig, *100 Best Selling Albums of the 50s*, (New York: Barnes and Noble Books, 2004), 40.

9. Billy Vera, "East Coast Blues: What That Is," essay in *The Mercury Blues 'n' Rhythm Story 1945–1955* (1996), CD Box Set, Mercury Records, 314 528 292-2, 55.

10. Jim O'Neal, "Midwest Blues: It's Just the Blues," essay in *The Mercury Blues 'n' Rhythm Story 1945–1955*, 10.

11. Dempsey J. Travis, *An Autobiography of Black Jazz*, (Chicago: Urban Research Institute, 1983), 192, 194.

12. NPR. https://www.npr.org/templates/story/story.php?storyId=3872390.

13. Tom Moon, *1,000 Recordings to Hear Before You Die* (New York: Workman Publishing Company, 2008), 10.

14. Will Friedwald, *A Bibliographical Guide to the Great Jazz and Pop Singers* (New York: Pantheon Books, 2010), 535.

15. Aretha Franklin, and David Ritz, *Aretha: From These Roots* (New York: Villard Books, 1999), 87–88.

16. Wilentz, *360 Sound*, 182.

17. Leonard Feather, *The Book of Jazz: From Then till Now*, (New York: Horizon Press, 1965), 155–56.

18. CNN online. https://www.cnn.com/2013/10/16/us/obituary-gloria-lynne/index.html, accessed October 18, 2013.

19. Scott Yanow, review of CD recording "Lorez Alexandria on King 1957–1959 (Fresh Sound Records)," *Los Angeles Jazz Scene* (August 2019), accessed online at http://www.scottyanow.com/LAJSCDRevAug.html.

20. Ashley Kahn, *The House That Trane Built: The Story of Impulse Records*, (New York and London: 2006), 97.
21. Bruce Crowther and Mike Pinfold, *Singing Jazz* (San Francisco: Miller Freeman Books, 1997), 150.
22. Carolyn Glenn Brewer, *Changing the Tune: The Kansas City Women's Jazz Festival, 1978–1985* (Denton, Texas: University of North Texas Press, 2017), 39–40.
23. Brewer, *Changing the Tune*, 40.
24. Abbey Lincoln, interview taken from *How It Feels to Be Free* [2021], streaming video, PBS American Masters.
25. Jacey Falk, from *How It Feels to Be Free*.
26. Kenny Berger, "Coleman Hawkins," *The Oxford Companion to Jazz*, ed. Bill Kirchner (Oxford and New York: Oxford University Press, 2000), 189.
27. *How It Feels to Be Free*, 2021.
28. Kwami Coleman, "*Free Jazz* and the 'New Thing': Aesthetics, Identity, and Texture, 1960–1966," *The Journal of Musicology*, Vol. 38, Issue 3, (Summer 2021), 273.
29. *Straight Ahead*, Abbey Lincoln, Earl Baker, and Mal Waldron, songwriters.
30. Tom Moon, *1,000 Recordings to Hear Before You Die* (New York: Workman Publishing Company, 2008), 368.
31. Jon Hendricks is one of the creators of "vocalese," the practice of adding lyrics to existing jazz melodies and improvised jazz solos. Hendricks and Eddie Jefferson are considered the fathers of vocalese, even though Jefferson is acknowledged to be the first singer to actually perform in that style.
32. Dr. Judith Schlessinger, review of CD recording by Nancy Wilson, "Turned to Blue" (Justin Time Records), *All about Jazz* website (August 17, 2006). https://www.allaboutjazz.com/turned-to-blue-nancy-wilson-review-by-dr-judith-schlesinger.
33. Richard Skelly, biography of Marlena Shaw on Blue Note Record's website. https://www.bluenote.com/artist/marlena-shaw/.
34. Friedwald, 389–90.
35. Dianne Reeves on Twitter. https://twitter.com/diannereeves1/status/1073457894782169088?lang=en.

CHAPTER THREE: "THE SIDEWINDER"

Barry Harris, the pianist on the album *The Sidewinder*, passed away in December 2021, just shy of his ninety-second birthday and just after the first draft of the manuscript for this book was completed. The author dedicates this chapter to Dr. Harris.

1. It is important to note that even though the record labels covered Black rhythm and blues using white singers, white teenagers would, in many cases, seek out the original Black artists. Even though Pat Boone outsold him, Little Richard had many white fans as well.
2. Herbie Hancock. https://www.herbiehancock.com/biography-full-page/, accessed March 19, 2021.
3. Herbie Hancock and Lisa Dickey, *Possibilities* (New York: Viking Press, 2014), 19.
4. Hancock and Dickey, *Possibilities*, 47.
5. Hancock and Dickey, *Possibilities*, 50.
6. Julie Malnig, "Introduction," in *Ballroom, Boogie, Shimmy Sham, Shake: A Social and Popular Dance Reader*, ed. Julie Malnig (Urbana and Chicago: University of Illinois Press, 2009), 3.

7. Eileen Southern, *The Music of Black Americans: A History* (New York and London: W. W. Norton and Company, 1983), 23.

8. Samuel A. Floyd Jr., *The Power of Black Music* (New York and Oxford: Oxford University Press, 1995), 57.

9. Nadine George-Graves, "Primitivity and Ragtime Dance," in *Ballroom, Boogie, Shimmy Sham, Shake: A Social and Popular Dance Reader*, ed. Julie Malnig (Urbana and Chicago: University of Illinois Press, 2009), 59.

10. Albert Murray, "'Art Is about Elegant Form': Interview with Wynton Marsalis," in *Murray Talks Music*, ed. Paul Devlin (Minneapolis and London: University of Minnesota Press, 2016), 21.

11. Murray, "'Art Is about Elegant Form' Interview," 21.

12. David H. Rosenthal, *Hard Bop* (New York and Oxford: Oxford University Press, 1992), 5.

13. Michelle Mercer, *Footprints: The Life and Work of Wayne Shorter* (New York: Tarcher/Penguin, 2004), 104.

14. Mercer, *Footprints*, 88.

15. Michael Cuscuna, notes to *Blue Note: A Study of Modern Jazz* (1997), CD, Blue Note Records, 7243 8 59229 2 3.

16. Richard Havers, *Uncompromising Expression* (San Francisco: Chronicle Books, 2014), 262.

17. Gene Seymour, "Hard Bop," in the *Oxford Companion to Jazz*, ed. Bill Kirchner (Oxford and New York: Oxford University Press, 2000), 383.

18. Mark Anthony Neal, *What the Music Said: Black Popular Music and Black Popular Culture* (New York and London: Routledge, 1999), 34.

19. Havers, *Uncompromising Expression*, 208.

20. John Scofield, notes to *Works for Me* (2000) CD, Verve Records, 314-549-281-2.

21. Ben Ratliff, "Billy Higgins, 64, Jazz Drummer with Melodic and Subtle Swing," *New York Times*, May 4, 2001.

22. David H. Rosenthal, *Hard Bop* (New York and Oxford: Oxford University Press, 1992), 8.

23. Gene Seymour, "Hard Bop," in the *Oxford Companion to Jazz*, ed. Bill Kirchner (Oxford and New York: Oxford University Press, 2000), 388.

24. Tom Moon, *1,000 Records to Hear Before You Die* (New York: Workman Publishing Company, 2008), 521.

25. Rosenthal, *Hard Bop*, 9.

26. Rosenthal, *Hard Bop*, 9

27. Neal, *What the Music Said*, 34.

CHAPTER FOUR: 33S AND 45S

1. Ray Charles, recalled by David Ritz, notes to Ray Charles, *Pure Genius: The Complete Atlantic Recordings (1952–1959)* (2005), Box Set, Atlantic Records.

2. Charles, recalled by David Ritz, notes to Ray Charles, *Pure Genius*.

3. The term "labels" is synonymous with record companies.

4. Quincy Jones, *The Complete Quincy Jones: My Journeys and Passions* (San Rafael, CA: Insight Editions, 208), 12.

5. Jones, *The Complete Quincy Jones*, 13.

6. Ashley Kahn, *The House That Trane Built: The Story of Impulse Records* (New York and London: W. W. Norton & Company, 2006), 39, 42.

7. Fredric Dannen, *Hit Men* (New York: Random House, 1990), 111.
8. Richard Havers, *Uncompromising Expression* (San Francisco: Chronicle Books, 2004), 94.
9. Gene Seymour, "Hard Bop," in *The Oxford Companion to Jazz*, ed. Bill Kirchner (Oxford and New York: Oxford University Press, 2000), 384.
10. Michelle Mercer, *Footprints: The Life and Work of Wayne Shorter* (New York: Tarcher/Penguin, 2004), 105.
11. Havers, *Uncompromising Expression*, 84.
12. Havers, *Uncompromising Expression*, 84.
13. A personal note: this album, more than just about any other, exemplifies all that is great regarding jazz in the sixties. It seemed to be played nonstop throughout 1965 by the author's father, and for that I will never be able to thank him enough.
14. Peter Keepnews, "Rudy Van Gelder, 91, Audio Engineer Who Helped Define Jazz Sounds on Records, Dies," *New York Times*, August 25, 2016.
15. Frank Tirro, *Jazz: A History (Second Edition)*, (New York and London: W. W. Norton & Company), 265.
16. Verve Records. website: http://www.ververecords.com/content/about.
17. Chris McGowan and Ricardo Pessanha, *The Brazilian Sound* (New York: Billboard Books, 1991), 53.
18. McGowan and Pessanha, *The Brazilian Sound*, 53.
19. McGowan and Pessanha, *The Brazilian Sound*, 54.
20. Moon, *1,000 Records to Hear Before You Die*, 309.
21. Sean Wilentz, *360 Sound: The Columbia Records Story* (San Francisco: Chronicle Books, 2012), 193.
22. Roy Carr, *A Century of Jazz: A Hundred Years of the Greatest Music Ever Made* (London: Hamlyn Press, 2005), 151.

CHAPTER FIVE: THE "IN" CROWD GOES TO THE CLUB

1. Except for Ellington at Newport, all the other live performances outlined can be viewed on YouTube. The Ellington performance was not filmed; thankfully, the recording gives you all that you need to understand how vital it is as a live performance.
2. Terry Teachout, *Duke: A Life of Duke Ellington* (New York: Gotham Books, 2013), 289.
3. Sean Wilentz, *360 Sound: The Columbia Records Story* (San Francisco: Chronicle Books, 2012), 147.
4. The story of Philadelphia pianist Jimmy Smith going into the woodshed for a year in 1954 in order to master the Hammond organ is recounted in the *Organ Jazz* chapter of this book.
5. Terry Teachout, *Pops: The Wonderful World of Louis Armstrong* (London: JR Books, 2009), 63.
6. Teachout, *Pops*, 64
7. Jonathan Gill, *Harlem* (New York: Grove Press, 2011), 267.
8. Ted Fox, *Showtime at the Apollo* (New York: Holt, Rinehart and Winston, 1983), 87.
9. Fox, *Showtime at the Apollo*, 87.
10. Jim Dawson and Steve Propes, *What Was the First Rock 'n' Roll Record?* (Boston and London: Faber and Faber, 1992), 1, 2.
11. Dawson and Propes, *What Was the First Rock 'n' Roll Record?*, 3.

12. Consider most recordings of jazz in the 1920s—rare is the record that has drums on the recorded track. Before microphone technology was perfected, musicians played into cones strategically placed in a studio, and drums would wipe everything out on the recording. On most old jazz recordings, you hear drummers playing on temple blocks, drum rims, or cymbals and gongs.

13. Dawson and Propes, *What Was the First Rock 'n' Roll Record?*, 4.

14. Dawson and Propes, *What Was the First Rock 'n' Roll Record?*, 4.

15. Geoffrey C. Ward and Ken Burns, *Jazz: A History of America's Music* (New York: Alfred A. Knopf, 2000), 379.

16. Stanley Dance, notes to Erroll Garner, *Concert by the Sea* (1955), CD, Columbia Records, CL 883.

17. Arthur Taylor, *Notes and Tones* (New York: Perigee Books, 1977), 92.

18. Taylor, *Notes and Tones*, 95.

19. Tom Moon, *1,000 Recordings to Hear Before You Die* (New York: Workman Publishing Company, 2008), 301, 302.

20. Erroll Garner. https://www.errollgarner.com/biography, accessed August 4, 2021.

21. Art Blakey, from *A Night at Birdland, Vol. 2*, 1954. Blue Note, 5038.

22. Moon, *1,000 Recordings to Hear Before You Die*, 302.

23. Richard Havers, *Uncompromising Expression* (San Francisco: Chronicle Books, 2014), 87.

24. Charles Mingus, intro to "Folk Form, No. 1," on *Charles Mingus Presents Charles Mingus*, Candid Records, CJS 9005, 1960.

25. Cannonball Adderley, intro to "Azule Serape," on *The Cannonball Adderley Quintet Live at the Lighthouse*, Riverside Records, RLP 244, 1960.

26. Miles Davis and Quincy Troupe, *Miles: The Autobiography* (New York: Simon and Schuster, 1989), 192, 193.

27. Davis and Troupe, *Miles*, 192.

28. Ashley Kahn, *Kind of Blue: The Making of the Miles Davis Masterpiece*, (New York: Da Capo Press, 2000), 116.

29. In 1961, Adderley was tapped to narrate the album *A Child's Introduction to Jazz*. Adderley proves to be every bit the equal of Leonard Bernstein in his "Young People's Concerts," and this now out-of-print album can be used today in a curriculum unit on jazz. It can be found online at https://www.openculture.com/2012/05/a_childs_introduction_to_jazz_by_cannonball_adderley_with_louis_armstrong_thelonious_monk.html.

30. *The Cannonball Adderley Sextet in New York* (1962), LP, Riverside Records, RLP 9404.

31. Dempsey J. Travis, *An Autobiography of Black Jazz* (Chicago: Urban Research Institute, 1983), 134, 135.

32. Travis, *An Autobiography of Black Jazz*, 131.

33. *The Encyclopedia of Chicago*, s.v. "Nightclubs."

34. Purvis Spann and E. Rodney Jones can be heard on B. B. King's classic 1965 album *Live at the Regal*.

35. E. Rodney Jones, notes to the Cannonball Adderley Quintet, *Mercy, Mercy, Mercy! Live at "The Club"* (1967), LP, Capitol Records, T 2663.

36. Paul K. Williams, "The Bohemian Caverns Nightclub AKA Crystal Caverns." http://househistoryman.blogspot.com/2012/05/bohemian-caverns-nightclub-aka-crystal.html (May 7, 2012), accessed August 21, 2021.

37. Williams, "The Bohemian Caverns Nightclub AKA Crystal Caverns."

38. Steve Larson, "Lewis, Ramsey (Emmanuel Jr.)," *The New Grove Dictionary of Jazz*, ed. Barry Kernfeld (New York: St. Martin's Press1996), 697.
39. Mark C. Gridley, *Jazz Styles: History and Analysis* (Englewood Cliffs, New Jersey: Prentice Hall, 1994), 352.
40. Gridley, *Jazz Styles: History and Analysis*, 352.
41. Gridley, *Jazz Styles: History and Analysis*, 301.
42. Eric Snider, "Still Part of the 'In' Crowd: Ramsey Lewis Keeps Grooving with a Saturday Afternoon Tradition," *Jazziz*, June 2021. https://www.jazziz.com/still-part-of-the-in-crowd-ramsey-lewis-keeps-grooving-with-a-saturday-night-tradition-exclusive/.
43. Snider, "Still Part of the 'In' Crowd."
44. Julie Coryell and Laura Friedman, *Jazz-Rock Fusion* (New York: Delta, 1978), ix.
45. Coryell and Friedman, *Jazz-Rock Fusion*, ix.
46. Herbie Hancock and Lisa Dickey, *Possibilities* (New York: Viking, 2014), 127.
47. Ramsey Lewis, to Eric Snider, "Still Part of the 'In' Crowd."
48. Ramsey Lewis, interviewed by Arun Rath on NPR, May 16, 2015. https://www.npr.org/transcripts/407077725.
49. Lewis, interviewed by Arun Rath.
50. Matt Micucci, "A Short History of . . . the 'In' Crowd," *Jazziz*, July 25, 2017. https://www.jazziz.com/short-history-crowd-billy-page-1964/.
51. Julie Coryell and Laura Friedman, *Jazz-Rock Fusion* (New York: Dell Publishing, 1978), x.
52. Coryell and Friedman, *Jazz-Rock Fusion*, ix.
53. Al Clarke, notes to the Ramsey Lewis Trio, *The "In" Crowd* (1965), LP, Argo Records LP-757.
54. The author of this book was fortunate to see Ramsey Lewis perform a couple of times in the late seventies and eighties. Lewis was classy, elegant, and entertaining, and a tremendous piano player!
55. *The Cannonball Adderley Sextet in New York* (1962), LP, Riverside Records, RLP 9404.

CHAPTER SIX: "WHEN YOU GO, LET 'EM KNOW THAT DADDY-O TOLD YOU SO"

This chapter is dedicated to Merri Dee (1936–2022), a Chicago radio and television legend and the ultimate survivor!

1. Herb Kent, on the website *The History Makers*. https://da.thehistorymakers.org/story/17529;q=Herb%20Kent%20Daddy-O%20Daylie.
2. Daddy-O Daylie, to Dempsey Travis in *An Autobiography of Black Jazz* (Chicago: Urban Research Institute, 1983), 264.
3. Daddy-O Daylie, to Dempsey Travis in *An Autobiography of Black Jazz*, 265.
4. Aaron Joseph Johnson, *Jazz and Radio in the United States: Mediation, Genre, and Patronage* (PhD dissertation, Columbia University, 2014), 224.
5. Johnson, *Jazz and Radio in the United States*, 114.
6. Nelson George, *The Death of Rhythm and Blues* (New York: Plume, 1988), 12.
7. George, *The Death of Rhythm and Blues*, 40.
8. B. B. King, from *B. B. King: The Life of Riley* (MVD Visual), 2012.
9. Christiane Bird, *The Da Capo Jazz and Blues Lover's Guide to the U.S., 3rd Edition* (New York: Da Capo Press, 2001), 54.

10. *Golden Age of Black Radio*, website: Indiana University archives: https://artsandculture.google.com/exhibit/golden-age-of-black-radio-part-2-deejays-archives-of-african-american-music-and-culture/tQKCWDGh2AvJJw?hl=en.

11. Peter Guralnick, *Last Train to Memphis: The Rise of Elvis Presley* (Boston, New York, Toronto, and London: Little, Brown and Company, 1994), 38–39.

12. Guralnick, 369.

13. Dr. William T. McDaniel, personal interview (July 26, 2022).

14. McDaniel, personal interview (July 26, 2022).

15. Elaine M. Hayes, *Queen of Bebop: The Musical Lives of Sarah Vaughan* (New York: Ecco, 2017), 86.

16. Travis, *An Autobiography of Black Jazz*, 480.

17. Rob Finnis, notes to *The Jazz Hits from the Hot 100 1958–1966* (2008), CD, Ace Records, CDCHD 1188.

18. Ashley Kahn, *The House That Trane Built: The Story of Impulse Records* (New York and London: W. W. Norton & Company, 2006), 36.

19. Kahn, *The House That Trane Built*, 36.

20. Roy Carr, *A Century of Jazz* (London: Hamlin, 1997), 165.

21. Aaron Joseph Johnson, *Jazz and Radio in the United States: Mediation, Genre, and Patronage* (PhD dissertation, Columbia University, 2014), 227.

22. Nelson George, *The Death of Rhythm and Blues* (New York: Plume, 1998), 111–12.

CHAPTER SEVEN: PULLING OUT ALL THE STOPS

For Dr. Lonnie Smith (1942–2021), and Joey DeFrancesco (1971–2022).

1. Dempsey J. Travis, *An Autobiography of Black Jazz* (Chicago: Urban Research Institute, 1983), 176.

2. Mark Anthony Neal, *What the Music Said* (New York and London: Routledge, 1999), 30.

3. History of the Hammond organ, accessed online. https://www.youtube.com/watch?v=iBjp2ZDA8A0.

4. Leonard Feather, *The Book of Jazz: From Then till Now* (New York: Horizon Press, 1957, revised 1965), 141.

5. Tom Moon, *1,000 Recordings to Hear Before You Die* (New York: Workman Publishing Company, 2008), 717.

6. David H. Rosenthal, *Hard Bop* (Oxford and New York: Oxford University Press, 1992), 112.

7. Richard Havers, *Uncompromising Expression* (San Francisco: Chronicle Books, 2014), 94.

8. Author unknown, notes to *Blue Note: A Story of Modern Jazz* (1997), CD, Blue Note Records, CDP 7243 8 59229 2 3.

9. Ira Gitler, notes to Jimmy Smith, *Home Cookin'* (1961), LP, Blue Note Records, 4050.

10. Roy Carr, *A Century of Jazz* (London: Hamlin Publishing, 2005), 155.

11. Bob Porter, "The Blues in Jazz," in *The Oxford Companion to Jazz*, ed. Bill Kirchner (Oxford and New York: Oxford University Press, 2000), 76.

12. Michael Ullman, notes to *Jimmy Smith's Finest Hour* (2000), CD, Verve Records, 314 543 598-2.

13. Carr, *A Century of Jazz*, 154.

14. Stanley Dance, "George Benson: Guitar in the Ascendancy," in *DownBeat: The Great Jazz Interviews*, ed. Frank Alkyer and Ed Enright (New York: Hal Leonard Books, 2009), 122.

15. David H. Rosenthal, *Hard Bop: Jazz and Black Music 1955–1965* (New York, Oxford University Press, 1992), 114–15.

16. Carr, *A Century of Jazz*, 156.

17. Bob Perkins, "They Made Philly the Jazz Organ Capital." https://www.wrti.org/post/they-made-philly-jazz-organ-capital (2015), accessed February 14, 2020.

18. NPR, *Home Cooking: The Jazz Organ Tradition in Philadelphia* (Jazz Night in America, 2018). https://www.npr.org/2018/01/02/396691354/home-cooking-the-philadelphia-jazz-organ-tradition-in-concert.

19. Havers, 170.

20. Havers, 169.

21. Tom Moon, *1,000 Records to Hear Before You Die* (New York: Workman Publishing Company, 2008), 883.

22. Ira Gitler, notes to Stanley Turrentine, *Hustlin'* (1965), LP, Blue Note Records, BLP 4162.

23. Pete Fallico. http://www.dvrbs.com/people/camdenshowbiz-RichardGrooveHolmes.htm.

24. Rob Finnis, notes to *The Jazz Hits from the Hot 100 1958–1966* (2008), CD, Ace Records, CDCHD 1188.

25. Finnis, notes to *The Jazz Hits from the Hot 100 1958–1966*.

26. Marr went on to become an associate professor of music at Ohio State University, and there are scholarships given out in his name to young musicians pursuing music as a profession. One of those scholarships was awarded to the author's son, who is now a professional jazz musician.

27. Ultimate Classic Rock Online: https://ultimateclassicrock.com/keith-emerson-appreciation/.

28. Jon Lord, interviewed by Joe Lalaina for *Modern Keyboard*, January 1989. https://www.thehighwaystar.com/interviews/lord/jl19890100.html.

29. Julie Coryell and Laura Friedman, *Jazz-Rock Fusion* (New York: Delta, 1978), 144.

30. Christopher Washburne, "Miscellaneous Instruments in Jazz," in *The Oxford Companion to Jazz*, ed. Bill Kirchner (Oxford and New York: Oxford University Press, 2000), 657.

31. The author of this book was thrilled to meet Jack McDuff at one of his performances in Chicago in 1984. When the organ great and his longtime drummer Joe Dukes honored the request to play "Soulful Drums," the author had to fake an allergy attack to hide his tears of joy!

32. NBC News Online. https://www.nbcnews.com/id/wbna6941860.

33. *New York Times*. https://www.nytimes.com/2022/08/26/arts/music/joey-defrancesco-dead.html.

34. Mark C. Gridley, *Jazz Styles* (Englewood Cliffs: Prentice Hall, 1994), 214.

35. David H. Rosenthal, *Hard Bop* (New York and Oxford: Oxford University Press, 1992), 115.

36. Mark Anthony Neal, *What the Music Said* (New York and London: Routledge), 31, 33.

CHAPTER EIGHT: MEAN GREENS, FRIED NECKBONES, AND HOME COOKIN' AT THE GREASY SPOON

1. This chapter uses lots of album and song titles. This is a good place to make note that in this chapter, as well as throughout this book, album titles are *italicized*, whereas song titles are surrounded by "quotation marks."

2. Ira Gitler, notes to Jimmy Smith, *Home Cookin'* (1961), LP, Blue Note Records, BN 4050.

3. Gitler, notes to Jimmy Smith, *Home Cookin'*.

4. Mark Kurlansky, *Ready for a Brand New Beat* (New York: Riverside Books, 2013), 199–200.

5. Albert Murray, "A real conservative? I'm not one. I'm an avant-garde person," in *Murray Talks Music: Albert Murray on Jazz and Blues*, ed. Paul Devlin (Minneapolis and London: University of Minnesota Press, 2016), 110–11.

6. Hank Marr called the place "The Greasy Spoon"; Les McCann preferred calling it *Bucket o' Grease*; Willie Bobo named it *Spanish Grease*, but after watching Benson and Burrell, Willis Jackson began calling the joint *Grease 'n' Gravy*!

7. Emily J. Lordi, *The Meaning of Soul: Black Music and Resilience Since the 1960s* (Durham and London: Duke University Press, 2020), 19, 20.

8. Duke Ellington and Billy Strayhorn, "King Fit the Battle of Alabam," from *My People*.

9. Cannonball Adderley, introduction to "This Here," on *The Cannonball Adderley Quartet in San Francisco* (1959), Riverside Records, RLP 12-311.

10. From the notes to *Miles Davis and Gil Evans: The Complete Studio Recordings* (CD Box Set), Columbia Legacy, 2-67397, 1996.

11. Richard Havers, *Uncompromising Expression* (San Francisco: Chronicle Books, 2014), 188.

12. Herbie Hancock and Lisa Dickey, *Possibilities* (New York: Viking, 2014), 42.

13. Geoffrey C. Ward and Ken Burns, *Jazz: A History of American Music* (New York: Alfred A Knopf, 2000), 456.

14. Richard "Groove" Holmes. http://www.dvrbs.com/people/camdenshowbiz-Richard GrooveHolmes.htm, accessed June 29, 2021.

CHAPTER NINE: "WHY AM I TREATED SO BAD?"..."COMPARED TO WHAT?"

1. Booklet accompanying the compilation "Really the Blues? A Blues History 1893–1959": West Hill Record Archives, WHRA-6028, 2010.

2. Booklet accompanying the compilation "Really The Blues?"

3. Peter C. Muir, *Long Lost Blues* (Urbana and Chicago: University of Illinois Press, 2010), 80.

4. Muir, *Long Lost Blues*, 80.

5. Terry Teachout, *Duke: A Life of Duke Ellington* (New York: Gotham Books, 2013), 328.

6. Albert Murray, "Murray's Final Nonfiction Statement," in *Murray Talks Music*, ed. Paul Devlin (Minneapolis and London: University of Minnesota Press, 2016), 220.

7. Most accounts say that Armstrong called Governor Faubus an "ignorant plowboy," but that was a quote that was cleaned-up because it was 1957. The real quote was provided by Larry Lubenow, the reporter who broke the story at the time, to Scott Simon, NPR host, for the fiftieth anniversary of the event. https://www.npr.org/templates/story/story.php?storyId=14620516.

8. Tom Moon, *1,000 Recordings to Hear Before You Die* (New York: Workman Publishing Company, 2008), 648.

9. Ashley Kahn, CD booklet to *Nina Simone: The Nina Simone Songbook* (2003), CD, Verve Records, 440 065 021-2.

10. J. C. Thomas, *Chasin' the Trane* (New York: Da Capo Press, 1975), 168.

11. Ashawnta Jackson, "Why MLK Believed Jazz Was the Perfect Soundtrack for Civil Rights," from *JSTOR Daily*, October 16, 2019. Accessed online June 11, 2021. https://daily.jstor.org/why-mlk-believed-jazz-was-the-perfect-soundtrack-for-civil-rights/.

12. From the album *Nina Simone in Concert*, recorded in 1964, Philips, PHS 600-135.

13. From the album *Nina Simone in Concert*.

14. New York Beat," *Jet Magazine*, April 9, 1964, p. 63. Accessed online at https://books.google.com/books?id=WMEDAAAAMBAJ&printsec=frontcover&hl=En&source=gbs_ge_summary_r&cad=0#v=onepage&q&f=false.

15. Greg Kot, *I'll Take You There: Mavis Staples, the Staple Singers, and the Music That Shaped the Civil Rights Era* (New York: Scribner, 2014), 108.

16. Martha Bayles, *Hole in Our Soul* (New York: The Free Press, 1994), 228.

17. Kot, *I'll Take You There*, 108.

18. Kot, *I'll Take You There*, 77.

19. Cannonball Adderley, from the song "Walk Tall (Baby, That's What I Need)," composed by Jim Rein and Joe Zawinul, from the album *74 Miles Away* (1967), Capitol Records, ST/T 2822.

20. Isaac Hayes and David Porter, *Soul Man*: Stax Records, 1967.

21. From the Stax Museum website. https://staxmuseum.com/content/uploads/2014/10/Sounds_of_Change_Lesson_1.pdf.

22. Ashley Kahn, *The House That Trane Built: The Story of Impulse Records* (New York and London: W. W. Norton & Company, 2006), 197.

23. Charley Gerard, *Jazz in Black and White* (Westport [Conn.]: Praeger, 1998), 81.

24. Miles Davis and Quincy Troupe, *Miles: The Autobiography* (New York: Simon and Shuster, 1989), 289.

25. Arthur Taylor, *Notes and Tones* (New York: Perigee Books, 1982), 143.

26. Kot, *I'll Take You There*, 102.

27. Kot, *I'll Take You There*, 124.

28. Davis and Troupe, 289.

29. Mark Kurlansky, *Ready For A Brand New Beat* (New York: Riverhead Books, 2013), 229–30.

30. Peter Guralnick, *Sweet Soul Music* (New York: Harper & Row, 1986), 355

31. Guralnick, *Sweet Soul Music*, 355.

32. Eileen Southern, *The Music of Black Americans (Second Edition)* (New York and London: W. W. Norton & Co., 1983), 547.

33. Southern, *The Music of Black Americans*, 547.

34. Herbie Hancock and Lisa Dickey, *Possibilities* (New York: Viking, 2014), 113–14.

35. Oliver Nelson, notes to his album *Black, Brown and Beautiful* (1969), LP, Flying Dutchman Records, FDS 10116.

36. Nelson, notes to his album *Black, Brown and Beautiful*.

37. Nelson, notes to his album *Black, Brown and Beautiful*.

38. From the *National Civil Rights Museum* website. https://www.civilrightsmuseum.org/from-the-vault/posts/ben-branch.

39. Nina Simone's spoken intro to *Why (The King of Love is Dead)*.

40. Sam Waymon, interview by Lynn Neary on *Weekend Edition Sunday*, NPR, April 6, 2008. https://www.npr.org/2008/04/06/89418339/why-remembering-nina-simones-tribute-to-the-rev-martin-luther-king-jr.

41. Carlos Santana, notes to Miles Davis, *The Complete Bitches Brew Sessions* (1998), CD Box Set, Columbia Legacy, 65570.

42. Miles Davis and Quincy Troupe, *Miles: The Autobiography* (New York: Simon and Schuster, 1989), 292.

43. Davis and Troupe, *Miles*, 293.

44. Davis and Troupe, *Miles*, 310.

45. Quincy Troupe, notes to Miles Davis, *The Complete Bitches Brew Sessions* (1998), CD Box Set, Columbia Legacy, 65570.

46. Gerald Early, notes to *Black Power: Music of a Revolution* (2004), CD, Shout Factory, D2K 37398.

47. Julie Coryell and Laura Friedman, *Jazz-Rock Fusion* (New York: Dell Publishing, 1978), xiii.

48. Troupe, notes to Davis, *The Complete Bitches Brew Sessions*.

49. Eugene McDaniels, interviewed on YouTube. https://www.youtube.com/watch?v=GC6LdIcmDQs.

50. McDaniels, interviewed on YouTube. https://www.youtube.com/watch?v=GC6LdIcmDQs.

51. Author unknown, notes to Les McCann and Eddie Harris, *Swiss Movement* (1969), LP, Atlantic Records, SD 1537.

52. Tom Moon, *1,000 Recordings to Hear Before You Die* (New York: Workman Publishing, 2008), 487.

53. Moon, *1,000 Recordings to Hear Before You Die*, 487.

54. Eugene McDaniels, interviewed on YouTube. https://www.youtube.com/watch?v=GC6LdIcmDQs.

CHAPTER TEN: HOW DID WE FORGET, WHY DID WE FORGET?

1. Miles Davis and Quincy Troupe, *Miles: The Autobiography* (New York: Simon and Schuster, 1989), 295.

2. Davis and Troupe, *Miles: The Autobiography*, 297–98.

3. Scott Yanow, *Bebop* (San Francisco: Miller Freeman Books, 2000), 43.

4. Scott DeVeaux, "Bebop and the Recording Industry: The 1942 AFM Recording Ban Reconsidered," *Journal of the American Musicological Society*, vol. 41, no. 1, 1988, 151.

5. DeVeaux, "Bebop and the Recording Industry," 152.

6. Mark Anthony Neal, *What the Music Said: Black Popular Music and Black Public Culture* (New York and London: Routledge, 1999), 17.

7. Cheryl Corley, *Critics Hit Chicago Public Housing Efforts*. https://www.npr.org/templates/story/story.php?storyId=12295323.

8. Preston Lauterbach, *The Chitlin' Circuit and the Road to Rock 'n' Roll* (New York and London: W. W. Norton and Company, 2011), 159.

9. Timuel D. Black Jr., *Bridges of Memory* (Evanston: Northwestern University Press, 2003), 161.

10. Mike Smith, written in 2007.

11. Terry Teachout, *Pops: The Wonderful World of Louis Armstrong* (London: JR Books, 2009), 64.

12. Charlet Gerard, *Jazz in Black and White* (Westport, Connecticut: Praeger Publishers, 2001), 2.

13. Gerard, 3.

14. Samuel A. Floyd Jr., *The Power of Black Music* (Oxford and New York: Oxford University Press, 1995), 140–41.

15. Eddie Jefferson, "See If You Can Git to That, from *Body and Soul* (1968), Prestige Records, PR 7619.

16. Albert Murray, "'Art is about elegant form': An interview with Wynton Marsalis," in *Murray Talks Music*, ed. Paul Devlin (Minneapolis and London: University of Minnesota Press, 2016), 20, 21.

BIBLIOGRAPHY

Abdul-Jabbar, Kareem, and Raymond Obstfeld. *On the Shoulders of Giants*. New York: Simon and Schuster, 2007.
Alkyer, Frank, and Ed Enright. *DownBeat: The Great Jazz Interviews*. New York: Hal Leonard Books, 2009.
Bayles, Martha. *Hole in Our Soul*. New York: The Free Press, 1994.
Berger, Kenny. "Coleman Hawkins." In *The Oxford Companion to Jazz*, 177–90. Edited by Bill Kirchner. Oxford and New York: Oxford University Press 2000.
Bergerot, Franck, and Arnaud Merlin. *The Story of Jazz: Bebop and Beyond*. New York: Harry N. Abrams, 1993.
Bird, Christine. *The Da Capo Jazz and Blues Lover's Guide to the U.S. (3rd Edition)*. Cambridge: Da Capo Press, 2001.
Black, Timuel D., Jr. *Bridges of Memory*. Evanston: Northwestern University Press, 2003.
Branch, Taylor. *Parting the Waters*. New York: Simon and Schuster, 1988.
Brewer, Carolyn Glenn. *Changing the Tune: The Kansas City Women's Jazz Festival, 1978–1985*. Denton, TX: University of North Texas Press, 2017.
Carr, Roy. *A Century of Jazz*. London: Hamlyn, 1997.
Clarke, Al. Notes to the Ramsey Lewis Trio, *The "In" Crowd*. LP, Argo Records LP-757.
Coleman, Kwami. "Free Jazz and the 'New Thing': Aesthetics, Identity and Texture, 1960–1966." *The Journal of Musicology*, Vol. 38, Issue 3 (Summer 2021), 269.
Collier, James Lincoln. *Ellington*. New York and Oxford: Oxford University Press, 1987.
Corley, Cheryl. "Critics Hit Chicago Public Housing Efforts." *NPR*.
Coryell, Julie, and Laura Friedman, *Jazz-Rock Fusion*. New York: Delta, 1978.
Crawford, Richard. *America's Musical Life: A History*. New York and London: W. W. Norton & Company, 2001.
Crouch, Stanley. "On the Corner: The Sellout of Miles Davis." *Reading Jazz*, 898–914. Edited by Robert Gottlieb. New York: Vintage Books, 1996.
Crowther, Bruce, and Mike Pinfold. *Singing Jazz*. San Francisco: Miller Freeman Books, 1997.
Cuscuna, Michael. Notes to *Blue Note: A Study of Modern Jazz*. CD, Blue Note Record, 1997.
Dance, Stanley. "George Benson: Guitar in the Ascendancy," In *DownBeat: The Great Interviews*. Edited by Frank Alkyer and Ed Enright. New York: Hal Leonard Books, 2009.
Dance, Stanley. Notes to Erroll Garner, *Concert by the Sea*. CD, Columbia Records, CL 883, 1955.
Dannen, Fredric. *Hit Men*. New York: Times Books, 1990.

Davis, Miles, and Quincy Troupe. *Miles: The Autobiography*. New York: Simon and Schuster, 1989.
Dawson, Jim, and Steve Propes. *45 RPM: The History, Heroes, and Villains of a Pop Music Revolution*. San Francisco: Backbeat Books, 2003.
Dawson, Jim, and Steve Propes. *What Was the First Rock 'n' Roll Record?* Boston and London: Faber and Faber, 1992.
Deveaux, Scott, and Gary Giddings. *Jazz (2nd Edition)*. New York and London: W. W. Norton & Company, 2015.
Deveaux, Scott. "Bebop and the Recording Industry: The 1942 AFM Recording Ban Reconsidered," *Journal of the American Musicological Society*. Vol. 41, no. 1, 1988.
Devlin, Paul. *Murray Talks Music*. Minneapolis and London: University of Minnesota Press, 2016.
Du Bois, W. E. B. *The Souls of Black Folks*. New York: Dover Publications, 1994.
Early, Gerald. Notes to *Black Power: Music of a Revolution*. CD, Shout Factory, D2K 37398, 2004.
Erlich, Lillian. *What Jazz Is All About*. New York: Julian Messner, 1962.
Farr, Joey. *Moguls and Madmen*. New York: Simon and Schuster, 1994.
Feather, Leonard. *The Book of Jazz: From Then till Now*. New York: Horizon Press, 1965.
Finnis, Rob. Notes to *The Jazz Hits from the Hot 100 1958–1966*. CD, Ace Records CDCHD 1188, 2008.
Floyd, Samuel. *The Power of Black Music*. Oxford and New York: Oxford University Press, 1995.
Ford, Phil. *Dig*. Oxford and New York: Oxford University Press, 2013.
Fordham, John. *Jazz*. New York: Barnes and Noble Books, 1993.
Fox, Ted. *Showtime at the Apollo*. New York: Holt, Rinehart and Winston, 1983.
Franklin, Aretha, and Davis Ritz. *Aretha: From These Roots*. New York: Villard Books, 1999.
Friedwald, Will. *A Biographical Guide to the Great Jazz and Pop Singers*. New York: Pantheon Books, 2010.
Friedwald, Will. *The Great Jazz and Pop Vocal Albums*. New York: Pantheon Books, 2017.
Gardner, Barbara. "Nancy Wilson: The Baby Grows Up." *DownBeat*, November 19, 1964.
Gates, Henry Louis, Jr. *The Black Church*. New York: Penguin Press, 2021.
George, Nelson. *The Death of Rhythm & Blues*. New York: Plume, 1998.
Georges-Graves, Nadine. "Primitivity and Ragtime Dance," in *Ballroom, Boogie, Shimmy Sham, Shake: A Social and Popular Dance Reader*, 55–71. Edited by Julie Malnig. Urbana and Chicago: University of Illinois Press, 2003.
Gerard, Charlie. *Jazz in Black and White*. Westport, Connecticut, and London: Praeger, 2001.
Gill, Jonathan. *Harlem*. New York: Grove Press, 2011.
Gioia, Ted. *The Birth and Death of the Cool*. Golden (CO): Speck Press, 2009.
Gitler, Ira. Notes to *Home Cookin'*. LP, Blue Note Records, BN 4050, 1961.
Gitler, Ira. Notes to Stanley Turrentine, *Hustlin'*. LP, Blue Note Records, BLP 4162.
Gitler, Ira. *Swing to Bop*. New York and Oxford: Oxford University Press, 1985.
Gitlin, Todd. *The Sixties: Years of Hope, Days of Rage*. New York: Bantam, 1993.
Gottlieb, Robert. *Reading Jazz*. New York: Vintage Books, 1996.
Greenfield, Robert. *The Last Sultan*. New York: Simon and Schuster, 2011.
Greig, Charlotte. *100 Best Selling Albums of the 50s*. New York: Barnes and Noble Books, 2004.
Gridley, Mark C. *Jazz Styles: History and Analysis*. Englewood Cliffs: Prentice-Hall, 1994.
Guralnick, Peter. *Last Train to Memphis: The Rise of Elvis Presley*. Boston, New York, Toronto, and London: Little, Brown and Company, 1994.
Guralnick, Peter. *Sweet Soul Music*. New York: Harper and Row, 1986.

Hancock, Herbie, and Lisa Dickey. *Possibilities*. New York: Viking Press, 2014.
Havers, Richard. *Uncompromising Expression*. San Francisco: Chronicle Books, 2014.
Hayes, Elaine M. *Queen of Bebop: The Musical Lives of Sarah Vaughan*. New York: Harper Collins Publishers, 2017.
Heile, Björn, Peter Elsdon, and Jenny Doctor. *Watching Jazz*. New York and Oxford: Oxford University Press, 2016.
Hentoff, Nat, and Albert J. McCarthy. *Jazz*. New York: Da Capo Press, 1978.
How It Feels to Be Free: PBS American Masters, 2021.
Jablonski, Edward. *Gershwin*. London: Simon and Schuster, 1988.
Jackson, Ashawnta. "Why MLK Believed Jazz Was the Perfect Soundtrack for Civil Rights." *JSTOR Daily*, October 16, 2019.
Johnson, Aaron Joseph. *Jazz and Radio in the United States: Mediation, Genre, and Patronage*. PhD dissertation, Columbia University, 2014.
Jones, E. Rodney. Notes to the Cannonball Adderley Quintet, *Mercy, Mercy, Mercy! Live at "The Club."* Capitol Records, T 2663, 1967.
Jones, LeRoi (Amiri Baraka). *Black Music*. New York: AkashiClassics, 2010.
Jones, LeRoi. *Blues People*. New York: Morrow Quill Paperbacks, 1963.
Jones, Quincy. *The Complete Quincy Jones: My Journey & Passions*. San Rafael: Insight Editions, 2008.
Katz, Mark. *Capturing Sound*. Berkeley and Los Angeles: University of California Press, 2004.
Kahn, Ashley. *A Love Supreme: The Story of John Coltrane's Signature Album*. New York: Viking, 2002.
Kahn, Ashley. *Kind of Blue: The Making of the Miles Davis Masterpiece*. New York: Da Capo Press, 2000.
Kahn, Ashley. *The House That Trane Built: The Story of Impulse Records*. New York and London: W. W. Norton & Company, 2006.
Kahn, Ashley. Notes to Nina Simone, *Four Women: The Nina Simone Philips Recordings*. CD, Verve Records, 440 065 032-2.
Keepnews, Peter. "Rudy Van Gelder, 91, Audio Engineer Who Helped Define Jazz Sounds on Records, Dies." *The New York Times*, August 25, 2016.
Kelley, Norman. *Rhythm and Business*. New York: Akashi Books, 2005.
Kerman, Joseph. *Contemplating Music*. Cambridge: Harvard University Press, 1985.
Kernfeld, Barry. *The New Grove Dictionary of Jazz*. New York: St. Martin's Press, 1996.
Kernfeld, Barry. *What to Listen for in Jazz*. New Haven and London: Yale University Press, 1995.
Kirchner, Bill. *The Oxford Companion to Jazz*. Oxford and New York: Oxford University Press, 2000.
Knopper, Steve. *Appetite for Self-Destruction: The Spectacular Crash of the Record Industry in the Digital Age*. New York: Soft Skull Press, 2010.
Kofsky, Frank. *John Coltrane and the Jazz Revolution of the 1960s*. New York: Pathfinder, 1998.
Kot, Greg. *I'll Take You There: Mavis Staples, the Staple Singers, and the Music That Shaped the Civil Rights Era*. New York: Scribner, 2014.
Kurlansky, Mark. *Ready for a Brand New Beat*. New York: Riverhead Books, 2013.
Larson, Steve. "Lewis, Ramsey (Emmanuel, Jr.)." *The New Grove Dictionary of Jazz*. Edited by Barry Kernfeld. New York: St. Martin's Press, 1999, 697.
Lauterbach, Preston. *The Chitlin' Circuit and the Road to Rock 'n' Roll*. New York and London: W. W. Norton & Co., 2011.

Lordi, Emily. *The Meaning of Soul: Black Music and Resilience Since the 1960s*. Durham and London: Duke University Press, 2020.
Malnig, Julie. "Introduction," in *Ballroom, Boogie, Shimmy Sham, Shake: A Social and Popular Dance Reader*, 1–15. Edited by Julie Malnig. Urbana and Chicago: University of Illinois Press, 2003.
Mandel, Howard. *Future Jazz*. Oxford and New York: Oxford University Press, 1999.
Martin, Rachel, and Vince Pearson. "More Than 'Kind of Blue': In 1959, a Few Albums Changed Jazz Forever." *NPR*, April 29, 2019.
McGowan, Chris, and Ricardo Pessanha, *The Brazilian Sound*. New York: Billboard Books, 1991.
Mercer, Michelle. *Footprints: The Life and Work of Wayne Shorter*. New York: Tarcher/Penguin, 2004.
Micucci, Matt. "A Short History of . . . The 'In' Crowd." *Jazz*, July 25, 2017.
Moon, Tom. *1,000 Recordings to Hear Before You Die*. New York: Workman Publishing Company, 2008.
Muir, Peter. *Long Lost Blues*. Urbana (IL) and Chicago: University of Illinois Press, 2010.
Murray, Albert. *Murray Talks Music*. Edited by Paul Devlin. Minneapolis and London: University of Minnesota Press, 2016.
Neal, Mark Anthony. *What the Music Said: Black Popular Music and Black Popular Culture*. New York and London: Routledge, 1999.
Nelson, Oliver. Notes to Oliver Nelson, *Black, Brown and Beautiful*. LP, Flying Dutchman Records, FDS 10116, 1969.
O'Neal, Jim. "Midwest Blues: It's Just the Blues." Notes to *The Mercury Blues 'n' Rhythm Story 1945–1955*. CD, Mercury Records, 314 528 292-2, 1996.
Owens, Tim. "Remembering Nancy Wilson: The Best of Jazz Profiles." *NPR*, December 12, 2018.
Peyser, Joan. *Bernstein: A Biography*. New York: Billboard Books, 1998.
Porter, Bob. "The Blues in Jazz." In *The Oxford Companion to Jazz*, 64–77. Edited by Bill Kirchner. Oxford and New York: Oxford University Press, 2000.
Pruter, Robert. *Chicago Jazz*. Urbana (IL) and Chicago: University of Illinois Press, 1992.
Ratliff, Ben. "Billy Higgins, 64, Jazz Drummer with a Melodic and Subtle Swing." *New York Times*, May 4, 2001.
Ritz, David. Notes to Ray Charles: Pure Genius: The Complete Atlantic Recordings. CD Box Set, Atlantic Records, 2005.
Rosenthal, David H. *Hard Bop*. New York and London: Oxford University Press, 1992.
Sales, Grover. *Jazz: America's Classical Music*. New York: Da Capo Press, 1992.
Santana, Carlos. Notes to Miles Davis, *The Complete Bitches Brew*. CD Box Set, Columbia Legacy, 65570, 1998.
Schlessinger, Dr. Judith. Review of CD recording of Nancy Wilson "Turned to Blue." (Justin Time Records). *All About Jazz* website. August 17, 2006.
Scofield, John. Notes to *Works for Me*. CD, Verve Records, 2000.
Seymour, Gene. "Hard Bop." In *The Oxford Companion to Jazz*, 373–88. Edited by Bill Kirchner. Oxford and New York: Oxford University Press, Author unknown, notes to *Blue Note: A Story of Modern Jazz* (1997), CD, Blue Note Records, CDP 7243 8 59229 2 3. 2000.
Skelly, Richard. Biography of Marlena Shaw. www.bluenote.com.
Snider, Eric. "Still Part of the 'In' Crowd: Ramsey Lewis Keeps Grooving with a Saturday Afternoon Tradition." *Jazz*, June 2021.
Southern, Eileen. *The Music of Black Americans*. New York and London: W. W. Norton & Company, 1983.

Southern, Eileen. *Readings in Black American Music.* New York: W. W. Norton & Company, 1971.
Stanfield, Peter. *Body and Soul: Jazz and Blues in American Film, 1927-63.* Urbana (IL) and Chicago: University of Illinois Press, 2005.
Stravinsky, Igor. *An Autobiography.* New York: W. W. Norton & Company, 1962.
Sudhalter, Richard M. "Hot Music in the 1920s: The 'Jazz Age,' Appearances and Realities." In *The Oxford Companion to Jazz,* 148-62. Edited by Bill Kirchner. Oxford and New York: Oxford University Press, 2000.
Tate, Greg. *Flyboy in the Buttermilk: Essays on Contemporary America.* New York: Fireside, 1992.
Taylor, Arthur. *Notes and Tones.* New York: Perigee Books, 1977.
Teachout, Terry. *Duke: A Life of Duke Ellington.* New York: Gotham Books, 2013.
Teachout, Terry. *Pops: The Wonderful World of Louis Armstrong.* London: JR Books, 2009.
Thomas, J. C. *Chasin' the Train.* New York: Da Capo Press, 1983.
Tingen, Paul. *Miles Beyond: The Electric Explorations of Miles Davis, 1967-1991.* New York: Billboard Books, 2001.
Tirro, Frank. *Jazz: A History (Second Edition).* New York and London: W. W. Norton & Company, 1993.
Travis, Dempsey J. *An Autobiography of Black Jazz.* Chicago: Urban Research Institute, 1983.
Troupe, Quincy. Notes to Miles Davis, *The Complete Bitches Brew.* CD Box Set, Columbia Legacy, 65570, 1998.
Tucker, Mark. *The Duke Ellington Reader.* New York and London: Oxford University Press, 1993.
Ullman, Michael. Notes to Jimmy Smith, *Jimmy Smith's Finest Hour.* CD, Verve Records, 314 543 598-2, 2000.
Unsigned. "Radio-TV." *Jet Magazine,* July 11, 1963, 66.
Unsigned. "New York Beat." *Jet Magazine,* April 9, 1964.
Unsigned. Notes to *Blue Note: A Story of Modern Jazz.* CD, Blue Note Records, CDP 7243 8 59229 2 3, 1997.
Unsigned. Notes to *Really the Blues? A Blues History 1893-1959.* West Hill Records, WHRA-6028, 2010.
Unsigned. Notes to Les McCann and Eddie Harris, *Swiss Movement.* LP, Atlantic Records SD 1537, 1969.
Unsigned, eddieharris.com.
Unsigned, "The Jazz Problem." *Etude Magazine.* August 1924.
Unsigned, herbiehancock.com.
Unsigned, errollgarner.com.
Vera, Billy. "East Coast Blues: What That Is." Notes to *The Mercury Blues 'n' Rhythm Story 1945-1955.* CD, Mercury Records, 314 528 292-2, 1996.
Vincent, Rickey. *Funk.* New York: St. Martin's Griffin, 1996.
Waldo, Terry. *This Is Ragtime.* New York: Da Capo Press, 1976.
Waldren, Clarence. "Nancy Wilson Celebrates 50th Year in Music with New CD *R.S.V.P.*" *Jet Magazine,* October 4, 2004, 60.
Ward, Geoffrey C., and Ken Burns. *Jazz: A History of America's Music.* New York: Alfred A. Knopf, 2005.
Washburne, Christopher. "Miscellaneous Instruments." In *The Oxford Companion to Jazz,* 653-67. Edited by Bill Kirchner. Oxford and New York: Oxford University Press, 2000.

West, Cornel. *Prophetic Reflections*. Monroe: Common Courage Press, 1993.
Wilentz, Sean. *360 Sound: The Columbia Records Story*. San Francisco: Chronicle Books, 2012.
Williams, Alastair. *Constructing Musicology*. Hampshire: Ashgate Publishing Limited, 2001.
Woodward, Richard B. "Kind of Blue: Jazz Competes with Its Past, Settles for the Hard Sell." In *Rhythm and Business: The Political Economy of Black Music*, 165–71. Edited by Norman Kelley. New York: Akashic Books, 2005.
Yanow, Scott. *Bebop*. San Francisco: Miller Freeman Books, 2000.

INDEX

AACM, 22, 173
A&M Records, 70, 76, 78, 80
ABC Records, 46, 47, 65, 66, 67, 133
Abner, Ewart, 20, 21
Abrams, Muhal Richard, 173
Adderley, Julian (Cannonball), 5, 9, 14, 17, 18, 38, 43, 51, 76, 84, 98, 99, 100, 101, 104, 109, 111, 142, 143, 156, 157, 162, 179, 182
Adderley, Nat, 100, 119, 153
Ahmad Jamal Trio, 104
Aimée, Cyrille, 52
Alexander, Joey, 104
Alexandria, Lorez, 45, 46, 52
Allen, Geri, 97
Allen, Jim, 132
Alpert, Herb, 34
Ammons, Gene, 86, 127, 130, 139, 147
Anderson, Fred, 173
Anderson, Thelma, 128
Angelou, Maya, 12
Argo Records, 11, 46, 51, 58, 68, 70, 76, 77, 86, 88, 89, 108
Armstrong, Louis, 13, 15, 23, 28, 35, 68, 93, 138, 150, 151, 152, 179
Art Blakey and the Jazz Messengers, 15, 21, 40, 59, 97, 139, 140, 142, 153, 157
Art Blakey Quintet, 97
Art Ensemble of Chicago, 173
Asch, Moses, 69, 70
Atlantic Records, 11, 21, 30, 32, 33, 44, 45, 58, 61, 63, 65, 66, 67, 68, 70, 73, 75, 76, 83, 86, 87, 88, 127

Auger, Brian, 132, 134
Auld, Georgie, 96
Avakian, George, 92, 96, 144
Ayers, Roy, 58
Ayler, Albert, 7, 9, 10, 14, 22, 31, 35, 68, 73, 179
Ayler, Donald, 31

Bach, Johann Sebastian, 24
Bad Plus, 105
Bailey, Benny, 167
Bailey, Donald, 171
Baker, Laverne, 39
Baraka, Amiri (LeRoi Jones), 12, 31, 32, 34, 120
Bar-Kays, the, 139
Bart, Ben, 178
Bartz, Gary, 17
Basie, Count, 35, 39, 50, 51, 68, 92, 96, 102, 124
Beatles, the, 3, 8, 10, 16, 21, 23, 78, 89, 124, 179
Beethoven, Ludwig van, 24
Bell, William, 160
Bennett, Tony, 52
Benson, Al, 54
Benson, George, 59, 127, 131, 138, 172
Berger, Kenny, 49
Bet-Car Records, 47
Bianchi, Pat, 134
Big Maybelle, 39
Bird, Christiane, 116
Bishop, Kate O., 135
Black, Timuel, 178
Black Arts Movement, 12, 31, 135
Blackwell, Ed, 76

Blake, Eubie, 35
Blakey, Art, 54, 68, 86, 97, 155
Blanchard, Terrance, 163
Bley, Carla, 134
Blue Note Records, 11, 14, 32, 33, 51, 54, 58, 59, 60, 61, 62, 68, 70, 71, 72, 73, 80, 81, 82, 83, 85, 86, 88, 98, 125, 126, 127, 128, 129, 136, 144, 145, 146, 168, 175
Bobo, Willie, 138
Bonfa, Luis, 84, 85
Booker T. and the M.G.'s, 34, 132, 160
Boone, Pat, 53
Bracken, Jimmy, 20, 70
Bradford, Carmen, 52
Branch, Ben, 127, 162
Brewer, Carolyn Glenn, 47
Bridgewater, Dee Dee, 52, 59
Brookmeyer, Bob, 85
Brooks, Roy, 171
Brown, Clifford, 76, 97
Brown, James, 14, 33, 46, 91, 94, 133, 139, 164, 165, 172
Brown, Oscar, Jr., 50, 142, 152, 153, 154, 182
Brown, Patti, 171
Brown, Ray, 171
Brown, Roy, 39
Brown, Ruth, 39, 40, 135
Brown, Sterling A., 12
Brubeck, Dave, 11, 16, 33, 68, 70, 95, 107, 132
Bryant, Rusty, 131
Buckinghams, the, 104
Buckner, Milt, 125, 130
Buffalo Springfield, 10
Burns, Ken, 8, 9, 23, 95
Burns, Ralph, 66
Burrell, Kenny, 41, 71, 81, 82, 127, 130, 131, 138, 139
Burton, Linn, 40, 118
Byrd, Charlie, 84
Byrd, Donald, 14, 54, 59, 144

Cadet Records, 11, 51, 63, 68, 76, 86, 89, 127
Calloway, Cab, 55
Camus, Marcel, 84
Candid Records, 49, 137, 152, 153
Cannonball Adderley Quintet (Sextet), 62, 94, 99, 101, 103, 111

Capitol Records, 3, 7, 11, 40, 43, 68, 89, 101, 103, 104
Captain and Tenille, 59
Carr, Roy, 9, 119, 128
Carroll, Diahann, 114, 115
Carter, Benny, 14
Carter, Betty, 47, 48, 49
Carter, Chris, 20
Carter, Ron, 172
Carter, Vivian, 20, 70
Cavanaugh, Dave, 40
Chambers, Joe, 171
Chambers, Paul, 46
Chandler, Gene, 106
Charles, Ray, 29, 33, 47, 50, 52, 65, 66, 67, 68, 130, 131, 133
Chess, Leonard, 70
Chess, Phil, 70
Chess Records, 46, 51, 68, 70, 86, 108, 178
Chick Webb's Orchestra, 39
Chinen, Nate, 16
Chisholm, Shirley, 165
Christian, Charlie, 24, 80
Christy, June, 40
Clapton, Eric, 83
Clark, Dick, 119
Clayton, John, 51
Clef Records, 84
Cobb, Arnott, 118
Cobb, Jimmy, 41, 46
Cobham, Billy, 172
Cohodas, Nadine, 42
Cohran, Kelan Phil, 173, 174
Cole, Cozy, 135
Cole, Freddie, 102
Cole, Nat King, 40, 50, 82, 95, 138, 179
Coleman, Kwame, 31, 49
Coleman, Ornette, 7, 9, 14, 16, 22, 23, 30, 33, 35, 60, 68, 75, 173, 179
Collins, Addie Mae, 154
Coltrane, Alice, 158
Coltrane, John, 7, 9, 14, 15, 16, 17, 22, 24, 30, 31, 33, 35, 43, 46, 58, 68, 82, 94, 100, 105, 133, 139, 142, 153, 154, 179
Columbia Records, 11, 21, 32, 44, 45, 68, 70, 85, 88, 92, 96, 143, 144, 145, 151, 152, 154, 175

Commodore Records, 151, 175
Connor, Chris, 40
Cook, Will Marion, 25
Cooke, Sam, 10, 133, 157
Cooper, Jack, 115, 117
Corea, Chick, 100, 106, 172
Cordell, Lucky, 103
Corley, Cheryl, 177
Coryell, Julie, 165
Cosby, Bill, 114, 115
Count Basie Orchestra, 104, 131
Crane, Bill "Butterball," 103
Cranshaw, Bob, 60, 61, 81, 82, 171
Crawford, Hank, 162
Crawford, Richard, 25, 26
Cronkite, Walter, 121, 159
Cropper, Steve, 34, 160
Crosby, Bing, 39
Crouch, Stanley, 23
Crowther, Bruce, 5
CTI Records, 11, 78, 86
Curtis, King, 139
Cuscuna, Michael, 59

Dalhous, Carl, 10
Dameron, Tad, 139
Damrosch, Frank, 26
Dance, Stanley, 96
Dannen, Fredric, 69
Davenport, Cow Cow, 35
Davis, Betty (Mabry), 144
Davis, Eddie "Lockjaw," 129, 180
Davis, Frances, 144
Davis, Jackie, 125
Davis, Miles, 7, 11, 14, 15, 16, 21, 22, 23, 24, 33, 35, 43, 46, 47, 50, 58, 60, 68, 70, 82, 84, 94, 100, 105, 126, 143, 144, 145, 156, 158, 159, 160, 164, 165, 166, 172, 182
Davis, Richard, 76
Davis, Sammy, Jr., 159
Dawson, Jim, 94
Day, Doris, 39
Daylie, Holmes (Daddy-O), 108, 113, 117, 118, 121, 123
Dearie, Blossom, 82
Debussy, Claude, 25
Decca Records, 11, 175

Dee, Merri, 117
Deep Purple, 132
DeFrancesco, Joey, 133, 134
Dells, the, 106
deMoraes, Vinícius, 84
Dennerline, Barbara, 133, 134
Deveaux, Scott, 14, 175
Diva Jazz Orchestra, 109
Dixon, Ben, 129
Dixon, Bill, 31
Doggett, Bill, 125, 131
Dolphy, Eric, 9, 49, 68, 71, 76, 77, 182
Domino, Fats, 53, 135
Donalson, Lou, 59, 62, 63, 97, 129, 144, 146, 147
Doors, the, 16
Dorham, Kenny, 95
Dowd, Tom, 83, 88
Du Bois, W. E. B., 30, 149, 158
Dukes, Joe, 127, 171
Dunn, Duck, 160
Durst, Lawanda "Dr. Hepcat," 117
Duvivier, George, 171
Dvořák, Antonín, 24, 25, 82
Dyett, Walter, 19
Dylan, Bob, 10, 45, 51, 85, 154, 179

Earland, Charles, 129, 131, 142
Early, Gerald, 165
Eckstine, Billy, 37, 102
Edison Recording Company, 69
Edwards, Gene, 132
Eisenhower, Dwight D., 15, 151, 152
Ellington, Duke, 4, 14, 15, 16, 17, 24, 25, 28, 35, 51, 55, 68, 85, 91, 92, 96, 103, 105, 114, 139, 141, 142, 150, 151, 155, 156, 157, 172
Ellis, Don, 14
Ellison, Ralph, 16
Emerson, Keith, 132
English, Bill, 171
Ertegun, Ahmet, 70
Ertegun, Nesuhi, 66
Etude Magazine, 26, 27
Europe, James Reese, 4
Evans, Bill, 14, 54, 68, 76, 100, 105, 106, 172
Evans, Gill, 14
Evers, Medgar, 6

Falk, Jacey, 48, 49
Fame, George, 126
Farmer, Art, 3
Farrell, Joe, 127
Faubus, Orval, 151, 152
Feather, Leonard, 37, 45, 47, 125
Feldman, Victor, 99
Ferguson, Bert, 116
Finch, Otis "Candy," 81, 82, 171
Finnis, Rob, 130, 131
Fitzgerald, Ella, 7, 14, 16, 33, 35, 39, 40, 42, 44, 50, 51, 55, 84, 178
Flack, Roberta, 167
Floyd, Bobby, 131, 134
Floyd, Samuel, Jr., 12, 57, 181
Flying Dutchman Records, 11, 86
Ford, Mary, 40
Fordham, John, 9, 14, 29
Foreman, Chris, 134
Forrest, Jimmy, 139
Frankie Valli and the Four Seasons, 20, 89
Franklin, Aretha, 16, 43, 44, 83, 105, 115, 139
Franklin, C. L., 115
Freed, Alan, 119
Freeman, Bud, 93
Friedlander, Lee, 73
Friedwald, Will, 8, 44, 52

Gambarini, Roberta, 52
Gardener, Barbara, 7
Garner, Erroll, 14, 96, 119, 130
Garroway, Dave, 40, 114, 118
Gates, Henry Louis, 12
Gaye, Marvin, 56
Genesis (band), 132
Gennett Records, 69
George, Nelson, 20, 115, 116, 120
George-Graves, Nadine, 57
Gerard, Charlie, 3, 158, 180, 181
Gershwin, George, 28, 51
Getz, Stan, 23, 55, 83, 84, 85, 95, 171
Gibson, "Jockey" Jack, 117
Giddings, Gary, 14
Gilberto, Astrud, 84, 85
Gilberto, João, 84
Gill, Jonathan, 4
Gillespie, Dizzy, 47, 68, 92, 95, 98, 175

Giovanni, Nikki, 12
Gitler, Ira, 49, 126, 129, 135
Gitlin, Todd, 6, 16
Glasper, Robert, 105
Gold, Ernest, 20
Goldings, Larry, 133, 134
Golson, Benny, 5
Gonsalves, Paul, 92
Gonzales, Babs, 123
Goodman, Benny, 15, 39, 55, 83
Gordon, Dexter, 55, 60, 61, 180
Gordy, Berry, 159, 162
Granz, Norman, 83, 84, 94, 95
Gray, Dobie, 86, 98, 108
Gray, Nettie, 108
Green, Grant, 14, 127, 129, 130, 131, 144, 155, 172
Greig, Charlotte, 41
Gridley, Mark, 29, 105, 106, 134
Griffin, Johnny, 15, 180
Guild, Jerry, 32
Guralnick, Peter, 117, 160

Haley, Alex, 116
Hall, Jim, 172
Hamilton, Chico, 62, 74
Hammond, John, 44, 45
Hammond, Laurens, 124, 125
Hampton, Lionel, 41, 47
Hancock, Herbie, 17, 18, 54, 55, 56, 57, 58, 60, 63, 68, 71, 80, 82, 100, 106, 107, 111, 147, 160, 172, 182
Handy, W. C., 26, 85, 150
Harris, Barry, 60, 61, 171
Harris, Eddie, 8, 19, 21, 22, 23, 29, 32, 35, 60, 68, 75, 107, 111, 138, 155, 166, 169, 171, 179
Harris, Wynonie, 39
Hart, Billy, 171
Hartman, Johnny, 46, 68
Hashimoto, Atsuko, 134
Hathaway, Donny, 163, 164
Havers, Richard, 80, 125, 128
Hawkins, Coleman, 49, 68, 83
Hayes, Elaine M., 38, 40, 118
Hayes, Isaac, 157, 160
Hayes, Louis, 171
Hazzard-Gordon, Katrina, 57

Index

Heath, Albert (Tootie), 171
Heath, Jimmy, 51, 62
Heilbert, Anthony, 156
Henderson, Joe, 59, 60, 61
Henderson, Jocko, 117
Hendrix, Jimi, 16, 91, 164, 165
Henry, Cory, 134
Herb Alpert & the Tijuana Brass, 34, 144
Hibbler, Al, 37
Higgins, Billy, 55, 56, 60, 62
Hill, Andrew, 68
Hines, Earl "Fatha," 38, 96, 103
Hinton, Milt, 171
Holiday, Billie, 7, 15, 39, 40, 41, 42, 45, 48, 94, 151, 152, 178
Holiday, Clarence, 94
Holland, Dave, 172
Holloway, Red, 127
Holmes, Richard (Groove), 29, 119, 126, 127, 129, 130, 131, 148
Holt, Isaac "Red," 108, 171
Horace Silver Quintet, 145
Horn, Jazzmeia, 52
Horn, Shirley, 50
Horne, Lena, 8, 44
Horowitz, Vladimir, 85
Hubbard, Eddie, 40, 118
Hubbard, Freddie, 55, 58, 73
Hughes, Langston, 12, 16
Humphries, Lex, 171
Hurston, Zora Neale, 12

Ike and Tina Turner, 133
Impressions, the, 106, 157
Impulse Records, 11, 32, 46, 67, 68, 70, 73, 74, 82, 86, 88, 130, 133

Jablonsky, Edward, 28
Jackson, Ashawnta, 154
Jackson, Hal, 117
Jackson, Jesse, 17, 162
Jackson, Mahalia, 150
Jackson, Michael, 91
Jackson, Willis, 127, 138, 139, 144
Jacquet, Illinois, 95
Jamal, Ahmad, 22, 23, 95, 96, 105, 107
James, Etta, 42

Jarrett, Keith, 105, 106, 172
Jazz Crusaders, 153
Jefferson, Eddie, 182
Jobim, Antonio Carlos, 84
Johnson, Aaron, 115, 119
Johnson, Ella, 39
Johnson, J. J., 67, 95
Johnson, James P., 35
Johnson, Osie, 171
Jones, Booker T., 34, 160
Jones, E. Rodney, 102, 104
Jones, Elvin, 172
Jones, Etta, 12, 42, 43
Jones, Hank, 5, 171
Jones, Ivan "Boogaloo Joe," 131, 142, 171
Jones, LeRoi. *See* Baraka, Amiri
Jones, Norah, 52
Jones, Papa Joe, 92
Jones, Quincy, 15, 41, 65, 66
Jones, Sam, 171
Jones, Thad, 15
Joplin, Scott, 25
Jordan, Louis, 35, 39, 138
Jordan, Sheila, 14
Joy, Samara, 52

Kahn, Ashley, 7, 31, 32, 67, 100, 119
Katz, Dick, 100
Keepnews, Orrin, 70, 76
Kelloway, Roger, 171
Kelly, Wynton, 21, 41, 46, 48
Kennedy, John F., 6, 161
Kennedy, Robert F., Sr., 6, 161, 163
Kent, Herb, 103, 113
Kent, Stacey, 52
Kenton, Stan, 14, 83
King, B. B., 45, 116, 117, 161
King, Coretta Scott, 158
King, Martin Luther, Jr., 3, 6, 120, 121, 139, 156–63
King Curtis and the Kingpins, 34
King Records, 46, 68, 131
Kirk, Rahsaan Roland, 131
Kot, Greg, 156, 158
Krall, Diana, 52
Kurlansky, Mark, 135, 159
Kynard, Charles, 131, 139

Lady Gaga, 52
Lambert, Hendrix & Ross, 14, 50
Larkin, Billy, 131
Lateef, Yusef, 101
Laws, Hubert, 51
Lazar, Sam, 131
Lead Belly, 150
Lee, Bill, 171
Lee, Julia, 39
Lee, Peggy, 8
Lee, Spike, 48
Legend, John, 52
Leslie, Don, 125
Leslie, Paul, 95
Lewis, Herbie, 171
Lewis, Ramsey, 5, 8, 13, 17, 18, 22, 23, 29, 83, 86, 105–11, 134, 157, 171
Liggins, Joe, 39
Limelight Records, 140
Lincoln, Abbey, 47, 48, 49, 136, 137, 142, 152, 155
Lion, Alfred, 58, 59, 62, 70, 82, 125
Little, Booker, 76, 182
Little Anthony and the Imperials, 78
Little Richard, 53, 56, 133
Lockwood, Robert, Jr., 115
Lomax, Alan, 69, 70
Lomax, John, 69, 70
Lord, Jon, 132
Lordi, Emily J., 139
Louterbach, Preston, 178
Lunceford, Jimmy, 96
Lutcher, Nellie, 39
Lynne, Gloria, 45

Mabern, Harold, 171
Macero, Teo, 165
Magnificent Montague, 117
Maher, Jack, 11, 119
Malcolm X, 6, 158
Malnig, Dr. Julie, 56
Mamas and the Papas, 78
Mandel, Howard, 7
Mann, Herbie, 13
Mansfield, Jayne, 48
Maricle, Sherry, 109
Marienthal, George, 107
Marienthal, Oscar, 107
Marr, Hank, 131
Marsalis, Wynton, 57, 109, 182
Martha and the Vandellas, 136
Martino, Pat, 131
Marvelettes, the, 136
Masakela, Hugh, 13
May, Billy, 43
Mayfield, Curtis, 106, 178
McCann, Les, 21, 29, 148, 166–69
McCoy, Sid, 21, 118
McDaniel, Hattie, 115
McDaniel, Ted, 82, 118
McDaniels, Gene, 166–69
McDermot, Galt, 144
McDuff, Jack, 8, 9, 13, 15, 62, 63, 86, 87, 105, 126, 127, 129, 130, 131, 132, 133, 134, 138, 139, 142, 157
McFarland, Gary, 85
McGowan, Chris, 84
McGriff, Jimmy, 87, 129, 130, 131, 132
McGuire, Barry, 10
McLaughlin, John, 129, 132
McNair, Denise, 154
McRae, Carmen, 39, 40, 48, 50, 158
McVea, Jack, 95
Medeski, John, 133, 134
Meeropol, Abe, 151
Mehldau, Brad, 105
Mendelsohn, Dorothy, 106
Mercer, Michelle, 21, 58, 80
Mercury Records, 11, 41, 50, 68, 100, 152, 153
Micucci, Matt, 108
Miles, Reid, 70, 73, 144
Milhaud, Darius, 26
Miller, Rice (Sonny Boy Williamson II), 115
Milton, Roy, 39
Mingus, Charles, 11, 14, 15, 16, 22, 30, 31, 33, 68, 95, 99, 152, 153, 155
Mitchell, Blue, 59, 62, 130
Mobley, Hank, 62, 63, 139, 179, 180
Monaco, Tony, 134
Monáe, Janelle, 91
Moncur, Grachan, III, 68
Monk, Thelonious, 11, 16, 68, 70, 85, 154, 175
Montgomery, Wes, 8, 24, 68, 76, 78, 79, 80, 85, 94, 131, 144

Moody, James, 135
Moon, Tom, 10, 30, 62, 85, 96, 98, 125, 129, 167
Morgan, Lee, 13, 14, 15, 23, 54, 58, 59, 60, 62, 63, 82, 130, 138, 142, 157, 171
Morgan, Tom, 103, 152
Morse, Ella Mae, 39
Morton, Jelly Roll, 35, 93, 138
Motown Records, 14, 20, 136, 137, 139, 159, 163
Muhammad, Idris (Leo Morris), 171
Muir, Peter, 150
Mulligan, Gerry, 68
Murray, Albert, 57, 138, 151, 182

Nadine, Slim, 95
Neal, Bob, 117
Neal, Mark A., 14, 59, 63, 124, 134, 176
Nelson, Oliver, 5, 15, 78, 80, 119, 128, 130, 139, 142, 153, 161, 162
"New Thing," 9, 10, 12, 16, 30, 32, 68, 173
Newborn, Phineas, 162

O'Day, Anita, 7, 17, 40
Ogerman, Claus, 78
O'Jay, Eddie, 117
Oliver, Joe "King," 93
Oliver, Paul, 150
O'Neal, Jim, 41
Original Dixieland Jazz Band, 26, 68
Oscar Peterson Trio, 107
Owens, Time, 7

Pablo Records, 95
Pacific Jazz Records, 11, 68, 70, 86, 89, 130
Palmer, Earl, 56
Parker, Charlie, 15, 24, 35, 47, 76, 93, 95, 96, 98, 100, 119, 124, 126, 133, 175
Parks, Rosa, 30, 151
Parlato, Gretchen, 52
Parlophone Records, 89
Patterson, Don, 126, 129, 131
Patton, Big John, 62, 63, 82, 126, 128, 129, 130, 133, 144
Paul, Les, 95
Payne, Freda, 46
Peer, Ralph, 69, 70
Perkins, Bob, 117, 128
Person, Houston, 130, 139, 141

Pessanha, Ricardo, 84
Peterson, Oscar, 14, 54, 95, 105, 107
Petrillo, James, 39
Pettiford, Oscar, 100
Phillips, Dewey, 117, 119
Phillips, Sonny, 129, 131
Pickens, Willie, 21
Pinfold, Mike, 5
Poitier, Sidney, 48, 115, 159
Ponder, Jimmy, 131, 171
Porter, Bob, 126
Porter, Cole, 51
Powell, Bud, 95, 105, 106
Preminger, Otto, 92
Presley, Elvis, 117, 166
Prestige Records, 11, 33, 42, 58, 61, 63, 68, 70, 76, 77, 82, 83, 85, 86, 88, 127, 129, 130, 141
Preston, Billy, 132, 133
Price, Lloyd, 129
Prokofiev, Sergei, 128
Propes, Steve, 94
Pruter, Robert, 20, 105
Purdie, Bernard, 171

Quinichette, Paul, 41
Quintet, the, 95

Raeburn, Boyd, 96
Ramsey Lewis Trio, 22, 46, 76, 77, 86, 88, 98, 106–9
Razaf, Andy, 51, 150
RCA/Victor Records, 85, 140, 175
Red Garland Trio, 139
Redding, Otis, 91
Reeves, Dianne, 52
Reprise Records, 68
Rhyne, Melvin, 131, 171
Richmond, Dannie, 152
Ridley, Larry, 171
Rivers, Sam, 68
Riverside Records, 9, 48, 68, 70, 76, 78, 79, 85, 86, 88, 100
Roach, Freddie, 126, 128, 131, 138, 144, 146, 182
Roach, Max, 48, 49, 95, 142, 152, 153
Roberts, Herman, 42
Robertson, Carole, 154
Rogers and Hart, 51

Roker, Mickey, 171
Rolling Stones, 133
Rollins, Sonny, 48, 58, 60, 82, 85, 95, 100, 152, 178
Rosenthal, David, 61, 62, 63, 127, 134
Ross, Annie, 50
Rouse, Charlie, 100
Russell, Catherine, 52
Russell, Curley, 97
Russell, George, 14

Sales, Grover, 24
Salvant, Cécile McLorin, 52, 109
Sam and Dave, 157
Sanders, Pharoah, 14, 68, 179
Santamaria, Mongo, 55, 57, 142
Santana, Carlos, 164
Savoy Records, 175
Seymour, Gene, 24, 59, 61, 78
Schiffman, Bobby, 8, 38
Schiffman, Frank, 8
Schifrin, Lalo, 128
Schlessinger, Dr. Judith, 51
Scofield, John, 61
Scott, Christian (aTunde Adjuah), 109
Scott, Rhoda, 131, 134
Scott, Shirley, 15, 81, 82, 105, 126, 127, 129, 130, 131, 134
Sebesky, Don, 78
Shaughnessy, Ed, 171
Shaw, Marlena, 51, 104
Shearing, George, 3, 107
Sheep, Archie, 31, 62, 68, 179
Shields, Del, 120
Shorter, Wayne, 21, 54, 58, 59, 68, 80, 142, 179
Shostakovich, Dmitri, 25
Signature Records, 175
Silver, Horace, 12, 33, 82, 86, 94, 97, 98, 135, 138, 139, 144, 182
Simon, Ernie, 40, 118
Simone, Nina, 7, 37, 38, 42, 85, 155, 156, 163
Sinatra, Frank, 8, 39, 52, 104, 164, 165
Sloane, Carol, 6
Sly & the Family Stone, 132, 164, 165, 176
Smith, Bessie, 138
Smith, Ethel, 124
Smith, Floyd, 132

Smith, Jimmy, 8, 9, 13, 14, 15, 29, 59, 63, 71, 74, 85, 111, 119, 123, 125, 126, 127, 129, 131, 132, 133, 134, 135, 136, 138, 144, 147, 171
Smith, Johnny "Hammond," 129, 131, 138, 139
Smith, Lonnie, 104, 129, 131
Smith, Lonnie Liston, 131, 134
Sousa, John Philip, 26, 27
Southern, Eileen, 57, 160
Spaniels, the, 20
Sparks, Melvin, 131
Spaulding, Esperanza, 52
Spencer Davis Group, 132
Springsteen, Bruce, 179
Stafford, Jo, 40
Staples, Mavis, 156, 158
Staples, Pops, 156
Staples Singers, 156
Starr Records, 69
Staton, Dakota, 40, 41, 42, 52
Stax Records, 14, 159
SteepleChase Records, 50
Stewart, Rod, 83
Stitt, Sonny, 15, 127, 139
Stravinsky, Igor, 25
Strayhorn, Billy, 51, 142
Sudhalter, Richard, 13
Sue Records, 11, 68, 86, 87, 89, 130
Sun Ra, 35, 173
Supremes, the, 147, 163

Tate, Grady, 80, 171
Tatum, Art, 15, 96, 105, 114, 133
Taylor, Billy, 24, 51
Taylor, Cecil, 30, 68
Taylor, Creed, 67, 70, 78, 119
Taylor, Gene, 163, 171
Teachout, Terry, 92, 151
Teagarden, Jack, 83
Temptations, the, 147, 163
Terry, Clark, 80, 155
Tharp, Sister Rosetta, 39
Thiele, Bob, 46, 175
Thomas, J. C., 154
Thomas, Leon, 59
Thomas, Rufus, 117
Threadgill, Henry, 173
Three Sounds, 144

Thurman, Camille, 52
Till, Emmett, 151
Timmons, Bobby, 86, 142, 153, 171
Tirro, Frank, 7, 22, 83
Tjader, Cal, 85
Torin, Sid, 118
Travis, Dempsey, 102
Treadwell, Oscar, 119
Troupe, Quincy, 165
Turner, Beauty, 177, 178
Turrentine, Stanley, 8, 17, 18, 81, 82, 86, 129, 144, 180
Tyner, McCoy, 14, 106
Tyson, Cicely, 144, 182

Upchurch, Phil, 171

Van Gelder, Rudy, 80–83, 98
Vaughn, Sarah, 38, 39, 40, 44, 50, 51, 103, 107
Vee-Jay Records, 20, 68, 70, 89, 178
Vera, Billy, 41
Verve Records, 11, 33, 47, 49, 50, 58, 68, 70, 71, 73, 74, 76, 78, 80, 83, 84, 85, 86, 88, 95, 126, 141, 144
Vick, Harold, 127, 130
Vinnegar, Leroy, 171
Vitro, Roseanna, 52

Waites, Freddie, 171
Waldo, Terry, 25
Waldron, Mal, 33, 76, 139
Wall, Dan, 133
Waller, Fats, 15, 51, 96, 114, 124, 150
Walton, Cedar, 171
Ward, Geoffrey C., 23, 30, 95
Warhol, Andy, 73
Warner Brothers Records, 69
Warren, Butch, 55, 56
Washington, Dinah, 7, 16, 39, 40, 41, 44, 45, 51
Washington, Grover, Jr., 17, 130, 180
Waters, Ethel, 150
Waymon, Sam, 163
Webster, Ben, 83, 130
Weinstock, Bob, 70
Wells, Mary, 136, 137
Wesley, Cynthia, 154
West, Cornel, 11

Wexler, Jerry, 66
White, Fred, 173
White, Maurice, 173
Whiteman, Paul, 27, 28
Wilentz, Sean, 39
Willette, Baby Face, 128
Williams, Alastair, 179
Williams, Bert, 149
Williams, Cootie, 41
Williams, Joe, 50, 102
Williams, Nat D., 116, 117, 118
Williams, Paul K., 105
Williams, Tony, 68, 100, 129, 172
Williamson, Sonny Boy, II, 115
Wilson, Alice V., 5
Wilson, Cassandra, 5, 52
Wilson, Earl, 5
Wilson, Gerald, 130
Wilson, Mary, 159
Wilson, Nancy, 4, 5, 6, 7, 8, 16, 17, 18, 38, 43, 44, 51, 52, 82, 94, 111, 118, 131, 171, 182
Wilson, Reuben, 129, 131, 133, 134
Wilson, Teddy, 5
Wilson, Woodrow, 5
Winding, Kai, 67
Wolf, Francis, 58, 59, 70, 73, 82, 125
Wolfman Jack, 119
Woodstock, 10
Woodward, Richard B., 24
Woody Herman's Thundering Herd, 83
Wooten, Victor, 59
Wright, Lizz, 52
Wynton Kelly Trio, 46

Yahel, Sam, 134
Yanow, Scott, 45, 175
Yes (band), 132
Young, Eldee, 108, 171
Young, Larry, 126, 128, 129, 131
Young, Lester, 41, 83, 118
Young, Snooky, 80
Young Rascals, 132

Zawinul, Josef, 41, 101, 102, 172
Zeitlin, Denny, 127

ABOUT THE AUTHOR

Photo courtesy of the author

Mike Smith has played drums in numerous jazz, soul, rock, country, and polka bands; he has performed as a jazz, rock, and choral ensemble vocalist; he has been an orchestral percussionist; and he has conducted jazz bands, concert bands, and orchestras across the country, including in New York's famed Carnegie Hall. Mike has been a music educator for more than forty years, with experiences teaching at every level from kindergarten through university. He has also been an arranger for numerous bands and ensembles, including jazz, rock, and pop bands; concert bands and wind ensembles; and marching and basketball bands. Mike enjoys presenting workshops and lectures on American music history in general, jazz and American popular music in particular, as well as arts integration for non-arts educators. Mike is an assistant professor of practice at Ohio State University, where he serves as coordinator of Jazz Studies, conducts the Jazz Ensemble and the Jazz Fusion combo, and teaches jazz history and jazz education classes.

www.ingramcontent.com/pod-product-compliance
Lightning Source LLC
Chambersburg PA
CBHW022017220426
43663CB00007B/1116